Neil Boyd is the pseudonym of Peter de Rosa, a former Roman Catholic priest who became a BBC producer and is now a full-time writer. Besides his best-selling books, *A Father Before Christmas*, *Bless Me, Father* and *Father in a Fix*, he has also written the scripts for the highly successful London Weekend Television series, *Bless Me, Father*, starring Arthur Lowe and Daniel Abineri.

Also by Neil Boyd

A FATHER BEFORE CHRISTMAS
BLESS ME, FATHER
FATHER IN A FIX

and published by Corgi Books

Father Under Fire

Neil Boyd

CORGI BOOKS
A DIVISION OF TRANSWORLD PUBLISHERS LTD

This book is for
Francis and Daniel
and their first cousins

Peter	Louise	Frances	Michael Francis
Paul	Sophie	Catherine	Patrick
Marisa	Andrew	Lucy	Nicole
Elizabeth	Paula	Clare	Zophia
Michael	Damian	Joanne	Stefania
Philip	Dominic	Matthew	Anna
Stephen	Simon	James	Katie
Robert	Richard	Juliet	Lucy Angela

FATHER UNDER FIRE

A CORGI BOOK 0 552 11628 9

Originally published in Great Britain by
Michael Joseph Ltd.

PRINTING HISTORY
Michael Joseph edition published 1980
Corgi edition published 1981

This book is set in 10/11 California

Corgi Books are published by
Transworld Publishers Ltd.,
Century House, 61–63 Uxbridge Road,
Ealing, London, W5 5SA

Made and printed in United States of America
by Arcata Graphics
Buffalo, New York

Contents

ONE

A Legend Comes to Stay

AT ST JUDE'S the impossible was commonplace. This meant that if you were wise and prepared yourself for the worst you were never very far wrong.

Almost the sole reason for this state of affairs was Fr Duddleswell, my parish priest. 'As twisted as a corkscrew and as slippery as sea-weed' was how our housekeeper, Mrs Pring, expressed it. 'As wily as a wagon-load of monkeys' was the verdict of Billy Buzzle, the friendly Bookie who lived next door.

How Fr Duddleswell came to acquire this reputation in the first place I had no idea. But enlightenment began to dawn at breakfast on the Monday of Holy Week 1951.

'Jasus,' Fr Duddleswell exploded, 'Father Abraham Cody has invited himself to stay.'

I looked at the letter in his hand and, highly sensitive now to disaster, enquired tongue-in-cheek if this was good news or bad.

He mockingly dabbed me with a fat finger across the table and rushed to the kitchen to tell Mrs Pring that the first parish priest he was ever curate to would be with us from Wednesday.

'As if Holy Week is not fierce hard enough already without this,' he shouted out, a mixture of gladness and gloom.

Father Abe was a legend and I was looking forward to meeting him. Fr Duddleswell's tales of him would have whetted any appetite.

'When Father Abe preached one of his hot sermons on

sex and marriage,' he reminded me on returning from the kitchen, 'no child was born in his parish for at least a year. And when the poor starved couples got at it again, did not even the married women hide their bulges from him as best they could?'

'Impressive,' I said, and I really thought it was, though I had heard the story a dozen times before.

'Impressive,' Fr Duddleswell whistled, 'he was that. All 225 pounds of him. He had a chestnut mare in those days, sturdy enough, true, but with him on her back the poor beast had a maximum speed of three miles per hour.'

'Like a London bus,' commented Mrs Pring, who had just come in.

'He took a broom with him everywhere, Father Neil, to scratch her underbelly with when she wouldn't shift.'

'Don't get any ideas,' Mrs Pring warned.

'Rumour was, though I never witnessed this meself, that once he had to carry the horse home himself.'

Mrs Pring and I looked at each other and, infected by his gaiety, laughed aloud.

'What a voice on him. When he turned round for the *Dominus vobiscum* at Mass he threw out his two arms like the antlers of a mighty stag and gave a great rutting roar.' Tears were streaming down his chubby cheeks unchecked at the memory of the joys of old. 'And his confessional whisper, ah I tell you, 'twould have split his box even were it made of stone.'

'This is Father Abe, lad.'

Fr Duddleswell made the introduction in his study. After all the legendary talk it was hard to believe that this diminutive, cassocked, harmless-looking figure in the armchair was *the* Abraham Cody. Expecting a giant of a man, I found something resembling an angora rabbit.

Father Abe had white silky hair brushed downwards to make a fringe. Beneath the fringe were white eyebrows, white moustaches and a white tufted beard. Gripped in his tiny white teeth was a big Havana cigar.

'I've heard a lot about you, Father,' I stammered.

8

From lips open and round, Father Abe exhaled a mouthful of smoke. As he did so, a vivacious smile spread across his lined, corduroy-like face.

'Shut the door, laddy,' he ordered. 'That draught would knock a nail in.'

I apologized and did as I was told. After which, from his armchair, the old priest sized me up. His voice had a habit of switching alarmingly from bass to treble and back again.

'Little Charlie here' – he speared the culprit with his cigar – 'tells me that you are closer to him than his vest and pants.'

'Father Abe, I did not say anything of the sort,' Fr Duddleswell objected.

Father Abe tapped the top of his cigar with his index finger and splurted ash in the direction of his former curate. 'Will you be silent, little Charlie, till I've said my fill.'

'I am truly sorry, Father Abe.'

'Don't be sorry, little Charlie, just fetch me a bottle of rum.'

'Father Abe,' Fr Duddleswell tutted unconvincingly, 'how d'you think we can get the price of a bottle of rum in this parish?'

'Your snug wee parish is rotten with the money. So lean over the gate there and whisper me where you keep the rum.'

Fr Duddleswell sadly shook his head. 'Father Neil will confirm that we have more debts than an Irish farmer.'

Having no choice I confirmed we were afloat with bills.

'Not that I am worrying on that score,' Fr Duddleswell said piously. 'Did not our Blessed Lord Himself say that the poor are happy in some deep sense?'

'Too deep for me,' Father Abe retorted.

''Tis true,' Fr Duddleswell came back, grinning, 'in spite of our Lord's words, I have never yet known a priest made miserable by a £5 Mass stipend.'

Father Abe ignored a remark intended to put him off the track. He stuck his cigar in the corner of his mouth and showed Fr Duddleswell the palms of his hands. 'Didn't I always teach you, little Charlie, these things are for giving.'

Fr Duddleswell momentarily lost his cool. 'For giving bread not stones, fish not snakes.'

'Ah,' Father Abe burst out, basso profondo, 'rank codology and you know it. Wasn't I daft mad to keep you with me those fifteen years, and teach you all I knew and feed you and clothe you and house you? Wasn't I? When you turned out a dirty little scab who pays me on the shins?' He swept his smoke aside with both hands like the curtains in the morning. 'Listen,' he piped disparagingly, 'I should have tested my friend before I needed him.'

Fr Duddleswell went on his knees by the armchair near which rested Father Abe's big brown suitcase and a small hessian sack, contents unknown.

'Father Abe, the doctor from the Priests' Home tells me that only a spider's web separates you from Heaven.'

'Don't sadden yourself at my death, little Charlie,' Father Abe said, touching Fr Duddleswell's arm tenderly, 'just fetch me the rum like a good lad.'

Father Abe took a liking to me from the first and I liked him. I agreed with Mrs Pring when she whispered to me, 'What a charmer. That one could get a spider to darn his socks for him.'

After lunch, while Fr Duddleswell was taking a siesta, Father Abe and I chatted in my room. He invited *me* to sit down with, 'Put your canal end down there, laddy.'

I was staggered to find that he was 'within a stone's throw of ninety', as he put it.

Ordained in 1888, he was already forty years a priest when I first saw the light of day. In fact, he was born before Gandhi and St Thérèse of Lisieux. When St Bernadette died in 1878 he was thirteen. When the poet Rupert Brooke died in 1915 he had reached his half-century.

'When I was fourteen years of age, laddy,' he said, 'we had a day off from school.' I shrugged to show I couldn't guess why. 'Because Newman was made a Cardinal, don't you know?'

'Of course,' I said, amazed.

'When he died in 1890, I said Mass for his soul. He wasn't such a bad feller in his own way, in spite of having once been a Protestant.'

'Which part of Ireland do you come from, Father?' I asked.

'New York,' he said. 'At any rate, I was born in the land across the herring pond. My parents took the boat there after the Famine. In those days the young Kerry men looked to the States as the old did to Heaven. Natural, I suppose, what with the Statue of Liberty in the next parish.'

Father Abe took a big puff and released the smoke slowly, meticulously, as if the shape of it had to be exactly right.

'My father, God rest him, adored America.'

'I suppose he died there, Father.'

'Not at all. He couldn't bear to finish his days outside Ireland. He came home like the salmon.'

I knew the jargon. 'So he was a Returned Yank, Father.'

He nodded. 'That's how I got my name, Abraham.'

'It's common over there, is it, Father?'

'Dear God, did little Charlie never tell you? I was born on 14 April 1865.'

'I'm sorry?'

'I was born on the day Abraham Lincoln got the bullet.'

'I *see*.'

'My first parish priest, Father Tim McCoy, never let me forget it. Every time I entered the room the Big Man started up on the Gettysburg Address.'

I must have laughed loud enough to waken Fr Duddleswell.

'Father Tim, he had the age all right. He was born in '23. Holy God, the tales *he* had to tell. About the Famine and *Uncle Tom's Cabin* when it first appeared and the definition of Papal Infallibility at the Vatican Council and the Charge of the Light Brigade and, of course, Abe

Lincoln, "a true-born king of men" he called him, being gunned down by that damned mad-man.'

My brain was beginning to reel from its proximity to ancient history when Fr Duddleswell poked his head round the door. Before he could speak, Father Abe said:

'If the Well of Hospitality is dry here, little Charlie, I want no word from you, not one.'

'But, Father Abe,' Fr Duddleswell began pathetically.

'Black luck to you, little Charlie, and goodbye.'

'But –'

'Pick up your feet and put 'em outside that door.'

Fr Duddleswell grimaced, from physical pain, I thought, muttered something about the only thing in common between Father Abe and Jesus on His cross was the thirst, and withdrew.

'As I was saying, laddy, Father Tim McCoy was a priest and a half. Of course, he was already sixty-five years old when I met him here in London. I tell you, he could whip Mass over faster than I could hear a child's confession.'

It occurred to me that Father Tim was another legend that closer inspection might have shrunk somewhat.

'I remember the Big Man well,' Father Abe continued, gesturing eloquently with his cigar. 'A tall, flat Frankenstein forehead. A big red slice of nose, then a longer piece added like an extension. A square jaw that always looked as if it needed a shave even after he shaved, which wasn't often, I grant. And the eyes. He could put in a walnut like a monocle, bring down his lid and crack, that was the end of that.'

'Quite a character,' I said. My delight in the description stimulated him further.

'A great porter drinker. His huge bald head always stuck in a nose-bag of beer. "Father Tim," I'd say to him, "you'd not stop from drinking your black oats even for the Angelus." "Abe," says Father Tim, "I'd finish me drink even if St Michael blew the Last Trump." And I believe he would.'

'He sounds great fun, Father.'

'Mad as a golfer. I recall the time we had a guest

12

preacher for the feast of Mary's Motherhood. This Passion-
ist was extolling the Holy Mother's virtues. "So humble
was she," says the preacher, "she didn't mind even washing her Son's socks." And didn't Father Tim jump up in the
pulpit and drag him out of there and himself crying, "You
blasted heretic, to think that our Blessed Saviour *needed*
having His socks washed." '

'I never heard that heresy mentioned in the seminary,' I
said.

'Ah, but he was a great patriot, was Father Tim. Why,
he died of loyalty to Ireland.'

I asked how.

'Well, y'see, laddy, it was all my fault really. He was
nearing his end when I, foolishly hoping to cheer him up,
started singing *The Wearing o' the Green.* And didn't a
lump rise in his throat so he choked to death.'

To get him to poke more embers in him into a flame I
said, 'You've seen a lot in your life-time, Father.'

'I have, laddy, and there's a lot still to see.'

I smiled and perhaps he interpreted it as disbelief.

'It's true,' he insisted. 'A tin-pot philosopher, Aristotle I
think, said once that life seems long to the young and short
to the old.'

'Doesn't it?'

'Holy God, not at all. I fully realize I'm on the north
side of age and destined soon for the boneyard. Yet I don't
feel in the least what you'd call old. The years are like sins,
I suppose. It's slyly they mount up.' He smiled broadly at
me. 'If I was told by an angel I had only five minutes left
me I would fill it with life. I would swallow huge chunks of
life. Those five minutes would seem endless' – his cigar
was at arm's length – 'marvellous and endless. And believe
you me, laddy, I wouldn't die quiet.' He shook his snowy
head. 'Noisy as an Italian tenor, that's how I would snuff
it.'

I murmured something silly about hoping he wouldn't
die soon.

'Thank you, laddy,' he said warmly. 'For me, each day
is a miracle. We old 'uns are the mountaineers, y'see. Each

13

step we take is priceless and perilous and, after it, we stop and tell ourselves, Oh how grand it is to be alive. And we see this big view and feel breathless with the climb and the sheer joy of staving off death thus far. And, like Moses, you could say, we're glad we reached the mountain peak.'

'A nice thought, Father.'

'But why bother anyway?' he said, as if all of a sudden he did not care a fig for a long life. 'If I die tomorrow, laddy, the grass'll still grow, the sun shine and the nights bring the cool. I don't matter a damn. I'll feed the soil that fed me, and that's all about it.'

With that he stubbed out his cigar, jumped up with surprising agility and went to the door.

'Going for a rest, Father?'

'Not at all. Come with me, laddy.'

I followed him downstairs. To my surprise, he opened the front door and marched down the street. From his cassock pocket he drew a real old Gawd-blimey cap, tartan-patterned, and pressed it on the back of his head.

'Hurry, laddy,' he called over his shoulder, 'so we don't have to rush.'

When we reached the High Street, he hailed a cab, bundled me in and gave the destination: 'The Royal Hospital, Chelsea.'

I had always wanted to visit the famous retirement home for old soldiers designed by Wren but why we should be going there now was beyond me. On the way, Father Abe provided no illumination. Instead, he lit up and filled the cab with fog.

The cabby dropped us off outside the main entrance of the Royal Hospital. I was clearly expected to pay the dues. But having been led from my study so abruptly I was in no position to do so.

'Never you mind, laddy,' Father Abe said soothingly. He took out a silver fob watch and dangled it in front of the driver's eyes. 'Will this do?' he enquired.

The cabby looked at the meter with seven shillings on it and grunted, 'I suppose it'll have to.' He grabbed the watch and drove off in a huff.

'I'm sorry you lost your watch, Father,' I said.

Father Abe shook his head as he lit up a fresh cigar. 'No matter. It wasn't worth a halfpenny. The damn thing stopped twenty years ago.'

'Why then, did you carry it around all this time?'

'Didn't it come in handy in an emergency?' he said, puffing away furiously. 'Mind you, it means I have to alter my will. I left it to little Charlie.'

Father Abe seemed to know his way around the place. Instead of giving me a tour of the chapel and the dining room, he walked me to an outhouse overlooking the Thames.

There we were greeted by a bluff old soldier with a puce-coloured face and huge grey moustaches. Clad in his dark, everyday uniform, he was pottering around among tomato plants. He and Father Abe greeted each other like long-lost brothers.

'This is Corporal Kennedy, laddy,' I was told. 'A hero of the War.'

I knew it wasn't World War II he was referring to.

'When the Corporal here wears all his medals he can't walk.'

The old soldier beamed. 'Come for a drop of the cratur, Father?'

Father Abe nodded. 'I'm as dry as a bean, Ted.' He touched his cigar. 'I'm told the smell of this would put a skunk on his back. Hope it won't destroy your plants.'

Corporal Kennedy emitted a throaty chuckle. 'Give 'em a bit of a lift, I shouldn't wonder.'

For a quarter of an hour, while they sipped the contents of a secret still, I listened to them discussing the War. I heard names like Mafeking and Ladysmith and increased considerably my repertoire of what in the seminary we called 'unparliamentary language'. The honk of the occasional barge going under Chelsea Bridge punctuated the conversation.

Then: 'Thank you kindly, Ted. Must be on my way.'

The Corporal accompanied us down the drive and to Chelsea Bridge Road where we flagged down a taxi.

'Do you have a decent convent in the parish, laddy?'

I said yes, understanding I was to give the address to the cabby.

As we drove off, Corporal Kennedy saluted us and Father Abe responded by waving his cigar.

'I shall tell the Mother Superior,' Father Abe said, turning to me, 'that I am a good friend of Father Duddleswell.'

'You'd do better,' I replied, 'if you told her you are his worst enemy.'

'Mother Superior,' Father Abe said, greeting the giant-sized Mother Stephen in the polished parlour, 'I am the worst enemy of the parish priest in these parts.'

'Be seated, Father Cody,' Mother Stephen ordered sweetly, smelling an ally. When we had obeyed: 'What can I do for you?'

Father Abe took out a crumpled piece of paper. 'The Superior at the Priests' Home where I'm living at present, she gave me this. A prescription for a dose of spirits to keep my rheumatics in check.'

'And Father Duddleswell refuses to comply with Mother's command,' Mother Stephen said shrilly.

'I am afraid that is the case, Mother.'

A minute or so later, Mother Stephen returned with a silver tray on which was a glass of rum.

Outside, where the taxi was waiting to take us home, Father Abe patted me on the back. 'Thanks for the tip, laddy. But for you, that visit would have been a waste of time. Like castrating a curate.'

'A good job you had that note from the nun, Father.'

'Wasn't it, just.'

His tone made me suspicious. 'It was genuine, I suppose.'

'Indeed. Though I have to admit, it was older than the watch I gave the cabby.'

At the presbytery, Fr Duddleswell was summoned from his study to settle up with the taxi driver. I heard him muttering, 'Jasus, this fist of mine is going to give Father Abe an early night.'

Father Abe was once more comfortably settled in my

study when Fr Duddleswell burst in. 'Listen here,' he began.

'Rum, little Charlie. *Sitio*, y'hear? I'm head-to-toe thirsty. I'll not tell you again.'

'The Bishop is coming to dinner.'

'Sponger O'Reilly,' Father Abe groaned. 'You're joking me. You really are a stinkpot.'

Fr Duddleswell beamed at the compliment.

'Little Charlie, may you melt off the earth like the snow off the ditch.'

'He got to hear of your visit, Father Abe, and like yourself issued himself an invitation.'

'I'll say the penitential psalms in readiness. Now leave us, if you'd be so kind.'

Obediently, Fr Duddleswell went away.

'Why "Sponger"?' I asked, sensing that Father Abe knew the Bishop better than was good for him.

'I had him as my curate before little Charlie came. The minute after he walked in the door I said to my housekeeper, 'Mary dear, that one is a real sod. One day he'll be a bishop.'

'Prophetic,' I said.

'He hasn't changed over the years. Still crying out to be the centre of attention like a baby's bottom.'

I was intrigued by this unexpected light cast on my father in God. 'What was the matter with him?' I asked.

'A queer article altogether and very solitary. As far as Sponger's concerned, one's company and two's a blessed nuisance.'

'Was he bright?'

'Not a splink of sense in him.' He gave a snoring sigh. 'A head thick as a Russian novel.'

'What were his special vices, then?'

'Vices? He had *none*. Neither had he any virtues. In fact, to give him a character reference I had only to tear a blank page out of a book.'

When I reacted to that, Father Abe continued, 'A middle of the roader was Sponger.'

'Very safe.'

'Not at all. Very dangerous like any feller who drives straight down the cats-eyes, so to speak. Another thing, now I come to think of it, he never lost his temper.' He winked at me confidentially. 'Never trust a feller who doesn't lose his temper. It means he's as full of himself as a ripe moon.'

I nodded.

'Sponger was always muttering to himself darkly like he was saying Mass, but no fireworks, know what I mean?'

Having lived for several months with Fr Duddleswell I knew exactly what he meant.

'Did the Bishop have a sense of humour, Father?'

Father Abe reacted as if I had tickled him under both arms. 'D'you know I once told him the old yarn about three hermits retiring to Connaught for prayer and meditation. After a year, the first says, "'Tis very peaceful here." A year later, the second says, "'Tis that." A year later still, the third of them says, "I'm going. You two talk too much." '

I roared again which pleased Father Abe.

'Sponger didn't see the joke at all. Every time I've met him since he's still scratching his poll trying to work it out.' Father Abe bowed his head in mock repentance. 'I shouldn't be talking like this at all. He's not so bad really, Sponger. Maybe I'm just agin the government as usual.'

I seized a golden opportunity before it faded. 'What was Father Duddleswell like as a curate?'

At mention of the name, Father Abe took a long drag of his cigar. The end of it shone orange like the sun behind a cloud. 'Little Charlie, you're asking about? Fitted in right away like paste in the tube.' He reflected further. 'A close wee feller, mind.'

'Tight as a cabbage.'

'You have him. He never wanted his hat to know what was in his head, as the saying is.'

'He's very mysterious,' I granted him.

'You've noticed. Never any different. His nose in every dark hole and corner like a plumber.'

'Hardworking?'

Father Abe nodded merrily. 'A good pair of shoulders on him. They could carry more than the handlebars of an Irish bike.'

'A lot of vices?'

'That is so, but isn't he riddled with virtues, besides?' I nodded agreement.

'Kindness comes easy to him like money from America.'

'He loses his temper sometimes,' I said ruefully.

'Oh,' Father Abe replied, his eyes wide open, 'he gets boiling mad with you, doesn't he? And yet he wouldn't do you a button of harm.' The old priest gestured roundly with his cigar. 'Many a time he called me all the black-guards, ruffians, whores and bastards – without any evil intent, mind. He must have learned the language at school because it wasn't taught him in the seminary.'

'Was he good with money, Father?'

'He collected the stuff in heaps and basketfuls. Not that he'd spend a penny on himself. He used to buy St Vincent de Paul suits.'

'Pardon?'

'All his clothes looked as if they were worn out before he got 'em.'

'A good appetite?'

'A regular bagman. Could eat the labels off the jars. And couldn't he pray?'

'With devotion, you mean?'

'Fast, laddy, fast. He has this magic speed on him like Father Tim. He could fit in a Hail Mary between two ticks of the clock. I reckon if a cloud burst and beads of rain raced down the window pane, little Charlie could say an Ave on every one.'

'You got on well with him,' I said.

Father Abe positively glowed. 'Who wouldn't? Out-wardly, mind, we were hardly loving as two doves on a ridge pole. But we were much to one another and will always be. Many another curate had I before and since but it was always little Charlie I kept in the centre of my palm.'

'Father Abe.'

Father Abe eyed the treasured intruder angrily. 'You are a tough gristle of beef and no mistake.'

'Would you like a cup o' tay?'

'Holy God, may the grass grow in front of your door. First, a glass of rum, you scabby feller.'

When little Charlie had retired, defeated, Father Abe said, 'Isn't he a darling considerate chap?'

I nodded, unclear whether this was irony or not.

'I reckon, laddy, he's worried in case I spill the beans about him.'

'Is that it, Father?'

'The truth is' – he gestured with his cigar for me to put my ear nearer his lips – 'little Charlie is not Irish at all.'

I blinked. 'You could have fooled me.'

Father Abe shook his head mischievously. 'When he first came to me fresh from the English College in Rome – English College, would you believe it? – he had an English accent. Dear God, it was something terrible.'

'Like mine,' I said, grinning.

He thumped his breast as if he wanted to knock a hole in it. 'I forgot entirely there is a British agent in the house. But it's true, laddy, I have to agree with you there. Anyway, in spite of his darling parents hailing from Cork, when little Charlie comes to me it's Pentecost in reverse. He speaks the same language as myself but I have the father and mother of a job following any damn word he says.'

' "Holy God, little Charlie," I said, "if you spoke a foreign language like Italian I could learn it." '

'So *you* are responsible for the way he talks, Father.'

Father Abe shrugged non-committally. 'Little Charlie is only stage-Irish.'

'Aren't all Irishmen?' I said.

Father Abe choked on his cigar till his face was red and his eyes watered. When he had recovered, he agreed there was something in my point of view.

'After I was finished with little Charlie he was as green as a thrice-dyed Irishman and mad keen to extend the Shamrock Empire. Why, the silly little feller wouldn't

20

even eat Danish bacon after what the Danes did to Brian Boru.'

'Sponger,' Father Abe said to the Bishop, 'how is every cartload of you?'

'Very well thank you, Father Abe.'

'Holy God, wouldn't the moon look pale next to you in all your finery.'

The Bishop, having just stepped out of his limousine, was embarrassed at this public revelation of his nickname. 'Father Abe,' he said, doing his best to smile, 'how are you with the years?'

'Fine and strong, Sponger. I can still sling an insult that would kill Goliath.'

'I'm sure you can, Father Abe.'

Fr Duddleswell stepped in hurriedly to stop the rot. 'A twin-handed welcome to you, me Lord.'

He led the Bishop from the hall into his study where I was waiting. I alone knelt to kiss the Bishop's ring. I was in favour at the time. He gave me a benign look.

When we were settled, the Bishop handed Father Abe two small parcels. The old priest opened them and found they contained a box of Havanas and a half-bottle of rum.

'Holy Mary, Sponger,' Father Abe exclaimed, 'here's me saying that when you die yours will be the only moist eye in the place and all the time you're a saint of God.'

'You're too kind, Father Abe,' the Bishop replied modestly.

'I never thought,' Father Abe mused, 'to have a bishop for my bottle man. If I had a handful of palms I'd strew them under your purple feet.' He pointed in a different mood at Fr Duddleswell. 'Squeezing a drink out of that one, now, is tougher than getting a Cardinal to ride a bicycle.'

'Go on,' Fr Duddleswell said, straining for a scrap, 'kick that leg in, I have another.'

Mrs Pring brought in the sherry. When she knelt to kiss the Bishop's ring, Father Abe said mockingly, 'I'm surprised at you, my Lord. Aren't you afraid that sort of thing'll give the ladies bad thoughts?'

After the Bishop had spoken a kind word to Mrs Pring, she went to put the finishing touches to the meal and I poured the sherries.

'A fine woman, your housekeeper,' the Bishop commented to Fr Duddleswell.

'Except, me Lord, she takes size twelve in tongues.' A familiar spark appeared in the blue eyes behind his glasses. 'You know, me Lord, how St Philip Neri levitated in prayer and had to hold on to the Papal chamberlain's whiskers to keep himself down.'

'I do, indeed, Father.'

'Well, that woman can lift me off the ground just by a blast of her mouth.'

'D'you two remember,' Father Abe said, 'my housekeeper, Mary?'

The Bishop and Fr Duddleswell signalled how could anyone forget that harridan. And the conversation switched to a certain Mary Turner who had them all persecuted and full to the chin with insults.

Fr Duddleswell had promised the company a fine leg of beef and prevailed on the Bishop, who fancied himself with the knife, to carve, when Mrs Pring knocked and beckoned me from the doorway to follow her.

She looked half-crazed. 'It's gone, Father Neil.'

'What's gone?'

'The joint.'

'The joint? Where?'

'I opened the window to let the smoke out of the kitchen, went to put the veg in the dining room –'

'Pontius?' I said hoarsely. 'Impossible. How could a dog run off with a steaming joint?'

I rushed into the garden and leaned over the fence. There was the answer. Billy Buzzle's black labrador had picked up the joint of prime beef by the string surrounding it and was dragging it carefully through the dirt.

I threw a stone at Pontius, taking care not to hit him, and returned to tell Mrs Pring the bad news.

'There's nothing else for it,' I said, and gave her orders what to do.

On rejoining the company I tried to whisper in Fr Duddleswell's ear but he silenced me. Father Abe was busy telling the story of three hermits who went to Connaught for the sake of peace and solitude.

No wonder the Bishop doesn't laugh, I thought. The poor bloke's probably heard it a hundred times before.

When we entered the dining room, choice vegetables were steaming in their china dishes. After grace, Fr Duddleswell reminded the Bishop of his promise to carve.

'This *is* Lent, my Lord,' I said, preparing the ground. 'Holy Week, in fact.'

The Bishop smiled paternally. 'I understand your scruples, Father Neil, but it's not every day of the year we are able to celebrate with Father Abe.' Crossing to the sideboard, he lifted the big silver dome of the meat dish and there was the piece of corned beef, fresh from its tin.

'Another of your little jokes, Fr Duddleswell?' the Bishop snapped.

'I am sure I beg your pardon, me Lord.'

The Bishop stood aside to show the disgraceful thing he had unveiled. Fr Duddleswell turned the colour of the Bishop's buttons.

'Pontius, Father,' I said by way of explanation.

'Not the damn dog,' the Bishop exploded, 'that nearly chewed me up when I blessed your bell!'

'I will chuck a dozen Dog-Bombs at that one,' Fr Duddleswell said grimly.

Fortunately, Father Abe was there to take charge. 'Holy God, boys, a donkey could carry the sense of both of yous easily. Go on like this and you'll end up as bed-fellows to Oliver Cromwell.'

Realizing it did not accord with a bishop's dignity to carve corned beef I volunteered for the job. It amused me meanwhile to hear Father Abe berating his former curates who, it struck me, were vying madly for the old priest's affections.

'In ancient days,' Father Abe sermonized, 'the chalices

23

were of wood and the men of gold. Now it's golden chalices and wooden men. As St Augustine or Savanarola said.'

First Fr Duddleswell apologized, then the Bishop. After that, it was a quiet meal of corned beef and Yorkshire pud with Father Abe directing the conversation into the safe channels of nostalgia.

'How is Canon Reardon, Sponger?'

'He passed on twelve months ago.'

' "Fronty" Reardon passed on, never! He must have gone terrible sudden.'

'He *was* eighty-nine,' the Bishop reminded him.

Father Abe looked at the Bishop and nodded. 'But I only saw him four or five years ago and there was nothing the matter with him then.'

'The years do age a man,' the Bishop reflected wisely.

By the end of the evening, I was convinced that Father Abe was a nice old boy, a trifle strange perhaps, but quite unlike the legends and tall stories his curates had weaved around him.

That is why I broke my sacred rule: I did not prepare myself for the worst. I had only myself to blame.

TWO
High Jinks at St Jude's

The next day was Maundy Thursday. Fr Duddleswell celebrated the late Mass and, during it, showed signs of acute
distress.

Twelve Chelsea Pensioners, imported for the occasion,
were seated in the sanctuary dressed, in their magnificent
ceremonial red uniforms. Their shoes and socks were off
and Fr Duddleswell's role, as Christ's representative, was
to wash their feet in memory of our Lord who washed His
disciples' feet at the Last Supper.

He worked his way along the line on his knees, washing
the feet, drying them, kissing them and handing each old
soldier a half-crown, the Maundy money.

Afterwards, he was unable to get up. He looked up at
me, pain wrinkling his eyes. 'I am hunkered by the lumbago, lad.'

I hoisted him to his feet and did my best to straighten
him out. He managed to finish Mass but I had to do the
heavy work for him.

'What're we going to do now?' I asked him at breakfast.
The next three days were the heaviest in the priest's calen-
dar, what with Good Friday, the Easter Vigil and Easter
Sunday to come.

'I can stay on the vertical for a few more days, Father
Neil.'

Mrs Pring told him that was a ridiculous idea. He had to
go to bed at once and stay there.

'Quiet, woman,' he growled, 'you are as talkative as an
altar boy.'

'And you,' she retorted, 'are more up the pole than Simon Stylites.'

'Father Abe will lend a hand,' I said.

'Jasus,' Fr Duddleswell exclaimed in pain and apprehension, 'Father Abe is too old and batty to bless a rosary.'

'He seems sound enough to me.'

Fr Duddleswell hissed through clenched teeth, 'You are wrong, Father Neil. He was not to be trusted twenty years since and now he is way beyond the use of reason.' He stopped speaking to ward off an attack in his lumbar regions.

'What about the wisdom of age?' I said, teasing him.

'Ah, core of me heart,' he said, the sap in him rising, 'me babe of grace, me big lump of a curate. Father Abe has bushels of wisdom but not one bloody grain of common sense to go with it.'

'I'll keep an eye on him,' I promised.

'If you had sixteen you'd never see that one, not if he gets it in his head that this parish is a dead leg of a place that needs livening up.' He sucked in his breath painfully. 'Above all, keep him away from the drink. That rum the Bishop brought, I hid it in the sacristy safe. If he swallows that, 'twill really put his head off its hinge.'

'Trust me,' I said, and saw the look of despair my remark occasioned.

Mrs Pring, having packed him off to bed, called Dr Daley. I waited until the doctor had completed whatever examination his prudish patient permitted before joining them in Fr Duddleswell's bedroom.

'What's the verdict?' I asked.

Dr Daley flicked an imaginary fly off his bald head. 'Himself won't be exactly lepping and skipping about for a while. It's lumbago, all right.'

'Caused by?' Fr Duddleswell wanted to know, trying without success to raise himself on the pillow.

'Who can say, Charles? Strain, sitting in a draught, rank decrepitude. A complex thing, the back. Muscles, discs, ligaments, spinal vertebrae, the lot.'

'And the cure, Donal? A quick one. I am not wanting to

start the long holiday of age so soon.'

'Rest in bed with plenty of exercise,' the doctor said, smiling. 'Not at the same time, of course.'

'Isn't that typical,' Fr Duddleswell groaned. 'I remember when last I complained of insomnia and you told me not to lose any sleep over it.'

'Keep yourself warm, Charles. If you cannot afford a lovely young woman like King David in his old age, a hot water bottle will do the trick.'

'Mrs Pring has given me three already.'

Dr Daley let out his breath as if the information had set his mind at rest. 'I didn't think you were sleeping alone, Charles.'

'Donal!'

'Sometimes a hard mattress helps or a piece of wood under a soft one. If you use a cross be sure not to nail yourself to it.'

'What about a door?' I said, trying to be helpful.

'Good idea,' the doctor responded. 'Not the church door, mind. That's too big and the ironwork would leave an elaborate tattoo on his Reverence's backside.'

'Will you be serious,' Fr Duddleswell insisted. 'I have to be up tomorrow to mind me parish.'

'Don't lift heavy objects, Charles, like the Sunday collection or Mrs Pring's plum pudding. Let the curate do all the heavy.'

'As usual,' I sighed.

'Above all, don't get excited when, as now, I take out my bottle of cod-liver oil and malt.'

The Doctor lifted his equipment out of his black bag, filled his glass and toasted the patient. 'The face of the good to you, Charles, and the back of the bad to you.'

'Amen to that,' Fr Duddleswell said glumly, holding himself where it hurt.

'Will you come into my study, Doctor?'

Father Abe waylaid Dr Daley and myself at the bottom of the stairs. I noted the ominous reference to Fr Duddleswell's study as his own.

We followed him in. 'Sit beside me so,' Father Abe said, and we sat by the fire which Mrs Pring had lighted to keep at bay the damp and chills of March.

'Little Charlie has told me all about you, Doctor.'

'Nice things, I hope, Father.'

'He didn't intend them to be but they were.'

'You mean,' the doctor said, summing up the situation rapidly, 'you would like a dose of the bromide.'

'I would. Little Charlie wouldn't give me any.'

'You'd as soon get wool from a goat.'

'Without it, the heart has gone out of my old feet altogether.'

'Why not?' the doctor said, going for the bottle. 'Wasn't it St Pat himself who first brought the whiskey to us.'

'The best medicine in a damp house, Doctor.'

'Our only guide, comforter and friend,' Dr Daley replied. 'Apart from the Holy Ghost, of course.'

As the drink tinkled into the glass, the old priest, with almost savage eyes, prayed heartily, 'Welcome God's aid. Isn't she the darlingest thing?'

Dr Daley prepared to toss it back. 'To all the wasted years.'

'Wait, now, Doctor,' and Father Abe held his glass at arm's length. 'May you have the health of a salmon, a woman to your taste, land without rent, a mouth ever wet and may you die in Ireland.'

They downed their drinks and smacked their lips in chorus. After which, Father Abe glanced at me a trifle guiltily. 'I'm only seeing the world the way the Apostle Paul used to see it, laddy.'

'How was that, Father?'

'Through a glass darkly.'

It came to me in a flash that while neither Dr Daley nor Father Abe were heavy drinkers they were always fishing for a drink. Why was this? It could only be because something about Fr Duddleswell made them want to pull his leg. The show went on even in his absence.

'One sip of this,' Dr Daley said, indicating the bottle, 'and a sparrow would spit in an eagle's eye.'

'I knew as soon as I saw you,' Father Abe said, holding out an empty glass, 'that I could safely drink with you in the dark.'

The doorbell rang and, to escape, I answered it myself. It was Billy Buzzle accompanied by Pontius. The bookie was dressed in his usual stripes, his zebra-suit, as Fr Duddleswell called it.

'Hello, Father,' Billy said breezily. 'Mrs Pring rang to say your Boss-man wanted a word with me.'

'Very likely,' I said, remembering the Bishop's visit, and led him upstairs.

'What's the smell in this house?' Billy asked, sniffing as he entered the sick-room.

'A visitor's cigar,' I said.

'Higher than pig-pong, that is,' Billy remarked.

Fr Duddleswell, overhearing, joined in. 'Higher than the convent wall, if you ask me.'

'Hello, Father O'Duddleswell. I didn't realize you were down on your luck. I'll get Pontius to lick your paw for you.'

Fr Duddleswell indicated his refusal.

Billy said, 'I can't understand why you're agin dogs, Father.' Nor could he. The notice he had recently fixed to his fence facing in our direction expressed his thoughts on Fr Duddleswell as an animal lover. It said: 'Don't bite the dog.'

'Oh, you can't,' Fr Duddleswell said wryly.

'Nope. When I was a nipper at Sunday School, they told us the story of that dog in the Garden of Eden.'

'The Book of Genesis speaks of no blessed dog in the Garden of Eden.'

'There was one,' Billy insisted, 'a black labrador. Just like my Pontius, here. When Adam and Eve ate the apple, our teacher said, God was so angry He yelled, That's the end of this nudist colony, and He made a ruddy great crack in the ground.'

'Ridiculous,' Fr Duddleswell snorted.

'Straight up. There was Adam and Eve on one side and all the animals on the other. The crack got bigger and bigger till this lovely dog couldn't stand it no longer. He bounded across the gap to be with his friends. And he's been loyal ever since.'

'That's a very nice story, Mr Buzzle.' I patted Pontius affectionately on the head, quickly withdrawing my hand when he snapped at it. It was my fault. I took him by surprise.

'Listen here,' an unimpressed Fr Duddleswell said, 'that pestilential dog –'

'That *what*? He's a rare Christian of a dog is my Pontius. He never bears grudges, did you know that? Not even when I accidentally tread on his foot.'

'That pestilential dog stole our joint last night.' Fr Duddleswell went on to explain the circumstances in some detail.

'Well,' Billy said, 'without admitting liability, I'll get you another leg of beef any time.'

'Forget it,' the invalid said. 'I have a favour to ask of you.'

The favour was this. Whenever Father Abe placed a bet with Billy, as he was bound to do, Billy was only to pretend to accept it. The old man had no clue about horses or greyhounds and it was sinful to take his money.

'What if he wins?' Billy asked.

'If he wins, I will pay up, Mr Buzzle. If he loses, you just hand over his money to me on the quiet.'

'You trying to muscle in on my trade?' Billy said laughingly. 'Okay, mate. For old time's sake.'

'What was that all about, Father?' I asked when Billy had left.

Fr Duddleswell spoke hesitantly. 'Father · Abe has always had a little, um, problem, lad.'

'Gambling?'

'He would bet on the tears falling down your cheek. I tell you, of late, ever since his mind started wavering, he has been accepting hundreds of Mass stipends.'

'And not saying the Masses, you mean?'

'That is so. Imagine, Father Neil, all those souls still suffering in Purgatory because dotty Father Abe, with no intention of offering the holy sacrifice, has squandered the money gambling.'

'O my God,' I exclaimed.

'Father Neil, you haven't – '

I had to admit that only that morning I had given Father Abe ten pounds out of the Holy Souls' box for forty Requiems.

'Never mind, lad,' he said kindly. 'It will all come back to me via Billy Buzzle.'

In fact, five pounds of it came back before the afternoon was out. I prayed the rest would return soon. Otherwise, I'd have twenty extra Requiem Masses to say without recompense.

That evening, I was hearing confessions. A large crowd of people was waiting to make their confession in preparation for their Easter Communion.

After an hour, there was a rap on my door. It was Father Abe.

'I've come to help you out, laddy.'

'No need, Father,' I implored. 'No need.'

'No trouble at all.' He stubbed out his cigar on the glass of my confessional and raised his voice to the penitents. 'Sinners,' he said, 'Fr Duddleswell has taken to his bed. I am hearing in his place.'

There was a stampede from my confessional to his. No doubt, the people hoped he was too old and deaf to hear a word they said.

All the same, there was quite a backlog of penitents waiting. Then, after another hour, I heard Father Abe piping up again:

'As you see, my dear people, there is still a black crowd of you waiting to be shrived.'

'Who the dickens does he think he is?' I groaned inwardly.

'There is but one solution,' he went on. 'Father Boyd and I will hear those with mortal sins tonight. Those with only venial sins on their soul can safely come back tomorrow.'

By the time I had given absolution to my penitent and broken out of my box there was no one left in church except Lord Mitchin.

'That one must be a desperate sinner,' Father Abe whispered aloud to me.

'He is as deaf as a post,' I shouted back angrily.

'I heard that,' Lord Mitchin said, having that very moment turned on his hearing aid.

It was impossible to harbour a grudge against Father Abe for long.

Later that evening, we were sitting by the fireside in Fr Duddleswell's study sipping cocoa. Father Abe said:

'It's a disgusting thing, laddy, but d'you know, I'm as fond of comfort as a cat.' He knocked cigar ash on to the coals. 'Old men's passions light few fires and that's a fact.'

'You've done your share of labouring in the vineyard, Father.'

'I reckon I have. Even so, now that my tune is nearly played, what am I wanting from life? A soft bed, a hard drink, baccy and a chance to air my backside at the fire.'

Sleepily, I said, 'You've enjoyed your years as a priest?'

'Indeed, laddy, and so will you. As a priest, I give you a for instance, as a priest you say a thing without thinking it and the words get lodged like bullets in someone's brain. And that someone, perhaps a little boy of seven summers, will carry those words with him to the grave. When he's an old man, he'll say, "Father Boyd, now, he was that grand priest at St Jude's when I was a lad, well, Father Boyd said – " and Father Boyd will be quoted as solemnly and accurately as if he were the prophet Isaiah foretelling the destruction of Jerusalem. And all Father Boyd actually said was, "Telling lies is very wrong," For that little lad grown into a toothless old man, Father Boyd is the teacher of eternal verities.'

I smiled self-importantly. Father Abe had once again ceased to be a legend and become a harmless old Irish storyteller sitting by the fire.

'You're very like little Charlie,' he said, 'not now that

the years have thickened him but when he first came to me.'

That surprised me. I wasn't sure whether it was wise to pursue the matter but I found myself asking, 'In what way?'

'You pray hard. Your kindness isn't showy but it's sure. And as yet you are innocent enough.'

'Thank you,' I said.

'You wouldn't happen to know,' he put in briskly, 'where little Charlie hid my bottle of rum.'

'I can't tell you, I'm afraid, Father.'

'The little feller likes you,' Father Abe said in a forgiving tone. 'I do believe he wouldn't give you up for the unification of Ireland.'

I reddened at the flattery. 'That's going a bit far, Father.'

'You're sure about that rum?' I shook my head. He continued, 'I felt the same ridiculous way about him, that's how I know.'

'But I'm *really* English,' I said, 'not stage-English.'

'Miracles happen, laddy. We Irish are curious forgiving folk. But, be God,' he came over confidential, 'a word of advice to you. Don't let little Charlie knock the hop out of you. If he fires a salvo at you, fire back at him.' He beckoned with his cigar. 'Come with me and I'll show you.'

He led me upstairs to Fr Duddleswell's bedroom.

'How're you feeling, little Charlie, are you ready for your wreath yet?'

'Almost.'

'That housekeeper of yours shelters you better than the rich man's cow.'

'You think so,' Fr Duddleswell said grumpily, laying his breviary aside.

'I do. Anyway, I've only come to ask if I can have my share of the Easter offering.'

'You cannot,' came the heated reply. 'You are a visitor here. Father Neil and I have laboured all the year for that.'

'Little Charlie, didn't I anoint you twice in the old days when your horse threw you?'

'No, Father Abe. And that is me final word.'

'Oh, I'll fell you like a Kerry ox, so I will.'

'Enough!'

'You are not worth a plate of frosted potatoes. You're wicked enough to end up in the Hot Place.'

'See you there.' Fr Duddleswell picked up his breviary again. 'Now will you get away out of here so I can bloody well suffer in silence with our Blessed Lord?'

On Good Friday, Fr Duddleswell stayed in bed. Father Abe offered to assist me at the afternoon service.

During the reading of the Passion according to St John, I twice had to send a server across to him. I didn't mind him sleeping but his snores were disturbing the congregation.

He helped me distribute Holy Communion but even this simple operation had its surprises. As was the custom, parents approached the altar rails in company with their small children. I saw Father Abe give the Sacred Host to three children in arms before their mothers and fathers could protest. Afterwards, I didn't dare ask how many children under five had made their first Communion that afternoon.

Fr Duddleswell swore that he would preach at the Easter Vigil next day even if he had to be wheeled in to the sanctuary in a barrow. It proved to be the only way to get him there.

From the bottom of the stairs I wheeled him through the hall, into the sacristy and then to the base of the sanctuary steps where a cushioned chair had been set aside for him.

'Dear God,' Father Abe whistled, 'you look like the Holy Father being carried into St Peter's on his *sedia gestatoria*.'

'More like a pig on the way to slaughter,' was Mrs Pring's comment.

Fr Duddleswell presided on his cushion throughout the long ceremony and preached, as promised, a sermon which ended like this:

'There was this feller, y'see, me dear people, kept getting a drop of water on his head. Wherever he went inside his house a constant drip-drip on his head.

'He sat in his kitchen: drip. He sat in his living-room: drip. He sat in the littlest room in the house: drip. When he went to bed: drip.

'It never happened to his wife or his ten kiddies, mind, only to himself. Whether it was raining cats and dogs outside or there were clear blue skies, always on his head and his alone: drip.

'This went on for so many years his head was like a pancake. Until a fairy woman told him why he was being victimized so. "Years ago," says she, "a little orphan came to your door asking for lodging. And did you show him any kindness at all? You did not. You pretended that with your own ten you had obligations enough."

'After listening shame-faced to the fairy woman, the man went in search of the orphan and brought him into his own house. And from that day to this, not a single drop of water has splattered on his head.

'Now, me dear people,' the preacher said, wrinkling his nose like a rhinoceros, 'we are in the holiest season of the year, Easter, and I am addressing you as the oldest orphan in the parish. So I tell you, if you want to avoid drips from above, show good will to me in the collection that is about to be taken. God bless you all for your generosity and a Happy Easter.'

He ended with a swift sign of the cross, after which he looked up, blinked and touched his eye as if a drop of water had fallen in it.

When the ceremony was over, I wheeled him back to his study where Mrs Pring served the three of us a snack.

'Well, Father Abe,' Fr Duddleswell said proudly, 'what did you think of me preaching?'

Father Abe shook his white head fondly. 'Little Charlie, little Charlie, who would've thought you remembered that begging sermon of mine after all these years. Now I'll let you in on a secret.'

'What is that, Father Abe?'

35

'I pinched that sermon myself from Father Tim McCoy.'

'You did?' Fr Duddleswell said, laughing. 'Who knows if one of these days Father Neil here will preach it himself in the presence of *his* curate.'

'Don't count on it,' I said.

Fr Duddleswell spent Easter Sunday in bed. He was reluctant to leave me in charge of the parish and Father Abe in charge of me. The pain in his back left him no alternative.

Father Abe gave little trouble at the two Masses he celebrated. First, he told the congregation that Fr Duddleswell was hunched up in bed like a cat and asked prayers for his recovery. Next, he preached a beautiful sermon on the Resurrection of Christ.

That would have been fine had he been content to leave matters there. But the date was March 25, the Feast of the Annunciation. He added a homily on the rosary which concluded with the words:

'When Jesus was a lad, my dear people, you mustn't think he wasted his days playing childish games. Indeed, not. He spent all his free hours in chapel on his knees before the Blessed Sacrament, saying His rosary.'

I had arranged two baptisms for that afternoon. Don and Jane Martin wanted me to christen their latest. They were naming him Neil in my honour since I had managed to be in on his birth and had comforted the mother. The other child to be baptized was Mary Jane, the daughter of the Martins' friends who came from Weymouth.

At the last moment, Father Abe pleaded with me to let him officiate.

'It may be my last chance, laddy,' he said.

I was disappointed not to christen my name-sake but how could I refuse the request? I explained the situation to the Martins and they agreed to let Father Abe have his way.

I watched him like a hawk throughout the ceremony. I told myself: 'I'm going to make damn sure he pours the water at the same time as he says the words.'

In this respect, Father Abe was faultless. Only, as he was baptizing baby Neil, he said, '*Maria Joanna, ego te baptizo . . .*' and the Martin boy was named Mary Jane. There was so much bawling at the time and Father Abe spoke the Latin words so fast no one seemed to notice. That's why I decided not to intervene. After all, I told myself, a mistake about gender hardly invalidates a couple of christenings.

At the reception afterwards, Jane Martin whispered to me:

'The boys think Father Cody is their great-grandfather.'

I knew that Francis and Danny, aged nearly four and nearly three, loved their Uncle Billy, as they called him, and were heartbroken at his death. They seemed to look on Father Abe as Uncle Billy come back again. He responded to them marvellously.

'Did you come down from a cloud?' Francis asked him.

'God love you, I did,' Father Abe said. 'I've spent most of my life, pet, up in a cloud.'

Francis gazed at the thick smoke from Father Abe's cigar. 'Do you make your own clouds, then?'

'All the time.'

Danny said, 'I've got a bad cough, Uncle Billy.' And he demonstrated for our benefit.

'You're a lucky feller,' Father Abe said chestily, 'I've only got a good cough.'

Francis pointed at his brother. 'Danny's got a rash all over him since you seen him last.'

'I wonder if he caught something,' Father Abe said.

'P'obably,' Danny speculated, 'I might have catched fire.'

Jane chipped in quietly to tell Father Abe, 'Danny's not really himself today.'

Francis overheard and said, with a worried expression on his face, 'But he looks like him, Mummy.'

Francis whispered loudly in Father Abe's ear. 'Uncle Billy, you know those railway lions we had for Christmas.'

'Of course, I do,' Father Abe replied.

'Well, Danny broked them. He shouldn't have done that, shouldn't he?'

Danny said, '*You* drawn all down Daddy's wall.'

'And up,' Francis said proudly.

'In we house,' Danny came back, 'Francis talks non-stoppily.'

Jane told Danny to eat his food like a good boy but he wouldn't.

'He can't be a General,' Francis said self-righteously, 'if he doesn't eat his sandwich, can he, Uncle Billy?'

'He'll eat it for me, won't you, Danny?' Father Abe said. At which the two boys had a race to see who could polish off his jam sandwich first.

After swallowing the last mouthful, Francis said, 'I ate it quicklier. I'm first. I'm first.'

Danny began to sob until Father Abe put in, 'Danny is the first to be second, aren't you, pet?'

Danny brightened up and took a bow.

'He's only little,' Francis said disparagingly.

'I'm growing up,' Danny insisted. 'I've got a big toe.'

When Father Abe saw him beginning to remove his shoe to exhibit it he assured him he had no doubts on that score. 'How old are you, Danny?' he asked.

'I'm nearly size three.'

'You are very big for size three.'

'Can I tell a story?' Danny said.

I left Father Abe in order to talk to the Martins and their friends. In half an hour the latter left and it was time for Neil to have a sleep. Father Abe was called on to bless the new Christian.

He took the child in his arms and held Neil's soft little hand in his. At that moment, a white butterfly appeared, where from I did not know, and settled on the pink, shell-like knuckles of Neil's hand.

'An angel dressed up,' Father Abe said, as the butterfly's wings came together like hands in prayer. 'God's grace on you, baby Neil, and may you never sin.'

Everyone, knowing the mischievousness of Francis and Danny, laughed politely. Don Martin nudged me.

'If he never sins, Father, he'll be a very special baby.'

'He does have the right name for it,' I whispered back.

'I'll pray for this child,' Father Abe promised, 'every day till I die.'

That evening, Father Abe blackmailed me again, this time into letting him officiate at Benediction.

'Who knows, laddy, this may be my last fling.'

After I had put the Sacred Host in the monstrance, Father Abe incensed it with a wild, shuddering swing. Afterwards, when I examined the thurible, the incense coals were not there. I was sure I had put them in before the ceremony began.

Father Abe was already giving out the rosary. 'The first glorious mystery, the Resurrection of our Lord Jesus Christ.'

The mystery didn't end. Hail Mary followed Hail Mary. Instead of ten, he must have got through twenty.

I tried to get his attention but failed. It was like flagging down a train.

Thirty Hail Marys. The congregation, including several nuns, which had been buzzing away steadily became more and more discordant.

I told an altar boy to put out a few candles, hoping this would make Father Abe realize that something was wrong.

He must have said about sixty Hail Marys when I called out, 'Glory be to the Father,' and brought to an end the longest rosary in the church's history.

Surely I wasn't the only one present who could smell burning. When I sneaked a look at the congregation I couldn't deny the fact that smoke was emerging from the folds of Mother Stephen's habit as she knelt, eyes-closed, in the front pew.

I rose and tiptoed up to her.

'Mother,' I said, touching the shoulder of this formidable being.

She awoke from her meditation with a start. 'Father?'

'I'm afraid, Mother,' I said, 'you're on fire.'

I led her into the sacristy where together we located the missing incense coals and extinguished them with holy water.

By this time, Father Abe had ascended the pulpit. Somehow he had acquired the envelopes in which the faithful had placed their Easter offering to the priests of the parish. Mercifully, I had removed the money but he had his own idea of what to do with the envelopes.

'The priests of St Jude's, my dear people, of which I am not one, would like to thank you heartily for your generous Easter offering.' And he proceeded to read out names and the sizes of contributions. This was 'cursing from the altar' with a vengeance.

'Mr and Mrs Brown and family, ten pounds – I beg their pardon, ten *shillings*. Mr Shillington, eight pounds.' Father Abe looked around him. 'Thank you, Mr Shillington, for your appreciation of what the clergy do for you, day and night, throughout the year.'

I knew for a fact there was no one called Shillington in the parish. Father Abe had made him up to shame any ungenerous contributors.

I signalled to Mrs Perkins, the organist, to strike up a hymn to drown him out and she obliged.

Afterwards, I took Father Abe to task. 'Have you never read about the widow's mite?' I asked.

'You must learn to take the world easy, laddy,' he said. 'I bet you there were lots of widow's mites in that Easter collection from folk who are not widows.'

He blew out the smoke from his cigar with the satisfaction of a man who felt his job was well done.

On Tuesday evening, I dropped in to church to say my rosary. Father Abe was there, hunched up in the front bench, lost in prayer. Or so I thought.

Were my eyes deceiving me or was he, like Mother Stephen before him, about to go up in flames. Then it dawned on me what was happening. He was diving like a duck from time to time into the depths of his confessional cloak, having a puff of his cigar, and coming up for air.

I prayed no parishioner would see him.

After a few minutes, he jumped up, genuflected piously and left. My watch showed it was opening time at 'The Pig and Whistle'.

In the last three days, Father Abe had cut quite a figure at the local. Fr Duddleswell was so worried he had made me draw up a rota of 'watchers' from the parish to keep an eye on him during opening hours.

One of the watchers was Tim Fogarty who had nine children, 'a quiverful of arrows', as Fr Duddleswell termed it. Tim had been at the Pig and Whistle the night before when Father Abe had tried his hand at darts. Tim must have stuck very close to his charge because he received a dart in his thigh.

I said to Tim, 'Could have been worse, I suppose.' Tim, a family man, thought hard before saying, 'I see what you mean, Father.' But I hadn't *meant* anything.

I didn't begrudge Father Abe his evenings' entertainment. In any case, he was so obviously a larger than life 'character', his escapades were easily forgiven by the locals.

I finished my rosary and walked towards the sacristy, intending to get the keys to lock up the church for the night. The sacristy door was barred from the inside. Father Abe must have pulled the bolt across before racing off to the pub.

I wasn't worried. I could still let myself out through the main door of the church, reaching the sacristy by way of the house. Except that the church door was also locked.

Dotty Father Abe must have taken it on himself to close the shop up so as not to scandalize any of the faithful who might otherwise see him at his devotions. He had used the rusty old iron key in the sacristy to lock the outer door and replaced it without me knowing.

I was in a real fix. Mrs Pring had taken the day off to visit her daughter. Fr Duddleswell was in bed with lumbago. No one, least of all Father Abe, would notice my absence. I might have to spend the night in church like one of the knights of old. I wasn't going to stand for it. I was famished and the church was chilly.

I banged furiously on the church door for five minutes without result. I contemplated throwing something through a window, a candlestick, perhaps. In the end, I settled for tolling the bell. I unhitched the rope and gave a huge pull, then another. As yet, no sign of assistance. I tolled the bell for another couple of minutes, ending with one mighty tug. In the instant, I found my arms being almost torn out of their sockets as I was catapulted into space.

It appeared that the bell's metal brake in the belfry had snapped. Fortunately, I had the presence of mind to let go the rope. If I hadn't, I would have soared thirty feet up the tower and smashed my skull either on the way up or the way down. As it was, I had a very painful fall from about twelve feet.

I landed on the small of my back and was stunned for several seconds. I was brought to my senses by the sound of people chattering, banging on the church door and ineffectually turning the handle.

I heard Billy Buzzle call out, 'Anybody home?'

I told him through the door what the problem was.

'No trouble, Father,' he said, 'the fire brigade's arrived.'

Fr Duddleswell told me subsequently that he was awakened from a drug-induced sleep by a steel-helmeted fireman who climbed through his window and demanded a key.

'Jasus, Father Neil, I thought I was finished and Michael the Archangel had come to take me home in the queerest of uniforms.'

When I related the full story he sent me off post-haste to the pub to fetch the old chap home.

In spite of the ache in my back, I raised a good speed on my bicycle. In the general panic, however, I had forgotten that my own brake blocks had worn thin and badly needed replacing. I reached the pub, only to find I couldn't pull up in time. My front wheel hit the kerb, buckled and over the top I went.

When I came to, a sympathetic crowd had gathered and Father Abe was standing over me, his right hand raised, bestowing on me absolution for my sins.

As the week went by, Fr Duddleswell made better progress than I did myself. Hot baths, he had discovered, were the best remedy for his complaint, and the sound of him singing Gilbert and Sullivan rang around the house.

'All will be well,' he chanted in the words of an English mystic, 'and all manner of things will be well.'

That was before Father Abe collapsed at the foot of the stairs. Fr Duddleswell helped me carry him to his bed and in the process suffered a recurrence of his lumbago.

Mrs Pring and I settled both invalids comfortably, then I telephoned the doctor.

I stayed while he examined Father Abe who was conscious but extremely pale. Dr Daley was clearly concerned at the state of his heart.

'How is it, Doc?' Father Abe managed to say.

'The drums are still beating loud enough.'

'I am tired,' Father Abe said, 'I am indeed. And a cold black wind blowing.'

We left him to sleep and dropped in on Fr Duddleswell. I, who had witnessed so many of his moods, had never seen him so emotionally disturbed.

'How is he, Donal? Has he a firm booking for the down train?'

Dr Daley shook his head non-committally. 'His ticker. But you knew that.'

'He's shamming like a fox, I shouldn't wonder.' Fr Duddleswell seemed almost angry that his beloved Father Abe was about to leave him. He made as if to get out of bed to go to him.

Mrs Pring prevented him. 'I told you to stay put, Father D.'

'Woman, your words go over me shoulder and down me back,' Fr Duddleswell retorted. But a further effort to move was unsuccessful. 'I'm cemented to me bed with this bloody lumbago. I will pray that he *lives*. Else I will never

43

pray again.' He looked upwards. 'D'you hear?'

I spent the next couple of days sitting at their bedsides by turns. Only once did I take a walk, drawn by the end of March sunshine.

After so many hours in the sickroom, I felt something of a convalescent myself. The world was wonderful again.

Everywhere, in window box and garden, there were signs of Spring. Yellow in the daffodils and in the forsythia bushes whose tops were already turning green. Sticky buds on the lilac trees, magnolias ready to burst into bloom. In the borders, primroses, and on the grass a few left-over snowdrops with masses of crocuses, blue, yellow and white.

It wasn't a sad time. Easter never was. Swallows zoomed at almost ground level, while on a telegraph pole a blackbird, lifting his yellow beak, blew beautiful bubbles of song. The penetrating scents of a new year filled the lungs: mown grass, turned-over turf, air you could really taste and smell.

Cherry blossom, fragile, pinky-white fluttered against the blue. As always at this season of the year, Housman's lines took over my mind:

> *Loveliest of trees, the cherry now*
> *Is hung with bloom along the bough,*
> *And stands about the woodland ride*
> *Wearing white for Eastertide.*

That evening, I heard Fr Duddleswell, half-asleep, praying, 'Lord, not my will be done necessarily, but something very like it.'

I smiled to myself.

Father Abe was in a kind of coma. He kept repeating what sounded like a riddle. 'God is a circle,' he whispered, 'whose centre is everywhere and whose circumference is nowhere.' Much later, I discovered he was quoting St Augustine.

Also: 'In life is marvellous homeliness, and in love is gentle courtesy, and in light is endless kindhood.' I heard him speak those words a hundred times. By all accounts, they would stand as a summary of his own priestly career.

Once Father Abe came to. He opened his eyes and in the light of a candle saw me sitting there, reciting my office. I don't know how long he had been awake before I noticed him.

He said, 'He likes you, laddy,' and I said, 'Thank you, Father,' and he said, 'Life is so gorgeous, the mystery is we are not always deliriously happy.'

These words fell on me like a heap of stones. Was he convinced that he had only five minutes left? I was tremendously glad I had allowed him a last sermon, a last christening, a last chance to lead the rosary, a last benediction. He had been over sixty years a priest. And because of me, he had had his 'last fling' before ascending to Heaven in a cloud.

Fr Duddleswell struggled out of bed and, on Dr Daley's advice, prepared to anoint him.

'What's this for, little Charlie?'

'Just in case, Father Abe.'

'You've said *Per istam sanctam unctionem* over me four times already, remember? This anointing is becoming a nasty habit.'

''Tis best to be safe, Father Abe.'

'I'm too damn lazy to die, you know that, little Charlie. I can't seem to put my mind to it.'

When it came to hearing Father Abe's confession, Fr Duddleswell nodded to me before hobbling out of the room. They were too close. It was not for him to hear the old man tell his sins.

So I put on a purple stole and listened to Father Abe's general confession. It took in his long life's span. When it was over, I gave him absolution and kissed the top of his head as I would kiss a child.

'I've eked myself out well enough, laddy,' he whispered. 'Now the hill is against me and I'll likely not make it to the top this time.'

'You will,' I said, 'if you hold on to the donkey's tail.'

'Send him in, then, laddy.'

Fr Duddleswell returned to complete the anointing and

45

give the papal blessing. Afterwards, Father Abe, happy, said:

'I am going off with myself, alone. We priests are used to that. But priests, I never knew this till now, die easiest of all.' He cleared his throat. 'When I took my vows as a young lad like Neil here, I never thought I was making an easy death for myself. Indeed, I did not. Strange it being easy, seeing I've always hated the frost.'

'Forgive me,' Fr Duddleswell said.

'What is there to forgive, little Charlie?'

'I asked the Bishop to come and see you.'

Father Abe managed a smile. 'That is the sin against the Holy Ghost, all right.'

The Bishop visited us that same afternoon. Fr Duddleswell had gone back to bed and I was answering a telephone call at the time. When Mrs Pring opened the front door to the Bishop, I signalled to him from Fr Duddleswell's study to go up on his own.

A few seconds later, I heard a tremendous crash upstairs and a cry of pain. The Bishop had opened the wrong door and Fr Duddleswell, next to it putting on his dressing gown, had been caught off balance and knocked flat. I quickly finished the phone call and rushed up to restore order.

When the Bishop emerged from Father Abe's room he was upset and dabbing his eyes. 'I'll say Mass for him tomorrow,' he said. 'Apologize to Fr Duddleswell on my behalf.'

'I will, my Lord.'

'It's about time, all the same, that someone other than myself suffered on my visits to St Jude's. If Fr Duddleswell proves too much for you, Father Neil, let me know and I'll see you are moved somewhere safer.'

'Thank you, my Lord.' I knew I would never volunteer to move from St Jude's.

When I next saw Father Abe he was in a deep sleep. Under his bed was the small sack he had brought with him. What made me think I had a right to look inside it? I don't know, there was no excuse. I untied the rope round the neck of the sack. It contained nothing but earth and a piece of paper on which was scrawled: 'Over me the soil of my Isle shall be cast.'

He carried with him everywhere the earth of his native land to cover his bones until Resurrection day. Right, I thought, if Father Abe's got to die somewhere, he's come to the right place.

Don Martin popped over to see me. He had heard of Father Abe's illness and pressed a pound on me to say Mass for his recovery.

'Insurance, Father,' he said. 'He promised to pray for our Neil every day of his life, so we don't want him pegging out too soon.'

Fr Duddleswell and I were in Father Abe's room quietly saying the evening rosary when the old priest joined in. '*Adsum,*' he said, like a child answering the roll call in school, when we noticed him. He seemed to be rallying. Dr Daley confirmed that he might not be stretched this time, after all.

Twenty-four hours later, Father Abe was fumigating his room with cigar smoke and claiming to be as strong as Oscar.

'A close-run thing,' he piped. 'I only beat death to the tape by an inch or two.'

'You did,' Fr Duddleswell said.

'Now fetch me a glass of rum, little Charlie, before I anoint each of your eyes with a hammer.'

Father Abe used me as his messenger to get Billy Buzzle. After his visit, Billy, wreathed in smiles, handed me a £5 note.

'That old bloke's all right,' Billy said. 'Give this flimsy to your Boss-man. Father Abe wanted me to put it on a gee-gee for him.'

When Fr Duddleswell saw the fiver, he snorted, 'That is the proof that Father Abe is on the mend and that everything else around here is about to be broken.'

'What damage,' I asked, 'can an old priest soon for the graveyard do?'

Billy Buzzle answered my question. He came in at

47

tea-time and demanded to see Fr Duddleswell. I went up with him to Fr Duddleswell's room, on tiptoe.

'Well, Mr Buzzle?'

Billy put his finger to his lips. 'Bad news, I'm afraid. Your little old priest's horse came up in the 3.30.'

'Jasus,' Fr Duddleswell whistled. 'Five quid but at what odds?'

Billy hesitated. 'Um, fifty to one.'

I saw the door handle turning noiselessly and Father Abe, in his dressing gown and belching forth smoke, stepped into the room. 'It seems, little Charlie, that you owe me £250.'

Fr Duddleswell put his arm over his eyes and turned his face to the wall.

THREE
The Deadly Rivals

'There she was flat in her coffin, Father Boyd, and what do you think she had on?'

I wasn't expecting to share in the secrets of the undertaker's trade. 'What, Mr Williams?' I gulped.

Freddie Williams, Director of the Co-op's Funeral Service, straightened out his long, sad face. He looked across to ensure that none of the mourners in the parlour after the funeral were in earshot before whispering, 'A tattoo.'

'A tattoo?' I questioned hoarsely, hoping for enlightenment.

'If her old man could have stripped *that* off I believe he would.'

'Do you mean to say – ?' I began knowingly, breaking off as if I had grasped, as any old campaigner would, exactly what he was getting at.

'Mean what, Father?'

No help there. 'Do you mean,' I repeated, taking the plunge, 'that I have just buried Mrs Robins in nothing but a tattoo?'

Mr Williams nodded solemnly. 'Naked came she into the world and naked, but for a little extra colouring, went she out of it again.' For my benefit: The 'Book of Job'.

'Why?' I spat the word out as if there was no fathoming the depths of modern depravity.

'He sold the lot, Father. *Everything.*' He swivelled his head back and forth in incredulity. 'Now, rings, expensive jewellery, a watch – that I can understand. But to remove every stitch of his wife's clothing, can you imagine?'

'This tattoo,' I said, foolishly thinking this might change the subject. 'Was it – ?' I was going to say 'professionally done'.

'I can't tell you about that, Father,' he broke in, 'either where it was or what it represented.' He made it sound as if I was prying. 'Undertaker's etiquette, you know. All I can repeat is that when I arrived in that bedroom up there –'

'To box her up?'

Mr Williams nodded. 'I said to Mr Robins, "Sir, couldn't we have a sheet for decency's sake?" He said to me, "She never minded." That was all. "She never minded." '

'Not very nice,' I said, sympathizing.

Mr Williams graciously turned down an offer of cucumber sandwiches for both of us, waited till the server was out of hearing and confided, 'It didn't occur to him *I* might be particular.' He made a face. 'He could at least have turned her on her tummy.'

Having exhausted my stock of disgusted grunts and raised eyebrows, I said, 'What difference would that make?'

'Don't you know?' he said.

'Of course,' I said, to stop him bothering. 'What did you do, Mr Williams?'

'I folded her arms. That helped a bit. Added a few forget-me-nots where it mattered. Then I got the lid on quick.'

A priest has a lot to do with dying and death. Also, therefore, with undertakers. And after the unforgettable day on which Freddie Williams joined Fr Duddleswell and me for a burial at sea he seemed to take an interest in me. It showed itself in the small confidences he shared with me when, according to local custom, we were invited together to 'partake' in the parlours of the bereaved.

'It's a raw time for the relatives, Father Boyd,' he said to me at one such gathering, sipping his tea.

I acknowledged the obvious, a bit put out that this amiable pessimist had collared me again.

'You have to be so tactful, you know. It's not easy being an undertaker when you can't even mention the word.'

' "Undertaker?" ' I said.

He shook his head. 'No, no, no.'

' "Death", Mr Williams?'

He shushed me as if I had just uttered an obscenity.

'It's part of my vocation,' he went on, when he had recovered his composure, 'to try to accede to the wishes and fancies of the bereaved.' He eyed me gloomily. 'You'd never believe what some people put in the coffins of their dear departed.'

I was learning not to hazard guesses in delicate personal matters.

Casting the occasional furtive glance over his shoulder, he itemised the luggage of corpses he had known.

'Bottles of whiskey, love letters, stuffed parrots, Bibles, garters.' He broke off momentarily. 'I've had most things in my career. Stamp collections,' he whispered on, 'a stapler, four-leafed clover, a tea pot, a fire extinguisher, a jar of pickled onions.'

That I couldn't resist. 'What for?'

'I didn't think it was my business to ask, Father.' Once more I felt properly put in my place. 'Naturally,' he added, 'I made quite sure the jar lid was screwed on tight.'

I put on an expression which said that I, for one, never doubted his professional competence.

'Death does funny things to people, Father Boyd.'

The speaker, on this occasion, was Mr Bottesford, owner of a private funeral parlour. Locally, he and Freddie Williams, of the Fairwater Co-op, were known as 'The Deadly Rivals'.

I was trying, as it happened, to find an excuse to get out of Bottesford's clutches in order to minister to the relatives. After all, I reflected, I don't want to spend every funeral talking to undertakers.

'Death does funny things to people,' he repeated.

I only half heard him. 'Apart from killing them, Mr Bottesford?'

'I mean it does some odd things to those who remain behind. Only the other day, a chap comes to my place and says, "I'd like my wife to be buried in her wedding dress." '

'Very touching, Mr Bottesford.'

'That's what I thought till we tried getting it on her. She had put on a hundred pounds or so since her wedding.'

I was quite interested by now. 'What did you do?'

'I asked the husband to get a tailor to pop round, take her measurements and alter the dress accordingly.'

'So that worked out all right, then.'

'No it didn't, Father. The husband must've forgot or was too embarrassed to mention that his wife had passed away. When the poor tailor saw her, he fainted, cracked his head on the coffin and was in hospital for ten days.'

I was spared comment as the undertaker took time off to hand a passing mourner one of his business cards. It said on it: 'Go to the Lord With Bottesford.'

'Advertising here?' I said, somewhat shaken.

'If not here, where?' he answered. 'This is the only place where people take death seriously. Besides,' he eyed me wickedly, 'there's an awful lot of humbug at funerals.'

'What do you mean?'

'Death isn't always as black as it's painted. There's as much rejoicing at many a funeral as there is at some weddings.' Before I could give him a piece of my mind, he added, 'One man's death is another man's inheritance.'

He reached out a long black arm and grabbed a *vol au vent*.

'People have no idea, Father Boyd, what skill we undertakers bring to our job.'

'I'm sure that's true,' I said. 'You're thinking of big, heavy people, I presume.'

'Even little 'uns,' he said, munching away, 'if they're the wrong shape.'

I realized it's not possible for undertakers to take every death personally but was it really necessary for Bottesford to wolf every edible in sight?

I asked him to explain this thing about shape.

52

'Well, there was the case I had last year of a bloke who was electrocuted in his tin bath.'

'Poor chap,' I murmured instinctively.

'The charlady found him six hours too late. *Rigor mortis*, to use the term favoured by the trade, had set in.'

'He'd gone stiff,' I said, horrified.

'Dead people do, you know.'

'I know,' I said.

'It's much worse than arthritis. They sort of *set*, like cement. Anyway, this bloke was a big 'un, all right, and he was completely wedged in his tub. He died with his bath on, so to speak.'

'How did you get him out?'

'I wanted to put a lid on him just as he was,' Bottesford said cheerily, 'but that wouldn't have been decent. No, we cut him out with a blow-lamp. That's when our troubles really began.'

Bottesford paused to pounce on a chicken drumstick.

'This part of the job, you see, Father Boyd, would've been bloody even if the corpse were a tiddler which he weren't.' He emptied his mouth to make his point more forcefully. 'How to get the perisher to lie down, that was the poser. When his legs were down his head was up. When we laid him on his back his legs shot in the air.'

'Rather like putting a non-folding chair in a box.'

'You've got the picture, Father. That's where the tricks of the trade come in, don't they?'

I realized the scoundrel was intending to leave me guessing. 'How did you flatten him out?' I demanded to know.

He smiled enigmatically above his chomping jaws.

'Did you use rubbing-oil? A crowbar? Blow-lamp?'

He wasn't telling.

'People who die of a heart attack sitting on the lav,' he continued, 'can be just as bloody.'

'Your life isn't easy, Mr Bottesford.' It occurred to me that, in his funereal company, neither was mine.

'Deadly,' he responded heatedly, 'and getting worse every year.'

53

'How's that?'

'It's these big apartment blocks they're putting up all over the place, Father. Ten floors sometimes, lifts that don't work, narrow winding staircases.'

'I never thought of that,' I admitted.

'Neither do the ruddy architects. They have no consideration for us undertakers when they design those places. They never think that the people who live in them will one day die in them and some poor blighters'll have to cart them out.'

'A helicopter might help,' I said.

'The other day, I took my team up 220 steps to pick up this body who weighed 250 pounds. That was without his box. I tell you, Father, he had no right to drop dead all that way up.'

'How did you manage, Mr Bottesford?'

'Felt like chopping him up in little bits, I don't deny, or lowering him out of the window. Took us twenty minutes to get him down to ground level.'

'You should have hired furniture removal men.'

Bottesford nodded his ginger-wigged head to acknowledge the pleasantry. 'To make matters worse, one of my blokes slipped a disc on the sixth floor and I had to lend a hand myself. Well, I'm a bit out of practice and on the last stretch, we lost our grip and the corpse got down before we did.'

I laughed.

'It wasn't funny, Father,' Bottesford said sternly. 'The lid was wrenched off and there was this big stiff lying spreadeagled on the pavement.'

'Oh.'

'Of course, the busybodies in the buildings got on the blower to the emergency services. Next thing I know, two police cars are screaming up. They took some convincing we weren't trying to cover up a murder and then, when we weren't looking, an ambulance took the body away. Took me two hours to find where it'd gone.'

With an effort I controlled myself. 'Dreadful. And I suppose, Mr Bottesford, your firm got the blame.'

He heaved a deep, wounded sigh. 'We've had no custom from that block since. And yet I guarantee you, Father Boyd, no one gives a better service in these parts than Bottesford's.'

'That is the key to it, Father Neil. Bottesford and Freddie Williams are touting for trade.'

This was Fr Duddleswell's interpretation of why the Deadly Rivals kept buttonholing me at funeral receptions. It was reinforced at a Bottesford funeral.

I was assisting Fr Duddleswell at the Requiem of an old parishioner, Jesse Tobin. Fortunately, there weren't many mourners present as Fr Duddleswell, at the head of the coffin, began reading the Epistle in English:

'Brethren, Behold I tell you a mystery: we shall indeed rise again.'

From within the coffin, right on cue, came the sound of an alarm clock. If dear old Jesse had blown a trumpet in there she couldn't have frightened us more.

In the sacristy Fr Duddleswell explained the happening. ''Tis not supernatural at all but Bottesford's doing. He wants to convince us that he is no longer robbing the departed.'

Apparently, Jesse had asked to be buried with one or two keepsakes. Bottesford had included her old alarm clock and set it to go off during the Requiem.

Fr Duddleswell said to me, 'I prefer the service given by Freddie Williams.'

I reminded him of the disastrous day of the burial at sea when Freddie had forgotten to weight the body down.

'Freddie is generally reliable,' he insisted. 'He tries to give the dead their moneysworth.'

I agreed with him. 'He does seem proud of his profession. In a melancholy sort of way.'

'Proud, indeed,' Fr Duddleswell said. 'At the Resurrection on the last day, Freddie will complain bitterly to the Almighty for undoing his life's work.'

I didn't really think there was a great deal to choose between the Deadly Rivals. One burial looked very much like another to me. But wanting to be fair, I decided to keep my eyes skinned to see which of them gave the better service. That way, I would perhaps be better able to whisper a word of advice in the ear of the bereaved and save them a bob or two.

'Meself,' Fr Duddleswell said cheerfully, 'I look forward to me death.'

Dr Daley, who had joined us in Fr Duddleswell's study after Jesse's funeral, looked at him, pop-eyed in disbelief. 'Why so, Charles?'

'Because, Donal, 'tis so much better than looking back on it.'

Dr Daley chuckled. 'Ah, death's not so bad. After all, the best people are dead. Jesus, for instance. And Saints Patrick, Columba and Bridget.'

'There is too much grizzle and grief around, Donal, and not enough of it expressed in a cheerful way to get it out of the system.'

'Wasn't that the reason for the wakes,' Dr Daley asked, twirling his half-empty glass.

'Oh 'twas, Donal. There was plenty of keening and singing and playing of the fiddle in the old days.'

'Also, Charles, don't forget the piles of snuff and tobacco for the white clay pipes and' – he drained his glass – 'a plentiful supply of the fire water.'

Fr Duddleswell stretched out his hand with the bottle in it. 'Go on, Donal,' he groaned, 'twist me arm much more and you will break the spring.'

'There was a keg of whiskey we had at one wake,' the doctor went on, 'which we were obliged to keep well away from the corpse.'

'Why was that?' I asked.

'Ah, Father Neil, a drop of that keg was used to moisten the lips of a dead man before.'

'And?'

'Didn't the corpse give such a kick that his shroud went from him up in the air like the white cloud at our Lord's Ascension?'

56

The three of us laughed and Fr Duddleswell slapped my knee with delight.

The doctor broke off to say, 'The whiskey gave rise to panegyrics, Father Neil. How could anyone speak ill of the dead with the dead man's porter or whiskey kicking like an unbroken horse in his insides?'

'Happy times those wakes,' Fr Duddleswell mused, 'happy times.'

'Happy for the bereaved in particular, Charles.'

'Indeed.'

'They were not lonely or tight-lipped in their mourning,' the Doctor explained for my benefit. 'They were not ashamed of their grief either but proud of it. They made a display of it.'

'They wanted everyone to know how happy they were,' Fr Duddleswell said, 'to have something to grieve about.'

'We Irish know how to die well and everything "dacent",' the doctor said.

'With the English, Donal, you would not know from their faces whether they were attending a funeral or a christening.'

'I remember,' Dr Daley said, 'how it was with funerals when I was but a lumpeen of a lad in Connemara. The wailing of the women with their long hair trailing like seaweed. Men lifting their homemade tweed hats. Tradesmen putting up the shutters on their shops. Everyone, even the kiddies, walking three steps after the corpse as the procession passed.'

'Like a carnival, Donal. Like a carnival.'

'I swear to you, Charles, if the devil himself died in Connemara he'd get a good Christian burial.'

Suddenly Dr Daley started almost to stutter with excitement as a boyhood memory came back to him.

'I remember once, Charles and Father Neil, I remember going to the graveyard where the Silent Majority were at rest.'

'As Homer put it,' Fr Duddleswell explained.

'And the custom was, d'you see, for everybody to take turns at digging the graves.'

57

'No professional gravediggers?'

The Doctor looked at me and shook his head. 'None. What could be more a labour of love than digging the grave of your fellow men? Mind you, the diggers did need some sort of recompense.'

Fr Duddleswell took the hint and freshened his glass.

'I remember it was the turn of my two eldest brothers. The night before this particular funeral they shovelled and swigged, swigged and shovelled till the job was done. And so, in a manner of speaking, were they. So drowsy did they become that they fell asleep in the grave with the bottles resting quiet and empty, like, on the upturned sod by the side of it.'

'Disgraceful,' Fr Duddleswell said, 'but so very understandable.'

'Bless you, Charles,' the doctor acknowledged gratefully. 'Anyways, next morning, Father Mac comes at the appointed hour, guiding the funeral procession. And what does he see when he arrives but my two brothers lying fast asleep inside? So Father Mac looks down from the height. "That is a good apprenticeship you are serving, lads, for a few years hence," says he. "But in the meanwhile, would you kindly vacate that hole so I can fill it with this corpse here who is entitled." Whereupon Father Mac stretches out his hands and the lads grab one each and he hauls them out.'

'A marvellous story, Doctor,' I said.

'Wait now, the best is still to be told. There happened to be three women over from the islands visiting a family grave at the time and they saw all this from afar but couldn't hear the words, and they, thinking my two brothers had been there and then resurrected before Judgement Day, fell fainting on the spot. And, wasn't it the talk for years afterwards on the islands that there was a priest on the mainland who had the power all right? "We've seen it with our own two eyes," the women said. "Even our Blessed Lord Himself only managed to raise one at a time." '

* * *

Death came by tandem to the parish on Fr Duddleswell's day off. He had warned me it might happen.

'If either of them slip another inch they will be over the edge.' But not to worry. He had already oiled them in readiness for death.

When the first phone call came, I cycled to the Comerfords. George Comerford, handsome, curly-haired, in his early forties, was the manager of a flourishing restaurant founded by his father. He was waiting at the door of his smart detached house to tell me that his father had passed away.

I went in to pray over the remains before having a quiet word with George in the kitchen.

'Don't worry about him, Father,' George said, as if he were consoling me. 'He had a good innings.'

'What was he, George, seventy-five?'

'It wasn't only he was old, Father. But since mum went, he was a long while facing west.'

'Everyone spoke well of him, George,' I said, and it was true.

'He had a lot of heart trouble but in the end he went quicker than you can pinch out a candle.'

'I'm glad,' I said.

'He didn't make no fuss about it, my dad. He just said, "I'm sorry, George, but it looks as if I'll have to be off." After that he didn't even have time to wave goodbye.'

I was thinking of George on the way home. How like his father he was and how bravely he was taking it. The whole parish knew he had passed over the prospect of marriage several times in order to look after his ailing father. He was bound to be feeling the wrench.

No sooner had I arrived back at the presbytery than Mrs Pring told me about Harry Carlin. 'He's gone, too, Father Neil.'

Without removing my cycle clips, I went to Stonehenge, the local nickname for Peabody Buildings, an old tenement block where the poor of the parish lived. The place always depressed me with its chipped steps, unnumbered doors and general smell of decay.

Freddie Williams was there ahead of me. His hearse was parked in the quadrangle and he, with one of his assistants, was already struggling up the narrow staircase with a coffin. Harry Carlin, who had been in a coma for days, must have been measured early.

When I reached them, Mr Williams was puffing and blowing. 'This isn't going to be the easiest, Father,' he said. 'There's no lift.'

I offered to lead the way since I knew where the Carlins lived.

Having arrived at the door, the first thing I saw was a note for the milkman. 'Only half a pint today, please.'

A lump rose in my throat. A small sign of how the bereaved had to adjust to the loss of their dear ones.

Not that Harry Carlin had been very dear to Marjorie. As I waited for Freddie to catch me up, I reflected on Harry's drinking problem and the violence that went with it. There were, fortunately, no children to share the domestic misery he had created. All the same, Mrs Carlin, still only thirty-five years old, would be mourning him at this moment.

'Ready?' I enquired of Mr Williams after he and Reggie his mate had rested the coffin for a few moments.

Freddie, breathing heavily, nodded and I knocked gently on the door. There was no answer. I knocked louder only to find the door swinging open on its own. I led the way into the darkened living room calling quietly, 'Mrs Carlin'. No reply.

'Perhaps she's popped out to see a neighbour,' Mr Williams suggested. 'I'll get on with my side of things, anyhow.'

We went together into the bedroom. The curtains were drawn. The only source of light was a night-light. They were very popular at that time, being a relic of the war years when people used them in the air-raid shelters.

I must admit to being shocked by what I saw. Harry's clothes were in a jumble on a chair just as he must have left them when he undressed for the last time. His shoes and socks were on the floor in full view and, most distressing of all, his teeth were in a glass of water.

The dead man was lying on his back in a big brass double bed, hollow-cheeked, old, forlorn-looking. Mr Williams and Reggie put the coffin down on the floor.

Freddie indicated the discarded clothes. 'Reckon his Missis wanted him togged out in those or in his pyjamas?'

I shrugged so that Mr Williams made his own decision. 'Let's pop him in the box, Reggie, as he is.'

As I was giving Harry my blessing, Reggie said in a startled voice, 'I think he's moving, Boss.'

'Don't be so daft, Reggie. It's the flickering light, that's what.'

I myself could have sworn I heard Harry snore.

As Mr Williams pulled down the sheet, the corpse jack-knifed and sat up in bed. 'What the bleedin' hell's going on?'

The two undertakers and myself were too terror-struck to tell him. When the dead man's eyes were accustomed to the light and he saw three tall gentlemen in black standing there, he, rigid as a pointer, simply said in a gummy fashion, 'My Gawd,' and fell back gasping on the pillow.

It didn't take me long to realize I had come to the right flat but on the wrong floor. It had happened to me once before in the seminary, another mammoth building where all the levels looked alike. I had entered 'my' room and seen a fellow student sitting, as I thought, at my desk by my window. But that never knocked the stuffing out of me like this.

The gentleman in bed savagely thrust his teeth in his mouth as Mr Williams, still stunned, was saying, 'You've not passed on, then, Mister.'

'No, I bleedin' well ain't,' the man said.

He explained in highly coloured language that he was a night-watchman and it was a bit much that a hard-working bloke like himself couldn't get a few hours kip during the day without three bleeding undertakers breaking in and trying to box him up while his wife was out visiting her mum's.

61

As we apologized and started to withdraw, the corpse said, 'And don't forget to take your bleedin' coffin with you.'

'Marjorie will be none the worse for losing Harry, Father Neil. One breath of wind will dry her tears,' Fr Duddleswell said that evening.

I had gathered as much. Mrs Carlin had handed me a ten shilling note for a Mass. 'I'll say a Requiem for him tomorrow morning,' I said, 'and I hope he's in Heaven by tomorrow night.' To which Mrs Carlin replied, 'No, Father, I want you to pray Harry stays in purgatory for a good long time.'

By all accounts, Harry deserved a stiff bout of purgatorial cleansing. He wouldn't go easy on the drink and the cigarettes in spite of Dr Daley's warning that with his chronic bronchitis he wouldn't be long for this world. In the event, he jumped the queue. Emphysema got him sooner than Dr Daley predicted.

He left a young, buxom widow, 'a very neat little lady,' Fr Duddleswell called her, 'and very well composed. She could have done better for herself than be wedded to a fixture like Harry Carlin and be forced to live in a Stonehenge flat with barely enough room for two cats to dance.'

George Comerford came to the presbytery to thank Fr Duddleswell for looking after his father throughout his long illness.

''Tis very kind of you to say so, George,' Fr Duddleswell said, gripping his arm. 'He got a grand death and no mistake.'

'Very successful,' George said simply, 'thanks to your anointing.'

'And didn't he deserve it, George? Was it not fitting that such a courteous fine gentleman should finish on a quiet note like a trout in the evening stream?'

As George's eyes misted up, I genuinely admired the way my parish priest could make small words sing when it was needed most.

'I'd be beholden to you, Father,' George whispered, overcome, 'if you would bury my dad, and if he was alive he'd say the same.'

'The funeral trade is in a blaze, all right,' Fr Duddleswell said, rubbing his hands. 'An ideal opportunity to check out these two undertakers' firms.'

Both funerals were arranged for the same day. Bottesford was burying Mr Comerford at 10.30 while the Co-op were attending to Harry Carlin at midday.

'If Bottesford tries any of his tricks,' I said, 'I'll be on him like a ton of bricks.'

'You do that, Father Neil. As far as I am concerned, that cold candle of a feller is as welcome here as the rent-collector.'

The bodies were brought into the church the evening before in preparation for the next morning's Requiems.

At six, Fr Duddleswell was at the church door to receive Mr Comerford's coffin. There was nothing I could see to criticize in the deportment of Bottesford and his men. Not surprising since Bottesford, like Freddie Williams, must have known that with two funerals from our church next day, a comparison was inevitable.

At eight, the Co-op team turned up. First, they removed the body of Mr Comerford from the catafalque in front of the High Altar and transferred it to another in front of Our Lady's altar. Then they brought in the remains of Harry Carlin. I had to admire, too, the polish and professionalism of Freddie's men. So far the honours were even.

When I had completed the short reception rite, I went across to the black, kneeling figure of Mrs Carlin. She was devout and tearful but not grief-stricken. I said a few words to her and told her I would see her at midday tomorrow.

When she left, the Co-op team transferred Harry's coffin to its resting place in front of the Sacred Heart altar for the night.

I made a final check. The purple drapes were neatly

spread over the coffins, the big candle sticks were positioned correctly and the respective wreaths looked decorous. I locked the church, extinguished the candles in case of fire and returned to the presbytery.

Fr Duddleswell had his usual cronies in for a fortnightly game of cards and a friendly drink. Dr Daley was there, of course, and Canon Mahoney, the bishop's theologian, and Father Kavanagh, nicknamed 'Nelson' because he had lost an eye serving as a naval chaplain during the war. A Scottish rating, it was said, threw a bottle at him.

The conversation, when I looked in, was clearly inspired by the prospect of two funerals at St Jude's.

'Anyway,' Canon Mahoney was giving out amid laughter and thick smoke, 'old Nelly wasn't having her husband be water-carrier to anyone in the cemetery. So she says to the driver of the hearse, says she, "Whip them horses up into a laver so my man gets there before Biddy's man." "I'm doing my best, Missis," said the driver. "I can see that," says Nelly, "but I'm wanting some improvement." '

'How like a woman,' Father Kavanagh said.

'Don't interrupt me, Nelson,' the Canon said, rubbing his nose with the back of a yellow index finger. 'So when Nelly gets to the cemetery she finds Biddy Malone and her folk already there with the remains of Biddy's husband. And what does Nelly do but pitch into the lot of them, laying low sixteen inside a few seconds.'

'Godalmighty' Father Kavanagh roared. 'Women!'

'Almost as bad as my housekeeper,' Fr Duddleswell said.

The Canon appealed for silence. ' "Now," says Nelly, viewing the destruction she just caused, "didn't I tell you my man is going to be buried first today? Take the lid off his blessed coffin." "Why?" says her driver. And Nelly says, "So's I can see the great laugh on the face of my man." '

There were huge guffaws and a few boozy cat-calls from the others. At which point, Fr Duddleswell felt called on to make his contribution as host.

'Dolly Melady died,' he began.

'Was that the Dolly Melady from Cork?' Father Kavanagh asked, a little the worse for drink.

'Could be,' Fr Duddleswell replied. 'Anyway, Dolly died.'

'I knew her dear mother,' Father Kavanagh interrupted again. 'Delphine. Lovely woman. She died, too.'

Canon Mahoney said, 'The flicking thing must run in the family.'

Father Kavanagh winked his good eye. 'There's a lot of it about, Seamus.'

'Anyway,' Fr Duddleswell continued bravely, 'when Dolly was coffined up in the hearse on the way to the 'yard, the wagon went over a bump at the corner and the jolt of it brought her back to life.'

'Is that a fact?' Canon Mahoney enquired.

'It happens quite frequently,' Dr Daley assured him. 'Especially in stories of this sort.'

Fr Duddleswell said, 'Three years after that, Dolly died again.'

'For the last time?' Dr Daley asked. 'It's good to know how much of the story is still to come.'

'For the last time, Donal. Now, the hearse was travelling the same stretch of road. And when it reached the very bit of rock that jolted her before, a terrible voice was heard from inside the coffin, crying –'

Before Fr Duddleswell could finish, his three cronies yelled in chorus, ' "Mind the corner," says she, "mind the corner." '

Fr Duddleswell pretended to hide the whiskey bottle out of pique.

'Death is not so bad,' Canon Mahoney said, lifting the discussion to a serious level. 'Without it there wouldn't be any birth, that's for sure.'

'Indeed, Seamus.' Father Kavanagh always sided theologically with Canon Mahoney. 'God has to thin out the old turnips to let the young ones grow.'

The mention of old turnips caused Fr Duddleswell to ask, 'And how is the Bishop, Seamus?'

'Very well at the moment. But while there's death there's hope.'

'*Vive la mort*, as we used to say in the Navy,' Father Kavanagh said.

Fr Duddleswell noticed I had come in and was standing quietly by the door. 'Did you see Harry Carlin safely in, lad?'

'Yes, Father.'

Fr Duddleswell turned to Dr Daley. 'I was instructing Father Neil only recently on the subject of corpses.'

'Saying what, Charles?'

'I was telling him, Donal, how the nails and hair go on growing in a corpse which proves something is still alive in there that's worth anointing.'

'Rhubarb,' Dr Daley said.

'It is so,' Canon Mahoney, the theologian insisted. 'That is why we anoint the dead, just in case. Unless the maggots have got 'em of course.'

'Then,' Dr Daley challenged, 'you'd better get out the holy oils and anoint each other this very second.'

'Why so?' the clergy demanded to know.

'Because death is going on inside you all the time. In fact, death starts at birth.'

'Will you unriddle that for us, Donal?' Fr Duddleswell said.

'It's a medical fact, Charles. Red blood cells, for instance, only last from two to three months at most. They die at the rate of a thousand per second. Brain cells are the same.'

Father Kavanagh scratched his woolly head. 'God forgive me, and I was blaming it on the drink.'

Dr Daley rubbed his hands together and little scales of skin showered off them.

'Jasus,' Fr Duddleswell said, 'your old paws are suffering from the dandruff.'

'Did you, know, Charles, a man has a hundred million million cells in the tissues of his body? They are dying and being reborn all the time. The nails and hair which you cite as going on living in a corpse are the very parts of us

66

which are made up of dead cells even in living people. The blood doesn't reach 'em, you see.' The Doctor showered the flakes of his skin on Fr Duddleswell's sleeve. 'So, bury that for me, if you'd be so kind, and see it gets to Heaven.'

Realizing that the great debate was likely to last till the early hours, I wished them all good night and read for a couple of hours before retiring to bed.

I slept in till 10.30 and was in church before eleven. There was a sizable congregation present because Mr Comerford had been a popular figure in the district. Among the mourners, I picked out the Mayor, a couple of other Councillors, Dr Daley, and Mother Stephen with three other sisters from our convent.

The Mass was over and Fr Duddleswell was reciting the Absolution. He circled the catafalque, sprinkling the coffin with holy water and incensing it. After that, he withdrew to the sacristy to prepare for the three-mile journey to the cemetery.

Bottesford led his men up the centre aisle. They removed the drape from the coffin and bore it with dignity to the hearse.

I knelt for a few moments in sleepy prayer. When I came to myself, the church was empty.

I was thinking that the Co-op would have to give an outstanding performance to improve on Bottesford's when I chanced to look across to Harry's coffin in front of the Sacred Heart altar. It wasn't there. But there was a draped coffin in front of Our Lady's altar where, the previous night, we had deposited the body of Mr Comerford.

No, I told myself. Even Bottesford can't be so damn stupid as to provide Fr Duddleswell and the first group of mourners with the wrong corpse. It's not possible.

But this was St Jude's . . .

I sprinted across the church, pulled the purple drape off the remaining coffin and read the name on the lid.

'Hell,' I shouted.

A storm was raging inside my head. Brain cells must have been dying in clouds. What was I to do? I could hardly let Harry Carlin be mourned and interred by the Comerfords, even supposing that no one but I noticed, which was most unlikely. I had to contact Fr Duddleswell.

I contemplated ringing the cemetery but that would only add to the embarrassment. Besides, I didn't know the number. I decided to get on my bike and hope I reached the grave before the burial.

I had travelled two miles when, to my joy, I caught sight of the funeral *cortège* at the traffic lights. I believe I would have overtaken it had not my bicycle chain snapped. There was nothing for it but to abandon the bike and run the last stretch.

Desperation meant that time-wise I didn't do badly, especially considering I hadn't had anything to eat or drink for twelve hours and I was impeded by my cassock. But I was close to being sick and nearly half dead myself when I came up to the mourners grouped with bowed heads at the graveside.

I had no breath left in me to explain. I pushed people aside roughly with oily hands and dragged myself to Fr Duddleswell's side where I looked down on him pleadingly.

It was the point in the ceremony where the coffin was due to be lowered. The very moment when the mistake would easily have been detected and rectified. Had I not distracted everybody by my sudden, crazed appearance.

'Father Neil, have your wits gone wandering in the next parish?'

I knelt down at Fr Duddleswell's feet, my chest heaving, and clung to his knees like a drowning man. I still hadn't enough puff to utter a single word.

It occurred to him that I might have something important on my mind.

'Has Mrs Pring been run over?' I shook my head. 'The church burned down?' A constant preoccupation of his. I shook my head again.

He was satisfied that whatever was worrying me it did not warrant this intrusion. He looked irritably at his watch and his voice was scythe-edged. 'D'you not realize,

Father Neil, you are due to bury Harry Carlin in half an hour?'

I nodded vigorously but otherwise didn't stir.

'This funeral is my business,' he hissed, 'so would you kindly take your head out of it?'

With his jaw he indicated to Bottesford that his men should start to lower the coffin.

I squeezed Fr Duddleswell's legs so frenziedly that he fell over backwards on the soft mound of earth. The first piece of luck that day. His cotta was covered with mud but he could so easily have fallen forward into the grave. The prayer, 'While we mourn our beloved brother here, we know we are most certainly soon to follow him,' would have been immediately fulfilled.

Dr Daley stepped forward from among the mourners. Gently but firmly he took my arm, convinced that I was demented.

'Poor Father Neil,' he purred, 'with that white face on you, you'd frighten a ghost to death.'

I was aware of a host of pitying eyes. Even the pallbearers, having pulled up the ropes, glanced curiously in my direction before withdrawing.

I pointed downwards so dramatically that Fr Duddleswell was forced to follow the direction of my finger. He read: *Harold Carlin 1911 – 1951 R.I.P.*

It wasn't easy explaining to the first set of mourners that a slight error had been made.

'That's okay by me,' George Comerford said charitably when I had finished.

'If you would like to take yourselves back to the church,' Fr Duddleswell said, 'we will put matters right first chance we get.'

Not that it was as simple to get the coffin out of the grave as to get it in.

It had settled comfortably in the mud and early attempts to get the rope under it failed. One of Bottesford's men jumped into the grave but his weight only made the coffin sink down deeper. Someone went off to fetch a pulley and a gravedigger appeared with a hose ready to wash down the coffin when it resurfaced.

Fr Duddleswell glowered at me as if he was reserving his prime comments for later. 'Look, lad, will you get off your ass and cart and hasten back to church to take charge.'

I pointed out that I had no means of transport. Since, by now, the mourners had left, Bottesford offered to give me a lift in the hearse.

'I won't be more than ten minutes,' he said to Fr Duddleswell. 'I'll be back for the coffin.'

Along the road, I saw my bicycle. A couple of school-boys were wheeling it away. If I let them, goodbye to the second bike within a year. I ordered Bottesford to stop.

As we screeched to a halt, I jumped out and grabbed the bike, without explanation, from the kids. Bottesford opened up for me and the kids gaped as I settled the bike sideways on the place where the coffin usually rested. To make it less obtrusive, I spread a few wreaths over it.

We had travelled another mile at a furious pace – too fast even for pedestrians to take their hats off – when we were flagged down by a police patrol car.

'Do you know what speed you were travelling at?' the policeman asked Bottesford.

'Sorry, Officer.' As Bottesford was saying it, he was taking out his driving license and slipping a £5 note inside.

I snatched it out of his hand before the policeman realized an attempt was being made to bribe him.

'You were doing fifty-five miles an hour in a built-up area, sir.'

'We're trying to get to a funeral,' I explained.

'Oh, yes, sir,' the policeman said, peering through the side window at my flower-strewn bicycle. 'You were very fond of that, were you?'

'I can explain, Officer,' I said.

'Save it for the magistrate,' he said, taking out his note-book. He scratched his head, suddenly seeing the funny side. 'First time I've ever stopped a ruddy hearse for speeding.'

'I'll lose my reputation,' Bottesford said pitifully, though after today I wondered what reputation he had left.

'Ah, well,' the Officer said, grinning as he put his notebook away. 'Don't do it again, eh, sir? Otherwise, you might kill someone.'

'Thank you, Officer, thank you,' Bottesford gushed gratefully. And we drove at a fitting funeral pace until we reached St Jude's.

It was remarkable how tolerant everybody was. George Comerford's only concern was for the poor widow whose husband had been buried before his time. But when Mrs Carlin heard what had happened, she was highly amused.

'This is the first time Harry's made me laugh in years,' she said. 'A second lot of burial prayers will do that one no harm.'

Fr Duddleswell whipped through his Requiem for Mr Comerford and I followed, quicker than usual, with a second Mass for Harry Carlin. The first group of mourners stayed in the cemetery to greet the second coffin. How cheerful everyone was.

After the committals, George insisted that everybody should accompany him to his restaurant where there was plenty of food and drink to go round.

'God,' Dr Daley cried, as he went hunting through the restaurant for the whiskey, 'after that, I could drink the sacking out of the mattress.'

I found an idle bottle for him. He thanked me profusely and, while pouring, muttered, 'Mustn't turn a treat into a chore, as the man said when he buried his wife only three feet deep.'

Even the Deadly Rivals, Bottesford and Mr Williams, were seen drinking a jar together.

The obvious gaiety prompted Fr Duddleswell to let me off lightly. All he said was, 'Who would have thought that out of all mankind, God should choose Harry Carlin to rise on the *first* day.'

'You were wrong, Charles,' Dr Daley called out to him

71

above the hubbub. 'The English do know how to behave at a funeral.'

Seeing the shining faces, Fr Duddleswell said prophetically, 'Like a wedding, Donal, like a wedding.'

It came as no surprise to me when, less than three months later, George brought Marjorie along and asked me to marry them.

'But for you, we would never have met,' George reminded me. 'Besides, we are practically family already, Marjorie and me. We even use one another's graves.'

FOUR
Holy Water

There was a special glint in Fr Duddleswell's eyes as he ascended the pulpit that Sunday morning.

'Me dear people,' he declared, 'this year in St Jude's there have been twelve less baptisms than last year. That means twelve less births. That means twelve less disciples for our Blessed Lord. And that means' – he looked down challengingly on the congregation as if demanding an immediate response – 'twelve married couples in this parish are not doing their duty of bringing new Catholics into the world.

'Which is why,' he continued, beaming, 'it delights me to announce there has been a little miracle in the parish. And I am responsible. In a manner of speaking.

'One of our number has conceived. A member of the entirely opposite sex to mine, I need hardly tell you.

'I know what you are thinking,' said the preacher, who never missed a nudge and fancied himself something of a mind reader. 'What is miraculous about a woman conceiving, especially when she has a husband healthy and willing and all? A shrewd question and no mistake.

''Tis because they tried for years. Tried hard, mind, not like some of yous who are only pretending. And still no sign of a little Catholic coming till I made the pair of 'em drink a drop of this.'

Fr Duddleswell held up a bottle. It was shaped and coloured, blue and white, like the statue of the Virgin of Lourdes.

'Lourdes water, me dear brethren, blessed by the Holy Father himself.' The preacher leaned over his pulpit

73

confidentially. 'Now, if any Catholic couples here present are having any difficulties in that respect, give a ring on the presbytery door.'

He winked confidentially and prepared to leave the pulpit when he had an after-thought. 'No charge. But you can, of course, make a little offering if you are so minded.'

'What did you make of that?' I asked Mrs Pring in the presbytery.

'If you ask me,' she said, removing her coat, 'Father D's off his tiny rocker.'

I laughed. 'How could he convince *you* that he can work miracles?'

'Easy. If he only sipped that stuff and it turned him into something like a human being.'

Fr Duddleswell heard as he was meant to. He had arrived, clasping his precious bottle, in the company of Dr Daley.

'Her teeth, Donal,' he broadcast cheerfully, 'wouldn't they do well as pokers to stir the fire?'

He invited me to join him and the doctor in his study.

'Imagine that,' Dr Daley was muttering incredulously, 'a woman needing holy water to conceive. That was never my dear mother's problem, God be merciful to her.'

I remembered what he had told me when I was in hospital. 'There were how many of you, Doctor, seventeen?'

He shook his hand as if he was trying to get sand off it. 'Round about that number.'

'And didn't you say your father was a nightwatchman?'

'But for that, Father Neil, God only knows how many of us there'd have been.'

We settled down comfortably as Fr Duddleswell began his explanation. It seems that six months earlier he had returned from a pilgrimage that took in, first, Lourdes, then, Rome. The bottle of holy water he had given in the first instance to Dr Daley.

The doctor nudged me. 'He had this strange notion, y'see, that it might cure me of the habit.'

'Did you even try it, Doctor?' I asked.

74

'Oh, I did. A wee sip. But could I keep the stuff down? I could not.'

'So you kindly gave it back, Doctor?'

'Don't get the wrong idea,' the doctor said with a twinkle, 'I'll certainly give up the gargle one of these fine days when I'm a bit older. Perhaps.'

Fr Duddleswell sniffed contemptuously and lifted his wirerimmed glasses on to his forehead in disbelief. 'A bit older, a bit older. You are not so young now that your toes can whisper in your ears.'

'I will do it,' Dr Daley insisted with a complete and endearing lack of conviction. 'I will.'

'And a broody hen, Donal, will one day fly backwards over the Irish Sea.'

Dr Daley touched the shoulder of his old buddy. 'See if there's a good turn in you and tilt your arm.'

'I will not.'

'Don't be fish cold with me, Charles.'

'You drink too much.'

The doctor opened wide his pink, sharp-rimmed eyes, amazed. 'On the contrary, Charles, my bitter life-long experience is I can never drink enough.'

Fr Duddleswell, in effervescent mood, suggested he try the softer stuff. 'Guinness, for instance.'

'Oh, Charles, I have only to look at the little clerical collar of froth on top of any beer and I cannot take even a sip.'

'Why, not, Doctor?'

'Because it puts me in mind of his Reverence here and gives me such a nasty feeling inside I can't begin to enjoy it.'

'Donal,' his Reverence said, already admitting defeat as he made for the cupboard, 'you should be hanging your head in shame like a cow's udder.'

Dr Daley bowed and dangled his bald head to oblige.

'Instead,' Fr Duddleswell continued, 'here is yourself emptying more glasses of whiskey than I can say Hail Marys.' He poured out a single which Dr Daley downed in one, his cigarette still lodged in the corner of his mouth.

75

'Why drink so fast?' Fr Duddleswell objected.

'If it's left too long it sticks to the sides, Charles.' Refreshed, he got down to business. 'Tell me, now, about this girl conceiving by the power of the holy water.'

'You will remember your advice to Deirdre Jameson, Deirdre Flynn that was.'

Dr Daley stroked his chin. 'The girl that was married six or seven years without increase.'

'The same.'

'The girl was never a patient of mine.'

'Nonetheless you advised me to tell her to go see a gynaecologist.'

'Standard practice, Charles.'

'For an unbeliever.'

'My guess was her tubes were blocked.' The Doctor pointed to his throat and coughed. 'Like mine at this moment.'

His host ignored the hint and held up, instead, his bottle of holy water. 'Even so, Donal, why trust to medicine when you have the facilities of the faith?'

'Because,' I chipped in, somewhat irritated, 'God works through medicines mainly.'

Neither seemed to hear me as Dr Daley took the bottle, unscrewed the top and sniffed.

'God, Charles,' he exclaimed, 'it smells like it came out of an old barrel. If the Jameson girl drank of that, the miracle is she's not dead.'

Fr Duddleswell snatched the bottle back before any of its contents were spilled. 'Not only is Deirdre Jameson not dead,' he snorted, 'she is six months alive and kicking with child.'

Dr Daley held out his empty glass. 'Let me be first to toast the bambino.'

Without being asked, I stretched out my hand and gave my ally a refill.

'Bishop O'Reilly, now,' the doctor countered, in defence of his profession, 'he's in hospital being operated on, isn't that so?'

Fr Duddleswell laughed grimly. ''Twould be too much

to expect faith in a bishop.'

'Oh, I don't know about that, Charles. Under all them layers of purple and fine linen, the Bishop is surely as naked as Jesus on His cross.'

'Anyway, Donal, Bishop O'Reilly is in hospital for a prostate operation.'

'There,' Dr Daley said, holding up his glass to the light, '*he* wasn't satisfied with sipping holy water.'

'With that complaint,' I said, 'he's not too keen on sipping anything.'

'How is the Bishop, by the way?' Dr Daley asked with professional as well as filial interest.

Fr Duddleswell frowned. 'His health is a cause of grave concern to the entire diocese.'

'Dear, dear, dear,' the doctor said. 'Is he that much worse?'

'He is nearly better, Donal.'

'Keep praying for him, then,' the doctor said with one of his nicely judged ambiguities.

'Well, now, Donal,' Fr Duddleswell said, seeing his old friend was in an accommodating mood, 'what does the Bible say about Sarah?'

'Sarah who?'

'Sarah, wife of Abraham.'

'She was nearly ninety years old,' I contributed, 'when God told her she would conceive for the first time.'

Dr Daley sipped and nodded as if he was listening to a deranged patient.

'Sarah laughed at that,' I added.

'And well she might,' Dr Daley said. 'But are you sure she didn't get her dates wrong?' Before Fr Duddleswell could explode, he said appreciatively, 'But isn't that a marvellous thing?'

'Sarah bore a son, Donal, nine months later.'

'And not one second more than fifty years overdue,' I said.

Fr Duddleswell was trembling in his anxiety to convert the doctor to his point of view. 'Have you thought about that, Donal?'

'Not a lot, Charles.'

'What does it prove, from the medical standpoint?'

The doctor whistled and tapped his middle finger on the desk. 'That when the Almighty puts His mind to it He does some very surprising things.'

'Y'see, Donal, Sarah took it for granted that at her age she never would have a child.'

'I wouldn't have raised her hopes.'

I said, 'She was certainly long in the tooth.'

'If she had any left,' the doctor said.

'Be serious, now,' Fr Duddleswell demanded. 'Abraham was himself pushing a hundred at the time. Imagine that.'

Dr Daley peered into his glass to avoid an eye to eye confrontation. 'I am doing my best.'

Not to be put off, Fr Duddleswell said, 'Did Abraham tell Sarah to go see a gynaecologist for him to poke his instruments around in her insides?'

'My guess is he did not.'

'So there, Donal.'

'But neither did he tell Sarah to drink a glass of Lourdes water blessed by Pius XII.'

Before Fr Duddleswell could deliver a broadside, Mrs Pring entered to announce a visitor. 'Mother Stephen.'

Fr Duddleswell called out to me in a hoarse whisper, 'Put the bloody whiskey away.'

Caught off guard, I said, 'Where, Father?'

'In the cupboard, Father Boyd.' Mother Stephen, tall, imperious, was already in complete charge.

'Of course, Mother.' And I did as I was told.

'Just heading for home, Charles,' Dr Daley said.

'You will all stay,' Mother Stephen ordered. And we stayed.

'I have come,' Mother Superior began in her chiselled English, 'about this miracle to Mrs Jameson.'

Fr Duddleswell was delighted. 'So *you* accept that 'tis a miracle, Mother.'

'I most certainly do. It belongs to me.'

Fr Duddleswell straightened out his face. 'I'm sure I beg your pardon.'

'Six months ago, Mrs Jameson came to the Convent and asked our sisters to pray she would have a child.'

Fr Duddleswell was shaken. 'She didn't, Mother. She couldn't have.'

'Are you calling me a liar, Father?'

'Oh, I believe you, Mother. Indeed, I do.'

Mother Stephen took out a now familiar locket from the folds of her habit.

'I gave her this relic of our holy Mother Foundress on loan. The child is our Foundress's first miracle. Only two more and the Holy Father will be able to declare her a saint.'

At breakfast, Mrs Pring echoed my own thoughts. Pointing to the bottle of holy water that now accompanied Fr Duddleswell everywhere, she said, 'I'll be glad when that thing's empty.'

'Your brain box is jealous of it, I suppose.'

'I agree with Mrs Pring.'

Fr Duddleswell picked up his bottle from the table and kissed it. 'You are blind, Father Neil, d'you know that?'

I blinked first one eye, then the other. 'My eyes seem all right, Father.'

'Yes,' Mrs Pring said, 'it's you who has to wear the glasses.'

'I was referring, Father Neil, to the eyes of your soul.'

'I'll get them examined first chance I get.'

Fr Duddleswell determined to stamp out my rebelliousness at once. 'Look, lad, a good Catholic is obliged to believe in miracles.'

I wasn't caving in that easily. I remembered Father Abe's words about firing back at little Charlie when he fired at me.

'The Church says,' I countered, 'that God works miracles whenever He likes. But, the Bible stories apart, we don't have to believe in any particular miracles.' For good measure, I added, 'Not even the miracles at Lourdes.'

'And mine,' he said, grinding his teeth, 'is not in that class?'

I shrugged my shoulders to show he could think what he liked.

'God demands we believe in mysteries which are beyond our comprehension.'

'You should have been a snake,' Mrs Pring said.

'Why so?'

'Because, Father D,' she replied, 'you're good at swallowing things bigger than your head.'

'Infidels, the pair of you. Only last evening, let me tell you, I smeared some of this holy water on me arm.' He raised his arm, lowered it and raised it again. 'And me rheumatics have completely disappeared.' Pain lit up his face as he felt the familiar twinge. 'Well, almost.'

Mrs Pring stood at the door, holding the metal tray like a shield. 'His brain is very fertile, Father Neil. It's a wonder he doesn't have a geranium growing out of his head.'

Then she left.

The two of us nibbled away in silence for a few minutes until I ventured to say:

'Father, if you insist on giving sips of that stuff to the young wives of the parish, the husbands are going to object.'

'Why so?'

I fixed him with a glance. 'They'll think you're trying to do their job for them.'

He purred condescendingly. 'Do not be so ridiculous, lad.'

'Undermining their virility.'

The usual irresistible smile spread over his small round face. 'Did y'ever hear such a thing?'

'Then don't be surprised if you get a brick through your window.'

His face darkened. 'That is not the attitude of Deirdre's husband, George. He is no doubting Thomas. He sent me a cheque for fifty pounds and he's a Protestant.'

'Why not claim that as a second miracle?'

He was riled. 'I might at that.'

I waited a moment before suggesting, 'He probably sent Mother Stephen fifty pounds as well.'

That did it. 'The miracle is no blessed good to me unless I have exclusive rights.'

I swallowed my coffee and rose to my feet. 'There you are. This so-called miracle of yours is already making you fall out with Mother Stephen.'

'Bloody nonsense,' he bellowed, biting cruelly into his slice of toast. 'You know that *everything* makes me fall out with Mother Stephen.'

I heard noises of scampering in Fr Duddleswell's study and the cry, 'Father Neil! Father Neil!'

I found him frantically opening and closing drawers and cupboards.

'Me bottle of holy water. 'Tis lost.'

I tried to check myself but failed. 'Have you prayed to St Anthony, Father?'

He was too distracted to reply. 'Here is meself with three young wives coming at midday for a booster.' He went to the door and yelled, 'Mrs Pring!'

'Perhaps,' I said, 'Mother Stephen broke in and stole it.'

A somewhat ruffled Mrs Pring showed in Dr Daley.

'Charles, me very dear friend.'

'Donal?' Fr Duddleswell was obviously not expecting him.

'When you phoned, Charles, to say the Jamesons were giving you fifty quid I thought I'd better pop round.'

'Me very dear friend,' Fr Duddleswell answered pleasantly, 'you cannot share in it.'

The doctor cleared his throat noisily. 'Bad news, Charles, I'm afraid. It isn't Lourdes water in that bottle at all.'

Fr Duddleswell rubbed his ears.

'I got rid of the Lourdes water, Charles.'

'Are you drunk as a Killarney boatman?' Fr Duddleswell gasped. 'That damned holy water has worked numerous first class miracles.'

'When you first gave it me, Charles, I disposed of it.'

'How?'

'In the usual domestic way.'

'Dear God above,' Fr Duddleswell said, his eyes scanning the heavens, 'is there no decency left in the world?'

'I wasn't attached to it, y'see, all water looking alike to me.'

Fr Duddleswell waited to get his breath back before: 'Let's get this straight, Donal. Six months ago, I gave you a full bottle of water and you gave me back a full bottle of water.'

'From out the tap, Charles. And the water in the whole reservoir can hardly be miraculous, can it?'

Fr Duddleswell shook his head so sadly it brought a lump to my throat. 'Which is why, Donal, you never took the miracle seriously.'

'Sorry, Charles. I feel so terrible about this my knees have turned to soda water.'

'Ah, well,' Fr Duddleswell said magnanimously, 'forget it, anyway. 'Twas God's will.'

'Kind of you to blame Him and not me.'

'I forgive you with all me heart,' Fr Duddleswell said with a smile which his voice did not betray. 'But you are an odd friend to me, I will say that.'

'True, Charles, you are almost as careless in your choice of friends as our Blessed Lord Himself.'

Dr Daley, though forgiven, had to make amends.

'Since 'tis your fault that I cannot now accept that fifty pounds,' Fr Duddleswell told him, 'I expect you to atone in a tangible way.'

'Certainly, certainly,' Dr Daley said, going for his wallet. 'Since you have taken the news as calmly as a heathen and without turning a hair, I'll scratch you out a cheque this instant.'

While he was writing, Fr Duddleswell was urging him on. 'Write clearly, now, that is not a prescription you are handing out.'

'There, Charles,' the doctor said, laying the cheque face-down on Fr Duddleswell's palm.

'Would you care for a short one, Donal?'

I could hardly believe my ears. Such an unsolicited

invitation was rare. Still rarer, Dr Daley's reply:

'Not today, thank you kindly. I've got to take to my scrapers.' And he moved hurriedly to the door.

'Thanks for this, anyway,' Fr Duddleswell called after him. 'God be on the road with you.'

'It should come in handy in an emergency.'

With that, Dr Daley was gone.

'Donal refusing a drink. What d'you think of that, Father Neil?'

'That's what I call a miracle,' I said.

'Now let's see what we have here.' He held the cheque up to the light. 'Handy in an emergency, he says. A cheque for one penny.'

Mrs Pring entered the room guiltily. 'Father, I've a confession to make.'

Off-hand, Fr Duddleswell said, 'Father Neil will be in his box next Saturday evening.'

'It's not a sin, only an accident.'

'Woman,' Fr Duddleswell said, 'at your age little accidents cannot happen.'

'Unless your name is Sarah,' I said.

'That water,' Mrs Pring managed to get out, 'is not Lourdes water.'

'Dr Daley just told us, Mrs P.'

Mrs Pring looked at me, wide-eyed. 'But I never told Dr Daley nor any living soul.'

'Told him what?' I asked.

'That when the Doctor sent the water back six months ago, I knocked it over.'

Nonchalantly, Fr Duddleswell said, 'I am not surprised at anything you do.'

'I was dusting at the time,' Mrs Pring went on.

'Do not bother me with your clumsiness, woman,' Fr Duddleswell said testily.

'You don't seem to understand, Father. The Lourdes water dripped on to the carpet. Every drop.'

'Don't worry, Mrs P.' I hoped to put her mind at rest. 'It doesn't matter now.'

In Fr Duddleswell's fertile brain, a seed had been sown.

'If the water was not from Lourdes, where was it from?'

'From the rain barrel in the garden.' From her pinafore, Mrs Pring drew out the missing bottle. 'I emptied it all out so you wouldn't be tempted again.'

When she left, Fr Duddleswell's seed germinated with uncanny speed.

'Not from the reservoir,' he mused, 'but from the rain barrel in the garden.'

Good at accepting disappointment on another's behalf, I said, 'It looks as if the miracle belongs to Mother Stephen, after all.'

That restored him to full vigour. 'Y'think that old Crow at the convent has put one over on me, do you?'

'I'm just relieved that this miracle business is over, Father.'

He bestowed on me a pitying smile. 'All over, Father Neil. All *over*. 'Tis only beginning.'

He went to the door to call Mrs Pring back. She was still in the vicinity.

'Come in,' he said kindly, 'come in.'

'I said I was sorry.'

'Whatever for, dear Mrs Pring? Am I saying harsh things to you?'

'No,' she admitted warily, 'are you ill?'

'Listen here. How much does that rain barrel in the garden hold?'

'About a couple of hundred gallons. Why?'

'Because, dear Mrs Pring, that barrel is miraculous, that's why.'

'O my God,' Mrs Pring gasped, as she turned to go. 'I can't take no more.'

He laid out his ambitions before me, instead.

''Twill be like having a Lourdes shrine in our own back yard.'

'No, Father,' I begged, shielding my eyes. 'Please, no.'

'Provided there's no drought, lad, an endless supply of holy water.' He had a far-away look. 'I can see it all. Pilgrimages from all over the world heading for St Jude's.'

'Barren women conceiving,' I said.

'Yes.'

'The sick hanging up their crutches in the church.'

'Yes, indeed.'

'Leaving their plaster casts in the Lady chapel.'

'Yes, yes, yes.'

'Goodbye, Father,' I said, heading smartly for the door. As I closed it behind me, I caught a glimpse of his dreaming seraph's face.

FIVE

Blessings from Heaven

'*Ave, ave, ave Maria; Ave, ave, ave Mari-ia.*'

A small afternoon congregation was belting out the Lourdes hymn while a line of young women knelt at the altar rails to receive Fr Duddleswell's blessing for a happy childbirth.

'O God,' he prayed, his right hand extended over them, 'who gavest a child to the aged Sarah and made the Blessed Virgin Mary fruitful, grant to all Thy handmaidens who seek Thine aid by partaking of this holy water the blessing of fertility. Through Christ our Lord. Amen.'

From my hideout in the shade of a pillar I watched Fr Duddleswell take a glass of water from a server, bless it and proceed to give a sip to each of the kneeling women. The server followed carrying a plate on which, after sipping, they placed their silent contribution.

Someone jogged my elbow: Billy Buzzle. 'I heard rumours, Father Boyd, now tell me what this lark is all about.'

I couldn't keep the tone of disparagement out of my voice. 'He thinks he's got a barrelful of miracles in the garden.'

'Ain't that mortal,' Billy said, the mischief in him bubbling over, 'so he was *praying* out the back. I thought he was throwing up.'

'It is rather sick-making, isn't it, Mr Buzzle?'

'You watch yourself, young 'un,' he said, surprising me. 'You ought to have more faith.'

'More *what*?' I replied sharply. 'You're not even a Catholic.'

86

'That's true but I recognize a good business proposition when I see one.' He gestured to the notes piling up on the plate. 'Look at all that lolly.'

'You ought to go into partnership with him,' I said.

Billy grinned broadly. 'Don't you be putting ideas into my head, my boy.'

A few days later, I found Fr Duddleswell in his study with his sleeves rolled up, funnelling water from a jug into small liquor bottles.

'For export, Father Neil,' he said without taking time off from his work.

'Export?'

'I am sending it to a few friendly parishes round about.'

I admired his altruism. 'That'll be expensive,' I said.

'Aren't you still as green, lad, as a leprechaun sitting on a blade of grass?'

'You're not *selling* holy water.'

He did his best to look hurt. It was almost believable. 'Of course not, Father Neil. I am charging but two shillings for the bottles.'

'You're giving water away free in two shilling bottles.'

'There, you have it.'

'But those bottles aren't worth tuppence.'

He waved my objection aside as if it weighed less than a smoke ring from Dr Daley's cigarette. 'You have to reckon on the labour costs, lad.'

'Whose?'

He filled up another bottle and screwed the top on before replying. 'Mine.'

'But this is disgraceful,' I said.

'Listen to me, lad. You have a Papal Indulgence hanging on your wall. Did you pay for it or no?'

'No, I didn't,' I responded heatedly.

'Yet you did pay for the parchment 'tis written on.'

I remembered that I also had a bone of St Thérèse of Lisieux in a reliquary that cost me ten bob.

'I suppose so,' I conceded. 'But I still think you're playing on people's credulity.'

87

His turn to be shocked. 'Is that what you think faith is, simple-mindedness?'

'I never said that.'

'As good as.' He softened a little, a tactic he frequently employed when he wanted to slip through my guard. 'The good people realize perfectly well that 'tis not the water in itself that matters.'

'No?'

''Tis what God does when they use the water with an ardent faith.'

'Why, then,' I wanted to know, 'do they need your water at all? Why don't they just pray?'

He gave me the pitying look he usually reserved for our discussion of Protestants. 'Why do we need water for baptism? Why did our Blessed Lord Himself use clay mixed from spittle to heal the eyes of the blind man?'

I hadn't the faintest idea but was saved from admitting it by the entrance of Billy Buzzle.

Fr Duddleswell put down his jug to greet him. 'Ah, Mr Buzzle, me dear neighbour, hail.'

'The bottles've arrived, then, Father O'Duddleswell.'

My suspicions were aroused. '*You* supplied the bottles, Mr Buzzle?'

'I took your tip, Father. We're partners, him and me.'

'That makes it worse,' I groaned.

'No, much better,' Billy insisted. 'I've got a good business brain, see. I'll take charge of market research, sales, transportation. *He* does the religion bit.'

To spiritualize matters, Fr Duddleswell put in, 'After the last water-drinking ceremony, Father Neil, did we not have two conceptions to our knowledge?'

'Father!' I cried. 'The first woman was just back from her honeymoon.'

He arched his eyebrows gothically as if I had hinted at something marvellously wicked. 'And what, pray, has that got to do with it?'

I ignored the question. 'And the second girl wasn't even married.'

He looked concerned. 'Is that a fact?'

'Now,' I said, hammering the nail home, 'she's trying to convince her parents it wasn't her boyfriend but your holy water.'

'There's one born every minute,' Billy said.

'That,' I said, 'is the danger.'

'Very well, Father Neil,' Fr Duddleswell assured me, 'in future we will only give it to the marrieds.'

Billy jumped in with, 'No need for that. The unmarrieds can put their bottles away with their trousseau.'

'Of course they can,' Fr Duddleswell said, relieved. He turned to me. 'We really do have to trust the young folk.'

That from a man who nearly burst a blood vessel whenever he saw a courting couple holding hands.

'If, in the end, the Bishop doesn't approve,' I pointed out, 'you're sunk.'

'We'll offer him ten per cent,' Billy said.

Fr Duddleswell didn't agree. 'You are far too generous with my money, Mr Buzzle.' He scratched his chin reflectively. 'I am thinking of asking a friend of mine to give the Bishop one of these little bottles for free.'

'Let's hope,' I said, 'it doesn't have the same effect on him it had on Deirdre Jameson.'

'Nobody was ever as good as Father D,' Mrs Pring observed tartly, 'except perhaps Jesus at the peak of His form.'

She was becoming understandably irritated by the constant stream of visitors and the endless phone calls. Everyone was demanding an interview with 'the faith healer of St Jude's.'

Apart from the ceremony for barren women, he conducted services of healing. Elderly people with rheumatism and arthritis, others with slipped discs, handicapped children, among them a ten-year-old deaf boy from the parish, Tommy Ferguson. They all found their way into the church of St Jude's where Fr Duddleswell cared for them, prayed over them and distributed rosaries and medals.

Mrs Pring was convinced he was making a huge profit. 'That one could sell rosaries to the Blessed Virgin,' she said. '*And* pigs and Sacred Heart statues to Jews.'

I wasn't sure about the profit potential myself, still less about the rights and wrongs of raising the expectations of the sick. I couldn't deny it gave some of them the chance of a rare outing. I once saw among the congregation three people in wheel chairs and a stretcher case. But wasn't it all motivated by rank superstition?

When I tried to discuss it with Fr Duddleswell he accused me of being a bit 'wanting' in the head.

'Can't you wait,' I pleaded, 'until the Bishop grants his approval?'

'Quiet, Saxon,' he said. 'Remember the old proverb, take Time by the forelock for he is bald behind.'

'But why should this water be so special?'

'Dear God, lad, your faith is so thin a sheep could nibble grass through it. Why is Lourdes water special? Why the water in any holy well in Old Ireland? Instead of asking why, why, why, you should drop humbly on your benders saying *Deo gratias*.'

He saw that I couldn't say Thank God for so dubious a benefit.

'You ask too many questions, Father Neil. Why were you born a Catholic and the lad next door a Protestant, tell me that? Why are you a priest and your best friend at school a harrassed married man with a power of kiddies?'

'I haven't the faintest idea.'

'Don't think ignorance is a sign of genius,' he snorted, disapproving of my tone. 'You consider the barrel in my garden is too wretched a thing for God to work wonders with, isn't that so?'

'I suppose so.'

'But wasn't our Saviour born in a stable with only an ox and an ass for companions? And didn't his fellow country-men say of Him, Can any good come out of Nazareth? And weren't His apostles fishermen, lowly folk without school certificates or university degrees?'

'And,' I chanted, already heading for the door, 'doesn't

God choose the foolish things of the world to confound the wise and the weak things of the world to confound the strong?'

I was almost out of earshot when I heard his final blazing retort:

'Will you stop running away on your sheep's trotters, boyo. Doesn't God do that sort of thing. Well, *doesn't He?*'

I was roped in, two evenings later, to make up a foursome at cards. Of the regulars, Dr Daley and Canon Mahoney had turned up but Father 'Nelson' Kavanagh had called off at the last moment with 'flu.

I was partnering Fr Duddleswell at whist and we were out of luck. After a hand in which we only made one trick I suggested that, while I dealt the cards, he tried to improve our prospects by using some of his holy water.

He seemed pleased that my faith was progressing. He went to his cupboard through the cigarette haze to fetch a small bottle, wet his thumb and signed his forehead. Meanwhile, I secretly exchanged the pack of cards we were playing with for another pack I had doctored before-hand. I would show up Fr Duddleswell's superstition for what it was.

Seeing him sign himself with holy water, Canon Mahoney expressed relief that he wasn't drinking the stuff.

Dr Daley noticed the inexpert way I handled the cards. 'I'm surprised,' he said, 'you can't play poker or gin-rummy.'

'Only whist, Doctor.'

'Is that so?' Canon Mahoney whistled through his jagged black teeth. 'I don't know what they teach the young lads in the seminary these days.'

'Trumps?' Dr Daley wanted to know and I told him, 'Spades.'

Out of the tops of my eyes I saw Fr Duddleswell picking up his cards with growing excitement. When Canon Mahoney said, 'My lead, I believe,' Fr Duddleswell touched his forearm with, 'No need, Seamus.'

91

'Aren't you playing any more, Charlie?' the Canon asked.

Without a word, Fr Duddleswell laid his cards on the table triumphantly. All of them spades.

'God,' Dr Daley exclaimed, 'the whole suit of trumps.'

'A miracle, Father,' I gasped.

Canon Mahoney said, 'You'd better let me have a closer look at that holy water, Charlie.'

I was really relishing the situation. Grown men, I thought, two priests and a doctor of medicine seriously looking on a 'chance' distribution of cards as evidence of the intervention of Almighty God in the affairs of men.

Dr Daley was saying, 'After a shock like that, Charles, I'm needing a sup of whiskey.'

'Whiskey,' Fr Duddleswell replied. 'Holy Moses, 'tis useless as hammering cold iron with a hair of me head.'

All the same, I could see he wasn't annoyed in the least, so delighted was he to have visible proof of the efficacy of his holy water. In the presence, too, of the Bishop's own theologian.

At the mention of whiskey, the card game broke up. We moved for refills to the desk where the liquor was set out on a tray with a jug of water.

Dr Daley was muttering, prayer-like, 'Wherever two or three Catholic priests are gathered together in His name, there is a bottle of whiskey in the midst of them.'

'You could knock the habit, Donal,' Fr Duddleswell announced gaily, 'if you only had faith.'

'Our Blessed Lord says,' Canon Mahoney put in, licking his rubbery lips, 'that if you have faith you can move mountains.'

'Who wants to shift mountains?' Dr Daley enquired.

'I do agree with you,' Canon Mahoney said. 'Besides, wouldn't it be terrible unsafe for mountaineers?'

Dr Daley's face registered an impious shock. 'That's blasphemious, Seamus.'

I poured Canon Mahoney a double and held the jug poised. 'Water, Canon?'

He snatched the glass from me. 'Thank you, no. I washed before I came.'

'I meant water for your whiskey, Canon.'

'Jasus, Sonny. The very sight of the filthy stuff is enough to bring me on a duodenal ulcer.'

Dr Daley intervened with professional solicitude. 'Then you mustn't drink it, Seamus, you must not.'

Canon Mahoney signed his breast with a big yellow thumb. 'Donal, you have my solemn word.'

Dr Daley switched to his host. 'To tell you the blessed truth, Charles, I did put a lick of your holy water here.' He touched the part of his scalp where his forelock used to be.

'Wait till I get my flashlight,' the Canon said.

'And nothing came of it,' Fr Duddleswell remarked, stating the obvious.

'Oh, it did, Charles. For a few days, I grew a thick, glossy patch of skin.'

Fr Duddleswell admitted, red-faced, that he, too, had made the same experiment, hoping against hope to grow a bit of fur.

Canon Mahoney roared with laughter. 'And you're both as bald as the prophet Elisha.'

'Better bald than headless, I reckon,' Dr Daley muttered, mourning his lost youth. Ash fell from his cigarette on to his brown jacket and red cardigan to signify that worse things than baldness were in life's pipeline for him.

'Now to business, Charlie,' the Canon said. 'Donal tells me there has been an epidemic of miracles in the parish here.'

Fr Duddleswell proceeded to give details. First, when Deirdre Jameson conceived, her husband George asked to become a Catholic.

Canon Mahoney butted in, a twinkle in his eye. 'The smart feller knows we priests have the power, y'see.'

'They're the best Catholics, the turned ones,' Dr Daley said, remembering perhaps his own sorry drinking record.

The Canon agreed with him. 'Indeed, Donal, they want to make up for lost time, like. Even so, I'm grateful to the Almighty God for giving me the Truth whole and entire first time round.'

'That's right, Seamus,' Dr Daley said, 'it's like being handed the whole bottle and not being rationed just to a meagre glass-full.'

'Then last week,' Fr Duddleswell said, anxious to continue, 'I gave Deirdre another sip of our home-made holy water and the hospital diagnosed twins.'

Dr Daley raised his glass 'To the both of them,' he said, and, having drunk, peered nostalgically into emptiness.

'After that,' Fr Duddleswell went on, 'George's two maiden aunts decided they want to receive instruction and they are or *were* on the committee of the Humanist League.'

The Canon held his glass aloft. 'As the whale said when he saw Jonas, "This'll take a bit of swallowing." '

'Don't give the girl any more of that holy water,' was Dr Daley's advice.

'Why ever not, Donal?'

'Because, Charles, there'll be so many queuing up for baptism, the devil included, there'll be a water-shortage in the diocese.'

Fr Duddleswell called for silence. 'I believe in "Multiply and fill the earth" more than most men, as me parish registers show, but I have definitely closed the bottle now to that Jameson girl.'

Dr Daley showed him his dry glass. 'In my experience, Charles, you are a winner at putting stoppers in bottles.'

'Wait now till I tell you,' Fr Duddleswell said, warming to his theme. 'Only the other day, Tricia Boswell who suffers something awful from arthritis drank some water and walked across the room.' He paused for dramatic effect. 'First time, mind, in three years.'

'And fell flat on her face,' I added.

Fr Duddleswell cold-shouldered me. 'But she walked, d'you hear?'

'She broke her jaw,' I said.

Having curdled my blood with a look, Fr Duddleswell turned to Canon Mahoney. 'What d'you think, Seamus?'

The Canon sucked a big black tooth. 'Perhaps you've just been lucky so far, Charlie.'

'Me lucky? When I am being persecuted by a Mother Superior whose tongue is saltier than Lot's wife after her accident.'

Dr Daley attempted to put things in perspective. 'Charles, your good fortune is such that if ever you get caught in a downpour it's sure to rain new potatoes.'

Before Fr Duddleswell could reply, Mrs Pring burst in.

'Mrs Pring,' Fr Duddleswell said, 'did I not tell you, no visitors?'

'Mother Stephen,' Mrs Pring announced.

Fr Duddleswell was on his feet in an instant. 'Apart from very important people, of course.'

'Do not get up,' Mother Stephen told the rest of us, her look intimating that she had uncovered a whole school of gin and sin.

Fr Duddleswell helped the Superior to sit and, sensing that his authority as parish priest was on trial, said:

'If you are here about Deirdre Jameson, Mother, I think I can prove that miracle belongs to me.'

Mother Stephen grew three or four inches in her chair. 'Tell me.'

'Deirdre is expecting twins, Mother.'

'You are mistaken, Father.'

'Oh?'

'A more careful examination of Mrs Jameson shows she is carrying triplets.'

'You are sure, Mother?' Seeing the coldness of her face, he hastened to add, 'No, I am not calling you a liar, Mother.'

It amused me that there should be a dispute over the responsibility for a baby's birth. 'Mother Foundress,' I said, 'is working her three miracles all at once.'

'I am pleased, Fr Duddleswell,' the Superior said, 'that your assistant is not siding with you.'

'I have written the Bishop, Mother, claiming the miracle for me holy water.'

95

'And I,' Mother Stephen said, rising like the Loch Ness monster out of dark waters, 'have written to our Cardinal Protector in Rome claiming all three miracles for Mother Foundress. Good day, gentlemen.'

We were too shaken to get up.

'Jasus, what a bleak mid-winter sort of a woman,' the Canon declared. 'She must've eaten sour grapes soaked in vinegar.'

Fr Duddleswell did his best to keep his morale up. 'I realize I was tough with her, Seamus, but that is the only kind of talk she understands.'

I nodded encouragement, once more firmly on the side of the home team.

"Tis enough to make a saint swearing-mad,' Fr Duddleswell fumed. 'That is the tenth time this week I've had to put up with her visitations.'

'Give me the plagues of Egypt any time,' the Canon said.

'She's more trouble than the ten commandments,' I said.

Dr Daley leaned over and capped it all. 'My sympathy, Charles. When you've your back to the wall, there's nothing for it but to turn and run.'

Mrs Pring came to tell us the coast was clear and to ask if she should make a cup of tea.

'Surely, my dear,' Dr Daley said, 'provided you don't bring it in here.'

Canon Mahoney seized the opportunity to ask Mrs Pring what she thought of the recent miracles.

'I do my best not to, Canon.'

'Be off with you, woman,' Fr Duddleswell growled. 'You are not worth the water eggs are boiled in.'

'Charlie,' the Canon said, patting his arm, 'you look as if you're going round in circles like a one-legged duck.'

Fr Duddleswell held out a bottle of holy water in desperation. 'You are a member of the Chapter, Seamus. Will you give Bishop O'Reilly this sample from me?'

'How much, Charlie?'

'No charge.'

'I mean for my services,' the Canon joked.

'One Our Father and one Hail Mary.' Fr Duddleswell winked knowingly at him. 'And by the way, Seamus, I wouldn't mention to the Bishop the miracle of the thirteen trumps.'

I seconded that, determined to tell Fr Duddleswell privately his mistake. 'We don't want the Bishop to know we waste time playing cards, Canon.'

'Not at all, Father Neil,' Fr Duddleswell said. 'I saw you change the pack for one you prepared beforehand.'

Seeing me blush, the Canon said kindly, 'The lad has taken the scarlet fever. But do you think your parish priest is an idiot, Sonny?'

'As a matter of fact – ' I broke off, smiling a big smile.

'We've got to brighten this mouldy old place up a bit.'

Fr Duddleswell was not at all put out by Billy Buzzle so describing his Lady altar. He unfolded the architect's plans.

'See here, Mr Buzzle. According to this, there will be six steps leading up to the altar, all of marble.'

'We've got to get a jazzier statue of our Lady,' Billy said.

'*Our* Lady,' I repeated. 'Your devotion is very touching, Mr Buzzle.'

'Look, Father,' he insisted, 'there'll be hundreds of charas turning up here every year and we've got to give value for money.'

'Besides,' Fr Duddleswell said, ''tis all for the glory of God, so we have to do this thing decent, like.'

'Where is this Lourdes place, by the way,' Billy wanted to know.

'In France.'

'Where exactly, Father O'Duddleswell?'

'Let me put it like this, Mr Buzzle. If Lourdes were in Ireland, 'twould be on the Cork-Kerry border. On the Cork side.'

A young lady crept up on Fr Duddleswell. I didn't recognize her.

'I've just bought this bottle of holy water, Father.'

To satisfy me, Fr Duddleswell asked, 'You *are* married, me dear?'

'Of course.' Fr Duddleswell nodded approvingly. 'Am I supposed to take it inwards or outwards, Father?'

'Howsoever you like, me dear.'

The young lady didn't yield ground. 'If I drink it, how many times?'

He smiled paternally. 'Four times a day after meals.'

'And if I rub it on me,' the young lady said shyly, 'where do I rub it?'

'Um, let me see now.' After a moment's reflection: 'Wherever you think it will do most good.'

The young lady was determined not to waste her money. 'Where's that, Father?'

'On second thoughts, me dear,' he said hastily, 'I think you'd best drink it.'

Mrs Rebecca Milton, an aged parishioner, took the young lady's place. With her rounded back, long neck and gummy jaw dropping down on her chin she reminded me of a tortoise. She, too, was clasping a bottle of holy water.

Fr Duddleswell pointed to it. 'Have you just bought that?'

Rebecca nodded. Gently but firmly, Fr Duddleswell took the bottle from her. 'That could be dangerous, Rebecca,' he said. 'You must have your money back, yes indeed. Father Neil.'

'Father?'

'Will you be so kind as to give this good lady a couple of bob?'

I dipped into my pocket, doubly grieved.

A couple of days later, I was with Fr Duddleswell in his study. We had been carrying carton after carton of bottles out to his garage for storage. Only one was left. He liked to keep it by him for the surprise visitor.

'Big day today, Father.'

''Tis that. Canon Mahoney will be here any minute

with the Bishop's official approval of our plans. Are you convinced yet?'

'Well, er . . .'

'Dear God in Heaven,' he said, 'I might as well be talking up the chimney.'

To shift attention from my unbelief, I pointed to his desk. 'Lots more mail, I see.'

'And few of them empty.'

'Empty' was his word for one without money. A letter 'with a pearl' was one with a generous contribution.

'Look here, lad.' He picked up the letter on top of the pile and read: 'Dear Father Dwirdles of St Jude's, My wife has been trying for years to have a little one. Could you help her?'

'What does he suggest, Father?'

Mrs Pring showed in Canon Mahoney who greeted us cheerily with 'Charlie' and 'Sonny'.

'Good to see you, Seamus,' Fr Duddleswell said, masking his excitement. 'Will you have a whiskey?'

Canon Mahoney waved the offer aside. 'I never drink before 11 in the morning on principle.'

'It's five past, Canon,' I said.

He studied his watch, shook it and put it to his ear. 'You are *right*, Sonny. Then give me a drop of the mountain dew.'

I was pouring when I heard Fr Duddleswell say in an awed whisper, 'That water I have, Seamus, 'tis very holy.'

'I'll still take the whiskey neat, thank you, Charlie.'

'I am thinking, Seamus, of opening up a kind of Lourdes shrine to our Blessed Lady.'

'Here in St Jude's?'

'Indeed. What d'you think, Seamus, honestly now?'

The Canon grabbed his drink to strengthen himself as the bearer of bad tidings. 'I tell you plainly, Charlie, Bishop O'Reilly wouldn't hear of it.'

'But you have the Bishop's ear, Seamus.'

'True, but have you ever met a bishop whose ear was connected up in any way with his brain?' The Canon whistled without meaning to. 'Bishops is wonderful things. God feeds 'em information direct, see.'

'Blessed bishops,' Fr Duddleswell fumed. 'But for the fact that we cannot do without 'em, they are no bloody use at all.'

'If this were Holy Ireland, now, Charlie, that'd be another kettle of fish. But it's a matter of definition almost that miracles cannot happen hereabouts.'

Fr Duddleswell tried telling him they had been happening right under his nose for weeks.

'A very Irish nose,' the Canon observed.

'Thank God,' Fr Duddleswell said in an empty voice, blessing himself.

'Take my advice, Charlie, and I won't charge you even the price of a Mass stipend. Bottle the water up and put some in your suitcase for when you next go to Cork or Kilkenny.'

'Over there,' I suggested, 'they appreciate the power of the holy H_2O.'

'Oh, they do,' the Canon agreed. 'Provided they don't have to swallow it.'

Fr Duddleswell grunted but seemed to realize nothing was to be gained by further protest.

'Remember, Charlie,' the Canon said, warming to his subject, 'the Pope had to canonize St John Fisher and St Thomas More without miracles. Even the English saints and martyrs don't like the flicking things. It makes the world too untidy, you see, Charlie, and English civil servants, who are full to the cork with white corpuscles anyway, don't know how to cope with them.'

Good for the English, I thought, without saying so.

The Canon raised his glass and generously, according to his lights, included me in his toast. 'May the shamrocks forever bloom and entwine upon your grave.'

'Thank you kindly, Seamus, but why did you not give his Lordship a sample to drink?'

'Oh, I did,' the Canon said, rising to go.

'*Deo* bloody *gratias*, Seamus, if you will forgive me Greek.' But seeing no reaction from the Canon, he murmured incredulously, 'And nothing happened?'

'Surely, I'm off this very minute to see him. Y'see, your man is back in hospital.'

'*Hospital*,' Fr Duddleswell and I said in chorus.

Canon Mahoney stood at the door, relishing our consternation. 'It gave him a powerful bout of dysentry.' With that, he left.

'I am played out,' Fr Duddleswell sighed. 'So ends the most glorious episode in the history of St Jude's.'

'With Bishop O'Reilly sitting on his throne.'

'The imagination boggles,' he said, dropping heavily into his chair. 'Ah, but 'twas sensational while it lasted, all the same.'

He stayed pensive for a few moments, looking out of the window as the Canon drove off.

'I'm sorry it's all over, Father, for your sake.'

He straightened his shoulders. 'Never spill tears for me, lad. I am of the Irish nation. I am used to being sniped at by me fellow countrymen.'

'I only wish,' I found myself saying, 'that you didn't do business with Billy Buzzle.'

'Billy? He gave his services free.'

'Oh,' I said, quite bemused. 'So you didn't share the proceeds with him.'

'Proceeds? There weren't any. It was costing me three to four pounds a day in overheads.'

The telephone rang. It was Mrs Ferguson to say her deaf son, Tommy, was making great progress with his speech therapy.

'Tis exceeding kind of you to put it down to me holy water, me dear, but really 'tis your own great faith that is doing the trick.'

Fr Duddleswell listened further and his eyebrows shot up. 'Now isn't that decent of him. Wonders of grace never cease.'

Afterwards, he told me that Billy Buzzle was contributing £100 to help send Tommy to Chicago for an operation.

I was staggered.

'I have a crow to pick with you, lad,' he said at length.

'Father?'

'I can understand why Dr Daley and Mrs Pring didn't see the miracles, and our much maligned Bishop, too, come to that. But you, Father Neil, me faithful apprentice . . .'

He broke off, a sad smile playing on his lips.

I tried to explain myself but didn't do well. 'I suppose, Father, you only see the miracles you believe in.'

'I realize, of course, Father Neil, there are miracles all round us. Sunrise every morning. The stars at night. Trees coming into leaf every springtime. Still, 'tis nice to think that God does special little favours for his friends from time to time.'

I nodded, saying nothing. I only felt that it wasn't really nice to think that, and that this difference created some sort of barrier between us which only time would reveal in all its immensity.

'And, then,' he went on, 'you were scandalized at me risking the accusation of playing on people's simplemindness.'

'True.'

'Didn't our Blessed Lord do the same, lad, healing people of their sicknesses from morn till night, giving them tangible proof of what faith can do for them, and promising that his disciples would do greater things?'

I wanted to defend myself and my point of view but the time was not right for it. Let him fire away, I thought.

'Faith, y'see, works in the strangest ways. It makes people feel important and that God still cares for them. Look, for instance, at Tommy's mother.'

I nodded agreement.

'Again, Father Neil, I've known many a woman who couldn't conceive because she or her man were too tense and worried. Often when they adopted a child the worries ceased and they had a baby of their own. Faith can work like that by removing worries.' He shook his head reflectively. 'Though how God acts I do not know nor do I pretend to know. One thing's for sure, incredible things happen when "simple-minded" people believe.'

102

I grabbed a bottle from the carton on his desk. 'Try working one last miracle, Father,' and I handed it to him.

'I couldn't possibly do that,' he said, unscrewing the top, 'could I?'

'Be a devil, Father.'

His high spirits returned. He wetted his thumb and signed himself as before. Just then, the door bell rang.

'There,' I cried enthusiastically. 'That could be a stranger wanting to make a huge donation to the parish.'

'Or Dr Daley promising to be eternally tee-total.'

'Or,' I yelled, 'Billy Buzzle asking to become a Catholic.'

When Mrs Pring came in, Fr Duddleswell beamed at her. 'Tell me the worst, Mrs Pring.'

'Mother Stephen,' she said.

Fr Duddleswell, realizing the game was finally lost, lifted the carton off his desk and deposited it in my arms. 'Yours for keeps, Father Neil.'

'You were expecting me, Father?' Mother Stephen asked.

'Not exactly, Mother. But sit yourself down all the same. As many welcomes to you as there are straws in the thatch.'

The Superior looked upwards suspiciously. 'But you have tiles on your roof, Father.'

'Tell me, Mother, to what do we owe the pleasure of this visit?'

'Our Cardinal Protector has written.'

'And?'

'He states quite categorically that the miracles of the babies must be attributed to our Lady and St Jude.'

Fr Duddleswell pursed his lips. 'Does he, now?'

'Obedience demands,' Mother Stephen began.

'Me dear child,' Fr Duddleswell interrupted her, making the most of his advantage, 'I command you under holy obedience to write back to that silly Cardinal in Rome at once. Tell him that Father Duddleswell, who is in complete charge of St Jude's, renounces the miracle in favour of your Foundress.'

Whether through astonishment at Fr Duddleswell's magnanimity or shock at being called 'me dear child', Mother Stephen was at a loss for words.

'Do you mean it?' she managed to get out at last.

Fr Duddleswell contemplated her sternly. 'Are you calling me a liar, Mother?'

'No, Father, no. But this is a great, great . . .'

'Miracle, Mother,' I said.

Mother Stephen gathered herself together. 'I must repay you, Father Duddleswell.'

He rubbed his hands together at the prospect of salvaging something. 'Well, if you happen to have your cheque book handy.'

'I was thinking, rather, of praying for you to our Foundress.'

That alarmed him. 'Please do not trouble her at all, Mother.'

'No trouble, Father.'

'She is dead,' I pointed out. 'She can't be too busy.'

'Our sisters will pray that you, Father, become a bishop.'

He sat back in his chair, chewing the inside of his cheek. 'Well, now, that *is* a thought.'

'Where you can do most good to souls.'

Fr Duddleswell was a dreamer again. 'Liverpool, perhaps,' he mused. 'Or Westminster itself.'

Mother Stephen said, 'I was thinking, Father, of deepest Africa.'

SIX

Beddings and Weddings

'There is too much of it around, Donal.'

'What is that, Charles?'

Fr Duddleswell was astonished that his old pal Dr Daley, didn't grasp his meaning at once, seeing he had been discussing *ad nauseam* the current outbreak of extra-marital misbehavings.

'Sex,' Fr Duddleswell said, his eyelids fluttering. 'Goings-on out of wedlock.'

We were guests for dinner at Dr Daley's ramshackle house. The meal was nearing its end. In that mischievous way he had, the doctor looked around his dining room like a short-sighted person searching for his glasses.

'I hadn't noticed, Charles, and that's a fact. But, then, only being a doctor, I wouldn't have your blessed opportunities for prying.'

'I am not referring to the confessional, Donal,' Fr Duddleswell insisted. 'Go into any public park and what do you find?'

'Bees fertilizing flowers,' the doctor mumbled, barely audible.

'You find randy young fellers on top of their girl friends, frenzied like they are doing brass rubbings.'

'Dear, dear, *dear*.'

'You have only to pick up your newspaper of a mornin'. Why, today there was that Hollywood film-star with a name like Micky the Looney who is just tearing into his fifteenth wife.'

'If I wasn't so outraged by him,' Dr Daley said, puffing like a steam engine, 'I might be envious.'

'Be serious, Donal.'

'He must be terrible fit.' Before Fr Duddleswell could intervene again, the doctor said, 'What was it St Augustine said in his *Confessions*, "Lord, give me chastity when I'm too old to notice." '

'Something like that,' Fr Duddleswell conceded.

'There you are, then, Charles.' The doctor stroked his grey, stubbly chin reflectively. 'Now I come to think of it, I haven't prayed for chastity in years.'

'Me neither. The need on me is not what it was.'

'Isn't it easy being virtuous, Charles, when vice brings more pain than pleasure?'

Father Duddleswell sighed his agreement. 'If you are patient, you do not have to turn your back on the divil, the world and the flesh, they turn their backs on you.'

Dr Daley gave a little giggle. 'Wouldn't it be nice to be tempted once again?'

Fr Duddleswell turned serious. ''Twould not,' and Dr Daley became miserable to keep him company.

'God, Charles, first the old eyes, then the ears, and now – '

'I know what you mean,' Fr Duddleswell said hurriedly to stop him finishing.

'It isn't fair, you know that, Charles. When the rest of you starts to fail, you can get yourself a pair of glasses and a hearing aid. Free, too, on the National Health. But as to the other – '

'Indeed, Donal, you have made your point.'

'Not entirely, Charles. In my experience, there is not too much indulgence in sex today but too little.'

Fr Duddleswell looked at him as if he had just dropped dead. 'You cannot mean it, Donal.'

'I do. Sex is like prayer or playing the fiddle. You need practice to be any good at it. But what with wireless and the cinema, there's less time and energy for it nowadays than since the era of fig leaves. And if this new television thing catches on in a big way, I tell you, there'll be almost no sex at all.'

'But, Donal, the number of young women these days

who are bedded before wedded! Why, 'tis worth considering banning Bank Holidays for fear of the avalanche of babies coming nine months afterwards.'

'Granted, there have always been young couples starting the world before they should, even as contrariwise, there have always been Irishmen who think it's sinful stripping down an engine.'

'Pity the poor girls in white,' Fr Duddleswell protested, 'who are pushing their wheel barrows up the aisle, trying to hide their bump with a bouquet.'

'Pity them I do indeed, Charles, from my heart. Yet that has always been the way of the world, has it not? Ever since the caveman dragged his mate home with him to add to the population.'

Fr Duddleswell was showing signs of exasperation. 'I tell you, Donal, things are far worse now than in our day and generation. There are even girls – God forgive me for mentioning it at this grand meal you have prepared for us . . .'

'Proceed,' the doctor said, with a gallant wave of his hand.

'There are girls approaching the altar rails, Father Neil will confirm it, with blouses that button up round their toes.'

Dr Daley smiled. 'The unlucky dip, as Seamus Mahoney calls it.'

'Indeed. And 'tis not their holy medals they're displaying.'

'Shameless as a herd of cows,' Dr Daley muttered impishly.

''Tis hard to tell whether they are wanting to take the Holy Sacrament or a hot bath.'

Dr Daley tried soothing him. 'Necklines are like the pound, Charles, up one day and plunging the next. It doesn't signify. Besides, as you always say yourself, the remedy is simple.'

'What is that?'

'If only the colleens joined their hands they'd find it easy to join their knees.'

107

"'Twas better in the old days,' Fr Duddleswell snorted, 'when men and women sat on opposite sides of the chapel.'

'But, Charles,' Dr Daley countered, 'didn't that holy arrangement leave everybody cross-eyed?'

Fr Duddleswell thrust his cheese plate away from him like temptation. 'I tell you, these are terrible days. I am marrying a couple one week and christening their offspring the next.

'Lucky for you a girl's never calved down the aisle.'

'I have sometimes wondered if the Matron of Honour is not really a midwife in disguise.' Fr Duddleswell shook his head vigorously. 'Sex is sweet to drink all right but bitter to pay for.'

'Like something else I know,' Dr Daley said, with a wink in my direction. 'I'll just fetch myself a drop of oil to keep the flame alive.'

He crossed to his cupboard.

'God,' he cried, 'the cupboard is bare.'

'You are like the foolish virgins, Doctor,' I said. 'No oil for your lamp.'

Fr Duddleswell said grumpily, 'They can't have been too foolish if they were still virgins.'

Back home, I took the opportunity of broaching a topic that was occupying my mind.

'Father, would you mind if I started a family group in the parish here?'

Fr Duddleswell hadn't heard of Family Groups, even though several nearby parishes had been running them successfully for months.

I explained that the priest encourages couples, usually young couples, to get together to discuss common family problems in a supportive atmosphere.

'Discussion, Father Neil?' I nodded. 'Don't you realize that explanation kills the pig? Besides, Catholics already know the Church's teaching on these matters.'

'But there are ticklish problems of relationship,' I dared to say. 'Problems about children, housing, neighbours, paying the rent.'

108

'There is no Catholic way of paying the rent, lad.'

'Then there jolly well ought to be,' I retorted.

'God help us,' he grumbled, still smarting over Dr Daley's alarmingly liberal views. 'I tried that sort of thing once when I was a young priest.'

'I'm surprised you can remember that far back.'

'It didn't work.'

'Your failures,' I said, blazing, 'are hardly a blueprint for my career.'

'Are they not?'

'No. There isn't any future in the past.'

'No future in the past,' he echoed mockingly. 'Who is this riddler in our midst: Lewis Carroll, Gertrude Stein, Virginia Woolf?'

'It isn't enough,' I said, calming down, 'to tell people the Church's teaching on marriage. They have to find things out for themselves.'

He relaxed and smiled. 'Like curates, eh?'

'Perhaps,' I said, stiff-lipped again.

'So be it, Father Neil. You can start next week.'

This took the wind out of my sails. 'You mean it, Father? You're not upset or anything like that?'

He shook his head benignly. 'How do we learn, Father Neil, except by our mistakes?'

I announced from the pulpit on Sunday that the first Family Group would meet at St Jude's on Thursday evening, 7.30 – 8.30. Engaged couples as well as married couples were welcome. Future meetings would be held in the homes of the participants, the host family providing light refreshments.

On Wednesday, Fr Duddleswell roped in my first couple. Batty Holohan and Dympna Tutty, he told me, were soon to be wed 'after a whirlwind Irish courtship of three years' and might benefit from contact with experienced married people.

I thanked him warmly. I had even more cause for gratitude the next evening. Batty and Dympna were the only couple to turn up to the meeting in the presbytery parlour.

'Well,' I said, glancing at my watch and seeing we were already a quarter of an hour late, 'time to get started.'

Batty sat down awkwardly. He had red hair closely cropped so it looked as if his head was enclosed in a rusty saucepan. He had red eyebrows and freckles. He was about forty.

Dympna wasn't much younger. She was dark, Latin-looking, with abnormally large hands which she didn't know what to do with.

'If any other couples arrive,' I said breezily, 'they can join in.'

'Suits us,' Batty said.

'Father Duddleswell tells me, Batty, that you are engaged.'

Batty nodded morosely. 'So is Dympna. Three year, Father.'

'And you are thinking of getting married.'

Dympna reached for her handkerchief. Inspired by Fr Duddleswell's recent comments, I was struck by the ungentlemanly thought that Dympna was pregnant and they were trying to find a way to say so.

'Is there any particular problem you'd care to talk about?'

Dympna gulped painfully, increasing my suspicions. 'There is, Father.'

'Please,' I said, gesturing with my hands to indicate they were free to bring anything up.

I waited for half a minute but in vain.

'You said you wanted to discuss a particular problem.'

Batty nodded but still said nothing. I realized I was going to have to conduct the conversation on the lines of confession.

'Is it about money?' I said, breaking the ice gently.

The couple shook their heads.

'A house?'

'We have a bungalow lined up,' Batty said.

Eighteen questions to go. To myself: Damn it, I won't beat about the bush. I said, 'It's about a baby, isn't it?'

110

They nodded and Batty mumbled, 'In a manner of speaking.'

I put on my most sympathetic mask. 'When is the little one due?'

'Never,' Batty said hoarsely.

'Never?'

'That's right, Father,' Batty confirmed, hanging his head.

What are they trying to tell me? I asked myself. Have they been at it out of wedlock and had no success? And do they think you can't get married *unless* a baby is on the way? They are peasant people, certainly.

'It's quite customary to get married *before* the baby is due,' I remarked hesitantly.

They gave me an odd look. I hadn't got it right yet.

I scratched my nose. 'Have you tried and, um, failed?'

'Oh, Father,' Dympna said, blushing madly.

Batty Holohan screwed up his courage. 'Dympna can't, Father.'

'She knows without trying?' I asked.

Dympna lifted her head. 'I love Batty very much, Father. He knows that. But the other thing.' She shuddered.

I was quite shaken by this revelation. I explained that what distinguishes marriage from every other form of relationship is its physical basis. It's a contract between a man and a woman by which they take on mutual bodily rights and duties. To approach the altar while withholding from the other partner the right to sex would invalidate the contract just as certainly as if one partner 'married' on a temporary basis or with the determination to exclude children for good by means of contraception.

'It would be like trying to play golf,' I said in summary, 'without a ball.'

'You mean, Father,' Batty said wretchedly, 'we can't have the words said over us, after all,' and Dympna, clutching at Batty's hand, said, 'I can't be buried with his people.'

'It says in the Bible that in marriage a man and a

111

woman become one flesh. Without that – ' I shrugged my shoulders.

'We've been so close,' Dympna said, weeping, 'and now we've got to part. After saving up all these years.'

'You can still be friends,' I said gently.

'Ah, it wouldn't be fair to Batty being just friends.'

I felt like saying that *I* wasn't preventing them being something more to each other.

As I showed them to the door, Batty said to Dympna, 'Come on, love, let's go into church to say the rosary.'

I was deeply upset. I was also annoyed. Annoyed with Fr Duddleswell for arranging to marry a couple when he hadn't bothered to make sure they fulfilled a basic condition.

Father D's an old fuddy-duddy, I fumed inwardly. He's past it.

I banged on his door and stamped in. He was at his desk, writing. He looked up.

'Your meeting is over already, Father Neil?'

'It is.'

'Well?'

I gave him a brief, fiery résumé, ending with Batty's remark about them not being able to marry, after all.

'You did not let them go home on that note, Father Neil?'

'Of course not. I consoled them as best I could.'

'What d'you mean, "consoled them"? You surely did not tell them they'd have to call the wedding off.'

'I didn't need to. They realized that themselves.'

'Dear God,' he cried, rising from his chair in a panic, 'you are as green as unripe corn.'

'Look, Father, I know the theology of marriage. I'm surprised you don't.'

'Get your coat on,' he thundered, 'and fetch that poor young couple back here this instant.'

'They're in church,' I told him.

He disappeared and in a few moments came back with Batty and Dympna, both of them crying. Fr Duddleswell looked at me grimly as if to say, See what you have done.

112

This, I thought, I must watch. If only to correct any further bloomer the old bloke makes.

'Sit yourself down, Dympna. You, too, Batty. There seems to have been a wee misunderstanding hereabouts.'

The couple gradually composed themselves.

'Now,' Fr Duddleswell said, 'Fr Boyd here tells me you are about to enter a most unusual and edifying marriage covenant.'

I was in turmoil. Why was he leading them up the garden?

'Father Boyd,' Batty began, 'he said –'

'Father Boyd,' Fr Duddleswell took up, 'was giving a general scholarly analysis of the theology of marriage. But yours is a special case.'

'Is it, Father?' Dympna asked, for the first time hopeful.

'Oh, 'tis indeed. Y'see, Dympna, you and Batty are marrying in exactly the same way as our Blessed Lady and St Joseph.'

I was as startled as Dympna was overjoyed.

'The fact is,' Fr Duddleswell went on, studiously avoiding my gaze, 'our Lady and St Joseph were genuinely husband and wife even though there was no physical side to their marriage.'

'So they were,' Dympna murmured brightly.

'Of course,' Fr Duddleswell said, 'they handed over to each other the right of bodily communion but they vowed at the same time not to exercise this right.'

'That's what happened, then,' Batty said, almost whistling.

'Not, Batty and Dympna, that I'd advise the pair of you to make a permanent vow. A temporary one renewed at the beginning of each calendar month is all that is required.'

Oh God, I admitted to myself, the old chap's right again. I had overlooked the possibility of a virginal marriage. I had applied to sex in marriage the generally sound Catholic principle that everything is forbidden until it is compulsory.

'Does that suit you, Batty?'

Batty nodded briskly.

'And yourself, Dympna?'

Dympna smiled her agreement.

'But remember, me dear young couple, that if at any time you change your mind, you have only to come and see me or give me a tinkle on the telephone.'

'We won't be changing our mind, Father,' Dympna said for the pair of them.

'If you do, you have only to say the word and I will dispense you immediately. I would have to give you a stiff penance to compensate, mind.'

'Of course,' Batty said, perhaps wondering what penance could be tougher than the one he'd got.

''Tis a very wicked and heinous sin to break your vow without my permission, *very* wicked.'

This was laying it on thick. I couldn't see why.

'Have you arranged your honeymoon, Batty?'

'We're flying to Spain for a fortnight, Father.'

'I could not think of a more suitable place,' Fr Duddleswell said, as he showed the happy pair to the door. 'I will start calling you next Sunday. And may you, Dympna, hear a hen sneeze on your wedding morn.'

This, I took it, was an Irish sign of good luck.

On his return, I apologized. Seeing me crushed, he was content to say, 'Did you not know, lad, that the parents of St Thérèse of Lisieux began their married life with that same vow?'

'No, Father.'

He fluttered his eyelids mischievously. 'And St Thérèse, you will recall, was the last of their thirteenth children.'

I laughed with relief.

'Will you do me one last favour, Father Neil? Promise you will not use your Family Group to split up any more happy couples.'

Another announcement was made at all the Masses on the following Sunday. On Thursday evening, I furtively looked through my bedroom window, praying no one would put in an appearance.

At 7.35, Freddie Williams drove up in the Co-op hearse. I took no notice because Freddie was a non-Catholic. Until I heard his voice in the hall.

'I've come for the Family Group, Mrs Pring.'

In the parlour, the sort of room Freddie and I were accustomed to meet in, he explained that he had received notification of these meetings through the letter box. He drew out a piece of paper on which had been pasted words of varying typography cut out of a magazine. It told of weekly meetings at St Jude's 'for those unlucky in love'.

'It's like a spy thriller in the films, isn't it, Father?'

I nodded, glad that Freddie was having a bit of excitement in his life. 'Who's responsible, Mr Williams?'

'I think I know. One of my pall-bearers is Eddie McEvoy.'

Eddie was one of our parishioners. A bit of a wag. Not that he could have expected Freddie to take the note seriously.

'How can you be sure it's Eddie?'

'Because I recognize the lettering. Bits and pieces from *The Undertakers Journal*.' He added characteristically, 'Always a very good read, Father.'

'And you're not annoyed?'

'I'm rather pleased, really. Eddie McEvoy is shrewd enough to know a problem when he sees one.'

'You and Mrs Williams, Mr Williams?'

His long, thin face went even blacker than usual. 'You guessed, Father.'

I delayed the start as long as I could, hoping that other customers would turn up and lend me support. None came. I'd have to go it alone.

'There's only one thing wrong with my marriage,' Freddie began.

'That's encouraging,' I said, wondering what he was doing, then, messing up my meeting.

'My Doris and I don't get on.'

I coughed in embarrassment. 'I don't suppose you can pinpoint the time when the trouble began?'

115

'I am tempted to say, Father, when all the guests had left. But I realize the rot had set in before then.'

I put on a smile but even without looking in the mirror I felt it didn't fit my face.

'I *was* romantic once, Father, that's why it hurts, you see. I bought a ticket for a dance.' There was a flame in Freddie's eye as he remembered. 'And there was this gorgeous girl, light as a fairy on her feet, with long fair hair, lovelier than a groomed horse. My heart galloped after her, so to speak, like a Derby winner.'

'You *were* romantic, Mr Williams, so you must have loved your Doris once.'

'Oh, that was before I met my Doris. I was talking about Mavis Dowling. She eloped with a milkman. I never really liked my Doris.'

I took a long breath. 'Why did you, er, marry her, then?'

'I had to.'

'You had to.'

'She made me. Or, at least, her father did.' Freddie looked as if the room had suddenly turned cold. 'A hard man, he was. I don't want to say anything nasty about Doris's dad but that one was a real bugger.'

I hadn't realized that Freddie Williams had a family. 'Do you have many children?' I asked.

'None.'

I worked it out that either Doris had duped him or the infant had died. Seeing my puzzled expression, he explained.

'Doris's dad owned the Funeral Service, Father.'

'Ah.' I still was none the wiser.

'I had a broad pair of shoulders on me – the best shape for coffins, too – but that was all. Depression years, they were. I hadn't any prospects. Neither had Doris unless one of the pall-bearers took her on.'

'And you were first choice?'

Freddie hesitated before replying. 'Not exactly. It wasn't till her father took me aside for a word that I realized why my three colleagues, all long standing, had lately been thrown on the dole.' He sniffed sadly. 'They refused the ultimatum.'

'So you asked her to marry you?'

'Asked? I suppose so. I kept my job as a dowry. But, to be honest with you, I was getting a bit desperate at the time.'

'In what way?'

'When you work as an undertaker you don't meet many women. Well, you do but not women in the marriage market, I mean. Either the tears are running down their cheeks or they're dead.'

I gave an understanding grunt.

'If, to take an example, you see a pretty young widow at the graveside you can't exactly introduce yourself, can you?'

'No.'

'In any case, what would you say to her? "Do you come here often?" or "Care for a night out at the pictures?" '

'Your wife, I don't suppose she secretly resents you being an undertaker?'

Mr Williams cast a look of admiration at me. 'Do you know, Father, I think she does. She didn't like her father and he was one.'

'Why didn't she like her father?'

'Mainly because he chose *me*, I shouldn't wonder.'

'Go on, Mr Williams,' I said.

'Well,' he said, fingering his new black topper, 'I never tried to hide the fact that I'm an undertaker and I like the job. Even when I was courting my Doris, I dressed like this.' With his hand he gestured down his professional attire. 'I was even married in this and used one of her father's best hearses for the wedding. We rearranged the inside a bit, of course.'

'Of course.'

'So she knew where my heart was and I think she was pleased with me at first. I provided her with the sort of life she was accustomed to. In our street, she was proud to be spoken of as the undertaker's wife. Always good for a few bob's credit at the corner shop. The third steadiest job

117

in the market place, we used to say.'

'The *third*?' I queried.

'The first is yours, Father.'

'And the second?'

'I'd rather not say, if you don't mind.'

I urged him to continue.

'It was the neighbours' kids that turned her against me in the end. My fault, I suppose, for leaving the hearse outside the front door at nights. The kids used to pass nasty remarks at her after that.'

'May I ask what sort of remarks?'

'They used to say, "That one" – meaning my Doris – "that one is married to a prune." '

'Not nice.'

'It was a bit thoughtless. Sometimes they referred to me as "The Big Stiff" or "The Removal Man" or' – he hesitated – ' "The Cockroach." '

I had to get beyond this name-calling to the roots of his marital difficulties. It was my duty as a priest. I launched out into the deep.

'Mr Williams.'

'Yes, Father?'

'Mr Williams, you don't think, er, the real source of your, er, problem, might be, how shall I put it . . .?'

'*No*, Father.'

'You are sure?'

'Absolutely. My Doris won't even hear of it.'

I changed slightly the direction of my attack. 'Do you sleep well at nights?'

'Not bad, Father. I sleep on top of my Doris.'

I cleared my throat. 'You do.'

'Always.'

'All night?'

'Yes, except when I have – '

'Do you have a double bed, Mr Williams?'

'Not since our honeymoon and even then I wasn't always allowed in.'

I was getting warm. 'You have two singles, then?'

'No.'

The wild thought came to me that they might sleep in separate coffins. I said, 'On the floor, Mr Williams?'

'We're not Japs, Father. Bunk beds. It's a habit we got into when we slept in the dug-out during the war.'

I nodded. My wild thought wasn't so wild, after all. What is a bunk but a coffin without a lid?

'You like the arrangement?' I said.

'At least we're near,' he said, 'but not too near.'

'And you sleep on the top bunk?'

'It gives my Doris reassurance, Father. Mind you, I don't like the set-up really.'

'You'd prefer a double bed.'

'I don't want to be ambitious. No, I mean I'd prefer the bottom bunk. To start with, I can't stand heights, that's why I keep away from the edge of graves, you may have noticed.'

'I hadn't, as a matter of fact.'

'Anyway, I have a recurrent nightmare. A sense of falling from a great height. Then I wake up with a thud. On the floor usually.'

'It doesn't sound very comfortable, Mr Williams.'

'If I'm to be totally honest with you, Father, it isn't. Especially as there's a wooden plank at one end of my bunk so I have to sleep with my knees up round my chin. I'm very tall. You may have noticed.'

I confirmed that I had. 'Couldn't you sleep the other way round, Mr Williams, so your feet go over the edge that way?'

He was astonished. 'Do you know, that's never occurred to me. Not in ten years.' His face clouded over. 'I'll ask my Doris if she has any objections.'

'Why should she?'

'She might wake up in the night and see these' – he pointed, thumbs-down, to his feet as if they were alien things – 'sticking out the end of the bunk. It wouldn't be a pretty sight, would it?'

'I don't know,' I admitted.

'You haven't seen 'em, Father. I reckon that next to

119

undertakers there's no one sees worse sights than a chiropodist.'

'Feet are never very beautiful at the best of times,' I said, in an attempt to cheer him up.

He came over confidential at this point. I had noticed before that sympathy brought out the worst in him.

'I've got corns, bunions, ingrowing toenails, the lot. Because of all the standing around I have to do. It's lucky for me we live in England.'

'Good chiropodists, you mean?'

'No, we wear shoes and socks. Otherwise, I reckon I'd have to stay indoors every day till it's dark.'

'Couldn't you wear bed socks, Mr Williams?'

His face burst with unconcealed emotion. It was like watching a sudden outbreak of boils.

'Do you know, I think you're *clever*, Father, I really do.'

I shrugged off the compliment in order to press on with the job in hand.

'How do your disagreements show during the day, Mr Williams?'

'Apart from her using my best cremation urns for vases?'

'I wasn't thinking of that particularly.'

Tears sprang into his eyes. 'Do you realize, Father, that my Doris has never been to one of my funerals? Not one.'

His professional pride was suffering a hurt whose extent it was difficult for a layman in these matters to calculate.

'I *am* sorry,' I said, not too sympathetically.

'Not even when Mrs Jennie White died.'

'Mrs White?'

'She was about the most vile, disgusting person I ever met.'

My nature got the better of me. I tried consoling him with, 'Maybe that's why your wife didn't attend her funeral.'

'Jennie *was* her best friend,' he insisted. 'No, she didn't turn up so as to spite me to my face. Another thing, Father. She . . . she insulted me horribly.'

'Yes?' I said, providing an opening if he wanted one.

' "If I die, Frederick," she said this to me last month, putting on a face like my left foot, "if I die, I'm not letting *you* bury me." ' Freddie wiped his eyes with the back of his hand. 'Well, what a thing to say to any undertaker, let alone your own husband.'

'It must have hurt,' I whispered.

'I've got my pride, Father. I said to her, "Doris, suppose I were to say to you, I'm not eating your cooking any more, what would you say?" '

'What *did* she say?'

'Nothing. But since then I've had to cook for myself.'

According to a marriage guidance book I had read I wasn't supposed to take sides in a marital dispute. All the same, Freddie secretly had my complete backing.

'She's a big woman, my Doris is, Father. Have you ever seen her?'

'I don't think so.'

'Then you haven't. Big is perhaps too small a word for her. She'll flatten some shoulders when she goes.'

I admired how, even in his depression, he still managed to view things professionally.

'She's enormous, really, Father. So it's not surprising she complains she doesn't feel altogether loved.'

'It's generous of you to say that, Mr Williams.'

He eyed me gratefully. 'Her body comes between us, so to speak,' he said, joking bravely and showing his white tomb-stone teeth. 'There is so much of her to love. I do my best. I put my arms around as much as I can reach at a time. I do it in relays and, that way, I cover most of her in about a week.'

Here, Mr Williams, his humour spent, broke off close to choking point. I decided it was kinder to both of us to bring the meeting to a close.

'You're the first person,' he said to me at the door, 'who's ever completely understood me. Know what I mean, Father?'

'Not exactly,' I said, blushing, but I thanked him for the

compliment. 'Any time I can be of help, Mr Williams.'

'Next Thursday at 7.30, then, Father.'

I reflected all week on Dr Daley's apparently crazy proposition that nowadays there was too little indulgence in sex. It was a proposition overwhelmingly supported by the only evidence I had. Batty Holohan and Dympna Tutty were intent on a virginal marriage while Freddie and Doris Williams's bedroom closely resembled a family vault.

On Thursday evening, I was thinking, 'Some Family Group! Only one member and he's an unhappily married man,' when attendance doubled. Enter Mr Bottesford.

'I have a family problem,' Bottesford explained in his whiny voice. 'My wife is threatening to come back to me.'

It was the gossip of the parish that Bottesford's wife had done the decent thing and left him for a commercial traveller.

I could hardly refuse Bottesford's application. As Fr Duddleswell pointed out, 'That one may swallow a rasher of a blessed Friday but he is a Catholic of sorts, whereas Freddie Williams is only Co-op.'

It did look a bit odd, all the same, having two rival hearses standing nose to nose outside St Jude's, especially as Bottesford's had a coffin in.

I played safe, that evening. We studied, in a less personal manner than before, the Catholic theology of marriage as set out in Pius XI's encyclical *Casti Connubii*.

We had been together nearly an hour when I was called out by an irate Fr Duddleswell.

'If this continues,' he said hoarsely, 'I am going to the Bishop to be fitted for a new curate.'

'What's the matter, Father?'

'I have had two callers at the door and three phone calls asking which of us has died, you or me.' He beckoned me. 'Come on, lad. If we don't act fast, we shall have all the old women of the parish buzzing around like flies on a cowpat.'

Having no clue to what he had in mind I followed him

outside to Bottesford's hearse. He opened the rear door and started pulling out the coffin.

'You can't do that,' I said.

"Tis empty, Father Neil. I am not having the bloody thing outside the presbytery late at night.'

The coffin was not empty. Something was sliding up and down inside it. Not heavy enough to be a corpse. We carried the coffin in to the hall and placed it on the floor near the grandfather clock.

'Next week, Father Neil, your Family Group will be meeting elsewhere. I am not having St Jude's turned into an undertakers' convention.'

With that, he returned to his study.

The doorbell rang and, being in the vicinity, I answered it. It was Mrs Rollings, my one and only convert. A pious lady and quite impossible.

'Good evening, Mrs Rollings,' I said, smiling pleasantly but firmly. 'You haven't come to join the Family Group.'

I was not asking but telling her.

'No, Father,' she replied to my relief.

'Perhaps you're here to see Father Duddleswell,' I said in hope.

'No, Father. I'm told I have to be confirmed and my Wilf says you're the priest to instruct me.'

I told Mrs Rollings I was about to bring a meeting to a close. After that, I'd consult my diary and fix an appointment.

'In the meanwhile,' I said, 'please make yourself comfortable.'

Before I could stop her, she sat down on the coffin, thinking it was some sort of presbytery bench.

I directed her to a more orthodox seat. 'That's a coffin,' I pointed out and took pleasure in leaving her before she could question me about it.

I had barely returned to the parlour when I heard a short, shrill cry followed by a thud. I hurried back into the hall where Mrs Rollings was stretched out cold on the carpet. Oozing from one end of the coffin was a thick line of blood. I nearly joined the lady on the floor.

'Help,' I called out weakly.

Fr Duddleswell popped his head round his study door and Bottesford and Freddie Williams came running to find out what the trouble was.

'Blood' was all I could say.

'I can explain,' Bottesford said.

'Later,' I told him angrily. 'Pick Mrs Rollings up, first.'

With Freddie he sat her on a chair while I rushed to get her a glass of water.

When she came to, she saw first me and Fr Duddleswell, and smiled. Then the two undertakers came into focus leaning over her and she passed out again.

'I think you had better go,' Fr Duddleswell told them, 'or this good lady is never going to recover.'

'It's only legs of lamb in there,' Bottesford whined, as Mr Williams loaned him a hand with the coffin.

That's it, I thought. That blasted Bottesford at his blackmarket activities again. Transferring meat in a coffin.

It was a splendid cover, I had to admit. The police would have to be pretty ghoulish to stop him and ask him to open *that* up.

The last picture I had of my Family Group that evening was of two undertakers walking together through our front door, solemnly bearing on their shoulders a coffin stuffed with leaky legs of lamb.

My hope was that Fr Duddleswell's veto on any further meetings at St Jude's had spelled the end of my Family Group. I had reckoned without the strength of Freddie Williams's despair. He rang to offer the use of his own home.

Without the publicity of the Co-op hearse outside the presbytery, I expected Bottesford at least to withdraw. Again, my hopes were dashed. He rang to enquire where the next meeting was to be held.

'At Mr Williams's place,' I told him, thinking that would dampen his enthusiasm.

'I'll be there, Father,' he said.

In the event, Doris Williams played ball. There was no denying the size of her. Legs like Shire horses, a bosom big enough to suffocate two guardsmen in at once and more double chins than a concertina. But she seemed an amiable creature.

A splendid hostess, Doris kept plying us with tea and home-made fruit cake as we men formulated the purposes and ends of marriage in a lounge festooned with pictures of Mr Williams posing beside tombstones. Doris herself wouldn't 'partake of a crumb' on account of her acute 'dyspepsia', a polite word, I presumed, for belly-ache.

When we had eaten enough, Doris sat quietly in the corner of the room, making up her face. She distracted me very much. When she powdered her nose, it reminded me of a snow-storm, and when she stretched her lips to rouge them I could think of nothing but someone getting in practice to paint a pillar box.

After that meeting, I had a word on the side with Freddie. He was delighted with progress so far.

'A really nice fellow, Bottesford,' he enthused. 'I had no idea.'

'Nor I,' I said.

'My Doris isn't doing so bad, either, is she?'

I could see he was fishing for compliments. 'She makes a nice fruit cake,' I said.

'I'll tell her that, Father, if you don't mind.'

'I don't mind,' I said.

'She's really thrilled that you're honouring us with your presence. She's partial to dog collars.'

He wasn't joking. With every meeting, Doris ogled me more and more. I was concerned lest the other two men were scandalized. They were probably too engrossed in their theological discussions to notice.

I found it hard to believe Bottesford was deeply interested in theology. Then, in a flash, I *knew* why he was coming to the meetings. He was hoping to persuade Freddie to defect from the Co-op and join Bottesford's Funeral Parlour. With Freddie's reputation for honesty and reliability, he would be able to sew up the trade of the whole town.

When I voiced my suspicions to Fr Duddleswell, he said, 'There is a distinct odour hereabouts, Father Neil, even if Bottesford is lying in lavender like Paddy's pig.'

The meetings had been continuing satisfactorily for a month when, one morning after Mass, I received an anonymous phone call. An Irish voice said, 'I t'ink you should know, Fairther. Poor Mrs Williams went in the night, Fairther. A big loss, Fairther.'

Before I could question him, the caller rang off. I recognized the voice as that of Eddie McEvoy, Freddie's pall-bearer.

I immediately told Fr Duddleswell that Mrs Williams's 'dyspepsia' must have been something far more serious.

'God rest her,' he murmured, signing himself. 'She'll make a full load for four.'

We jumped into the car and drove to Freddie's place.

As soon as Freddie answered the door, Fr Duddleswell gripped his arm. 'I am so sorry, Freddie.'

Freddie sniffed and rubbed the pouch under his eye. He had not had a wink of sleep, it was obvious.

'Come in, Fathers. Bad news is like a bad shilling, isn't it? It travels very fast from one to the next.'

He invited us in to his kitchen and I managed to whisper on my own behalf, 'My deepest sympathy.'

He smiled courageously. 'It was God's will, Father. Besides, she's happy now. At least, I hope so.'

'I'm sure she is, Freddie,' Fr Duddleswell responded.

'Her heart, you see,' Freddie said. 'How was I to know? She never told me a thing.'

'Steady,' Fr Duddleswell urged.

'To be honest with you,' Freddie said, 'I'm not altogether broken up. As you know, Doris and I never really hit it off and yet just as we seemed to be getting it together . . .'

'Don't blame yourself, Mr Williams,' I said.

'I'll try not to.' He poured tea for us. 'It'll take a bit of time to adjust. Twenty-five years is a long time.' He thought again. 'A *very* long time.'

'Can I go and see her, Mr Williams?'

He grabbed my arm. 'No, Father, there's nothing in the world will bring her back now.'

Fr Duddleswell asked, 'When is the funeral, Freddie?'

Mr Williams had the usual glazed look of someone who has suffered a sudden and sharp shock. 'Funeral?'

Knowing the background, I felt the terrible irony of the question. Doris had never attended any of Freddie's funerals on principle. It seemed she was about to break her rule at last.

'He'll do it now, won't he, Father? Bottesford.'

'When, Freddie?'

Freddie gazed at Fr Duddleswell, bewildered. 'When she dies, Father. That's normal.'

'Of course, Freddie. We mustn't hurry things along.'

A good effort from Fr Duddleswell, considering that no sooner was Doris dead, as far as he was concerned, than she rose again.

That's what Eddie McEvoy meant by his anonymous call. Doris had upped and left in the night and gone to live with Bottesford.

'Anyway, Freddie,' Fr Duddleswell said, 'I only came to say that if you need anything after your wife's departure, you can rely on me.' And, looking daggers in my direction, he left in a hurry.

'Wasn't it nice of him to call?' Freddie said.

I resolved to take full responsibility for the calamitous course of events.

'Mr Williams,' I said, 'this would never have happened but for my Family Group.'

He came across and shook my hand solemnly. 'I know, Father Boyd. I have to thank you most sincerely for the break-up of my marriage.'

'It's kind of you to say so,' I said, edging away from the compliment.

'I see it all now. Bottesford planned it all from start

127

to finish. It wasn't Eddie McEvoy who sent me the original invitation.'

'Bottesford? How do you know that?'

'Because when Doris left me last night, I went round to Eddie's place and offered him ten quid for all he'd done for me. It was news to him and he wouldn't take a penny. In fact, he must've felt a bit insulted.'

I rearranged my thoughts rapidly. Bottesford had invited Freddie to the Family Group in the first instance so he could get at Doris. When Fr Duddleswell threw us out of the presbytery parlour, Doris did her bit by offering the use of hers. And Doris's ogling of me was nothing but a front while she flirted with Bottesford.

'The whole thing is utterly despicable,' I concluded aloud.

'Not to worry, Father.' Never had I seen Freddie in such a buoyant mood. 'I wish Bottesford the best of luck. My Doris was an iceberg to me but if he can thaw her out there's enough of her to satisfy Solomon.'

My eyes misted up at the generosity of the man. Until he added:

'The fact is, Father, the reason I'm not cut up is because I've met a nice little widow.'

'You didn't meet her, how shall I put it, professionally?'

He nodded. 'I never thought I'd be so lucky.'

'Isn't that rather like a doctor falling for one of his patients?'

Freddie laughed aloud at my innocence. It was a very strange sound. Like a goose. 'No, Father. I'm not in competition with her former husband, am I?'

'I suppose not.'

'I gave him a good send off.'

'I'm sure you did.'

'That's why she fell for me, I think. Now, the thing is, Father,' – he winked at me – 'and this will please you, the lovely lady in question is a Catholic. I'd like to be fully instructed as one myself. Which is where you come in.'

'Let me have another think, Mr Williams,' I said, and

128

performed the feat frantically while he looked on. His infatuated smile didn't help.

First of all, I reflected, I break up Mr Williams's marriage to Doris. Doris runs off to live adulterously with one of our parishioners, Bottesford. And now Freddie wants to marry a Catholic widow, which is not allowed, while Doris is still alive, and to become a Catholic himself, which, in the circumstances, is inadvisable, to say the least.

Freddie cut across my thoughts just as it occurred to me that Fr Duddleswell was not going to be pleased with my performance.

'Father, before you say another word, there's something you should know about me. I've kept it dark for years but you've been so kind I don't want to hide anything from you.'

I returned to the presbytery prepared for another battering, this time from Fr Duddleswell. I allowed him to run through the litany of my failures, the most unpardonable of which was using my Family Group to break up a marriage.

Marriage, even between non-Catholics, is binding, he lectured me in a cold theological tone. It is not a slip-knot that the couple can wriggle out of when it suits them but a reef-knot that only God can cut with the sharp teeth of death.

It was straight out of a sermon of his which I had heard three times before.

'Did I not warn you, Father Neil, to leave marrieds alone? Now you will realize 'tis perilous to get between the tree and its bark.' He released an angry breath. 'And all the while Bottesford was pretending to be interested in religion he was feeding Doris up with false music.'

I heard him out, including his wry reflections on my youth and inexperience. Then, nonchalantly:

'You are talking out of the top of your biretta, Father.'

'What d'you mean, lad. Has Doris left Bottesford and gone back to Freddie already?'

'As a matter of fact, Father, Freddie and Doris were never married in the first place.'

'Who fed you that nasty rumour?'

'Freddie.'

Fr Duddleswell sat back in his chair, stunned. 'But Freddie is a model of rectitude, a pillar of Fairwater society.'

'He is.'

'Was he or Doris married before, then?'

I shook my head, and, to be merciful, explained.

'Mr Williams, Father, is a Catholic.'

'Never!'

'Doris's dad forced him to marry Doris in an Anglican church. After that, he never darkened the door of a Catholic church again, except for funerals, of course.'

'So,' Fr Duddleswell inferred, 'Freddie was never validly married in the eyes of the Church because, as a Catholic, – '

'He should have been married in the Church,' I said, like a lecturer, 'and wasn't.'

'That puts an entirely new complexion on things,' Fr Duddleswell admitted.

'It means,' I put in immodestly, 'that I have not broken up Freddie's marriage, merely stopped him living in sin with Doris.'

'Not that there was much of that involved from what I heard. Not with herself keeping her legs crossed like a tailor.'

I eased up. 'Freddie actually smiled, Father.'

'Must have been like a cat with a saddle on.'

'It was, rather.'

I was telling him of Freddie's plan to divorce Doris and marry his Catholic widow when the phone rang.

Fr Duddleswell answered it and said, 'Yes, I will hold.' To me: 'Long distance from Spain.'

'The Holohans?'

He smiled at me in a self-satisfied way, as if to say we all have our little triumphs. 'The second day of their honeymoon, lad. Let us hope the heifer is on heat, at last.'

'You're hoping, aren't you,' I taunted him, 'that they'll commit that wicked sin?'

'Real wickedness is quite irresistible, Father Neil. Besides, I rang up their tour operator to tell them that the Holohans are a honeymoon couple.'

'Why do that?'

'Because honeymoon couples are entitled to a bottle of cheap bubbly and a double bed.'

'Ah,' I said.

He had got his connection. 'Ah, yes, Dympna darlin',' he said in a velvety voice, 'what a lovely surprise hearing from you. . . . You want me to dispense you from your vow of virginity on your honeymoon. Let me think carefully, now.'

It didn't take him long. But, then, it *was* a long-distance call.

'Dympna, tell me, Batty did not force this decision on you? . . . Ah, I see, 'twas *entirely* your idea. Fine, fine.' He smirked at me. 'Well, Dympna, this is such a serious matter I will have to give you a stiff penance, but I did warn you about that. So before you go to bed next, whenever that is, I want you to kneel down and say three Hail Marys in honour of the Sacred Heart. . . . Don't mention it, Dympna. Now would you put Batty on the line.'

I couldn't take any more of Fr Duddleswell's smugness. I was at the door, ready to leave, when his smooth tone was replaced by one of utter agitation.

'But, Batty, you cannot do that. You *must* let me dispense you from your vow . . . 'Tis ridiculous for Dympna to be free to . . . to do things when you are holding fast to your vow . . . I know you have the holy example of St Joseph, spouse of our Blessed Lady, but St Joseph did not go to the bloody Costa Blanca for his honeymoon.'

My sides were splitting. When I left, Fr Duddleswell was still trying to convince Batty Holohan in Benidorm that it was imperative he renounce his vow of chastity for the sake of his marriage.

SEVEN

A Mixed-up Marriage

Before my first Christmas at St Jude's, in company with Fr Duddleswell and Canon Mahoney, I had attended an inter-faith Conference. It was held at the Anglican Vicarage of St Luke's. Our doctrines on Hell and Purgatory had made little impression on the Anglicans and Methodists. Still less on Rabbi Epstein, an émigré Pole, who seemed already to have one foot in the Hereafter. We priests agreed such conferences were a waste of God's good time and resolved not to attend any more.

Bishop O'Reilly was of a different mind. After reading the Canon's report, he told him that in England, every two weeks an Anglican clergyman was received into the One, True Church. What better forum for converting them than an inter-faith Conference?

'What about the Rabbi, my Lord?' Canon Mahoney had asked.

'Didn't our Blessed Lord Himself start out as a Jew,' the Bishop reminded him, 'before he turned?' And didn't He convert His Blessed Mother, a very pious Jewess, as well as His twelve lovely disciples, besides?'

Canon Mahoney couldn't deny that former Jews did have a big hand in getting Catholicism off the ground.

'There, then, Canon,' the Bishop went on, 'if our Blessed Lord had adopted your defeatist attitude, where would the Catholic Church be today?'

A second Conference was scheduled for the middle of May. The topic was a vexed one: Mixed Marriages. It was our turn to provide the position-paper, so the Canon handed over the task to Fr Duddleswell.

For days beforehand, he was busy, consulting heavy tomes and scribbling madly. After which, he sent a draft of his talk to the Canon who returned it with a brief comment: 'Courteous and charitable, Charlie. A model of intransigence.'

As Fr Duddleswell let me read the note, his eyes misted up with emotion. ''Tis not every day of the week, Father Neil, I receive praise of this calibre.'

The day before the Conference, the Canon cried off. His housekeeper rang to say he had gone down with 'flu. She had, she said, already telephoned his Lordship.

Fr Duddleswell and I were discussing this serious depletion of our forces when Billy Buzzle's voice floated in from the hall.

'Cheerio, then, Mrs Pring. I'll drop in again same time next week.'

Fr Duddleswell was at his study door in a flash with, 'Me dear friend, please come in, do.'

Billy looked around him. 'Talking to me, Father O'Duddleswell?'

'The very man. Come in.' And he almost dragged our neighbour in after him.

'Short of cash or something?' Fr Duddleswell shook his head. 'I've just been having a cup of char with Mrs Pring. Anything wrong with that?'

'Mr Buzzle,' Fr Duddleswell said, 'you wouldn't be free to attend a Conference at two tomorrow afternoon?'

'What for?'

'I would very much like to have the man-in-the-street's point of view on a delicate religious topic.'

Billy thumbed through his diary. 'Well, there's no race meeting. Okay, anything for a lark.'

Fr Duddleswell slapped him on the back, nearly knocking the breath out of him. 'That is the spirit, Mr Buzzle.'

'Can I bring my dog along? He's much better than me at religion.'

Fr Duddleswell shook his head, smiling as if he meant

it. 'We will have the dog-in-the-street's point of view another time.'

'He's real tame, my Pontius is. It's all I can do to get him to bite a dog biscuit.'

'He made a meal of my backside last Christmas,' he was reminded.

'Yeah, funny that. I always thought he had a sweet tooth.'

'The answer, anyhow, is still no.'

'Pity. But what are you discussing?'

'Mixed marriages.'

'Where one partner drinks and the other don't?'

Another benign smile. 'Something of the sort.'

'I'm all against 'em,' Billy said.

When he had left, I asked what Billy would add to the Conference.

'Confusion, Father Neil.' He explained that the Bishop didn't understand it's a waste of time talking to Protestants. 'Billy will prove me point, you follow?'

Mrs Pring announced the unexpected arrival of Mother Stephen.

Fr Duddleswell leaped to his feet, whispering hoarsely, 'Dear God, the Big Penguin.' Aloud: 'Mother Superior, an honour to have you visit us. Would you care for a cup o' tay?'

'Our rules, Father,' she said, sitting stiffly. 'Firstly, I have come about our Foundress's tibia.'

'Have you lost it, Mother?' I asked cheekily.

The Superior evidently considered it her solemn duty as Christ's representative to ignore me. 'I would like you, Father Duddleswell, to put it on display here in the parish church.'

Fr Duddleswell, uncharacteristically, was at a loss for words. 'What for, Mother?'

'To encourage devotion towards her, naturally.'

He stroked his chin thoughtfully. 'Is it fitting, Mother, that a lady as refined and cloistered as your Foundress should be showing a leg, so to speak?' Seeing a storm about to break on the Superior's face, he added, 'I speak with the utmost respect.'

'The holy tibia is encased in a reliquary of gold and semi-precious stones,' she said. 'Her modesty will be preserved.'

'All the more reason for saying no, Mother. The reliquary may be stolen, y'see.'

'And Mother Foundress will only have one leg to stand on,' I said. It was dawning on me that Mother Stephen was all bark and no bite.

'I will discuss the matter with his Lordship, Father.'

'Do that,' Fr Duddleswell said, happy enough to pass the buck.

'Secondly, Father Duddleswell, I will myself be attending the Conference tomorrow afternoon.'

'Strange, Mother,' he said, looking up the list. 'I do not recall sending you an invitation.'

'The Bishop did not forget, Father. His secretary telephoned the Convent half an hour ago, asking me to take Canon Mahoney's place and to send him a detailed report of the proceedings.'

As before, the Reverend Percival Probble attended with Michael D'Arcy and the fat John Pinkerton, his curates. The Methodists, Tinsey with the tin-whistle voice and the bearded Sobb, were also there, as was the Rabbi Epstein, a tiny island of a man, bony and mysterious.

Mother Stephen and I flanked Fr Duddleswell as he read his paper while Billy was next to me, slumped in his chair, devoutly asleep.

A biting wind blew inside and outside the room.

Fr Duddleswell explained clearly that the Catholic Church disapproves strongly of mixed marriages. She tolerates them between her own children and others, whether baptized or not, only on the strictest conditions.

First, the ceremony must be conducted before the parish priest of the place. Otherwise, it is not a valid marriage and the Catholic party is held to be living in sin.

Second, the bishop may grant a dispensation. The non-Catholic must however sign a document in advance promising not to interfere with the faith of the Catholic partner

135

and to allow all children born of the union to be baptized and brought up as Catholics.

When, after half an hour, Fr Duddleswell put his papers in order, Mr Probble had to restrain his junior curate. 'Please, John, remember your resolution.' He turned to Fr Duddleswell: 'I personally find your views most interesting.'

'Thank you, Mr Probble. I take it that means you, too, disagree with them.'

Mother Stephen's icy voice intervened. 'They are *not* Father Duddleswell's views.'

Thinking the Superior was impugning his orthodoxy, he insisted, 'Indeed they are, Mother. Mine *and* the Bishop's.'

'They are,' Mother Stephen affirmed, 'the views of Almighty God.'

'Precisely what I meant,' Fr Duddleswell blustered. 'And I trust, Mother, you will be so good as to tell his Lordship that in your report.'

Mr Probble suggested that perhaps the Catholic attitude might be considered a trifle severe, seeing that Methodists and Anglicans were themselves Christians.

The erudite Mr D'Arcy pointed out that in Victorian England it was quite customary for sons of mixed marriages to be brought up in their father's religion and daughters in their mother's.

'I'm sure the Catholic clergy fought that tooth and nail,' Fr Duddleswell said.

'On the contrary,' Mr D'Arcy said, 'the Catholic clergy went along with it. As they did in Silesia.'

I was out of my depths, knowing little Church history and having no idea where Silesia was.

'It is true,' Mother Stephen said, saving the day, 'that in a few places, Pope Benedict XIV's encyclical *Magnae nobis* of 1741 was neglected.'

'Indeed it was,' Fr Duddleswell echoed. 'In a very few places.'

'But,' Mother Stephen continued, making it plain that her learning needed no assistance, 'Pius VIII and Gregory

XVI reaffirmed that for Catholics to allow any child of theirs to be brought up as non-Catholics is against the law of God.'

'As much against God's law,' Fr Duddleswell added, 'as for a father to marry his own daughter.'

Fatty Pinkerton was all this time puffing hard on his cigarette and throwing out the occasional 'Iniquitous', 'Bigots', 'Pressurizing non-Catholics to become Romans.'

Fr Duddleswell picked up the last point. ''Tis true that most conversions to Catholicism, about 14,000 a year, are the result of mixed marriages.'

'That proves it,' Sobb said. 'Catholics take no account of the consciences of people outside their communion.'

'Indeed we do,' Fr Duddleswell replied. 'If these good people are troubled in their consciences they should not sign the document.'

'But that will only mean,' Sobb said, 'that they cannot marry Catholics.'

Fr Duddleswell smiled superiorly. 'The fact that they do sign, sir, shows that Methodists do not take the matter as seriously as Catholics. After all, you do not suggest that your people are so weak-kneed as to marry the person of their choice *against* their consciences?'

'We are suggesting,' Mr Tinsey whistled, 'that Methodists are Christians and that Catholics refuse to accept that fact.'

'And,' Pinkerton added, his resolution worn thin, 'the Catholics threaten their own flock if they disobey. As usual, with hellfire.'

That was the moment when Billy Buzzle jerked awake. 'Did I miss much of your Boss Man's speech?'

'All of it,' I assured him.

'Oh dear,' he whispered. 'That *was* lucky.'

The mention of hellfire turned Mother Stephen's thoughts to her Foundress, who, I recalled, had left her husband and children to found an orphanage. I hoped that Pinkerton was unaware of this.

'Our holy Mother Foundress once had a vision of

thousands and thousands of lost souls descending into the fiery pit.'

Billy leaned across me to console her. 'Shame, Mother.'

Mother Stephen, grateful for sympathy from any quarter in that frosty room, said, 'A *great* shame.'

'Did the doctor give her something for it?' Billy asked.

Pinkerton, blind to Mr Probble's warning glance, said, 'Why can't the Catholic Church treat Catholics as adults and let them decide for themselves whom they want to marry instead of talking about them endangering their faith and risking hellfire?'

'Myself,' Billy said, 'I like the idea of Hell.'

'How *very* interesting,' Mr Pinkerton said. He believed all opinions, however crazy, are free and equal.

'Yeah,' Billy laughed, enjoying being the focus of attention, 'think of the good company.'

Mr Probble wagged his head courteously. 'I hadn't thought of that.'

'All the gamblers and drinkers go there, don't they?'

The Methodists nodded vigorously.

'And just you imagine,' Billy went on, 'no more chilblains, no one strumming away on harps and a great big sign up,' – he made the appropriate gesture – 'FRYING TONIGHT.'

Billy laughed and, in spite of myself, I laughed, too.

To impress Mother Stephen, Fr Duddleswell enquired sternly, 'Father Neil, would you mind telling me why you are gurgling like a jackass?'

'Because he's got a sense of humour,' Pinkerton said, 'and you haven't.'

'No, dead serious,' Billy said, trying to stifle his amusement with scant success. 'I prefer Hell to being up there with all those clouds and clergymen.'

Pinkerton laughed to spite Fr Duddleswell.

Billy put on a straight face. 'Father O'Duddleswell, since my dog wasn't allowed in, can I ask a silly question?'

Fr Duddleswell pointed at Pinkerton. 'It cannot be any sillier than his.'

'The Bishop does not approve of silly questions,' Mother

138

Stephen remarked and Fr Duddleswell, remembering his plight, agreed with her.

'No, Mr Buzzle, of course you cannot ask a silly question.'

'You mean,' Billy complained, 'because I'm not wearing a clerical collar I can't ask silly questions.'

'You, sir, are not a clergyman,' Mother Stephen said.

Billy responded instantaneously. 'Neither are you, sir.'

'Mr Buzzle,' Fr Duddleswell said, controlling his mirth with difficulty, 'would you have the good manners not to insult Mother Superior while she is in the room.'

'Okay, Father O'Duddleswell, but I thought you invited me so I could ask questions.'

Mother Stephen turned on the chairman. '*You* invited him?'

'In the hope he would see the light, Mother.'

'I have,' Billy said, 'I'm not coming no more.'

'Swear,' Fr Duddleswell muttered grimly.

Billy roared. 'Who at, mate?'

'Never you mind.'

All the time these squabbles were going on, Rabbi Epstein had been silently gazing at his joined fingertips. The fingers were long and thin, translucent almost. As I looked at this lonely, seemingly lost little man, I called to mind a piece of doggerel we used to recite among ourselves at school: 'Get a bit of pork, Stick it on a fork, And give it to a Jewboy, do.'

'Rabbi,' Mr Probble said, attempting to draw him into the conversation. 'Have you any strong feelings about mixed marriages?'

The Rabbi shot upright as if his thoughts had been far away. His eyes as he spoke were dim, lustreless.

'What say the Talmud?' he murmured. 'Pardon. A dog speak gooder English.'

'It is perfectly intelligible,' Mr Probble said, 'and that's the main thing.'

'A happy coupling of male and female,' the Rabbi said, 'is hard for the Almighty like the parting of the Red Sea.'

'He managed it,' Pinkerton said cheerfully.

'Once,' the Rabbi conceded. 'I also remember that Abraham loved Sarah.'

Mr Probble was perplexed. 'Am I to take it, Rabbi, that you are agreeing with Father Duddleswell?'

'Reverend Father does not know what his talk is about.' Fr Duddleswell had time to open his mouth but not to utter before the Rabbi added. 'But he is quite right.'

'Of course,' Mr Pinkerton sighed.

'Father Duddleswell a funny man. He does not get married. But God say, Multiplify and fill up the earth.' The Rabbi clapped with his fingertips. 'How he so wise for an ignorant?'

'You are married, Rabbi?' Mr Sobb asked.

'Of certainly. I am a man.' Out of the corner of my eye, I saw Fr Duddleswell gulp. 'My wife . . . my wife is Edzia.' He seemed to have difficulty in speaking her name which he pronounced with a full Slavonic flavour. 'My Edzia. Like a fruitful vine. Our children, olive shoots around my table. Seven children, Beautiful, them all.'

'You certainly multiplied and fill the earth.' Fr Duddleswell's voice had genuine admiration in it.

'Yes,' the Rabbi said. '*Filled the earth.*'

Mr Probble felt it was his duty to bring the conversation back to the topic of mixed marriages. 'You said, Rabbi, that you agree with our Catholic hosts.'

'Not always. Not about, for an example, the divorce. Kings and patriarchs got divorces.'

This was so far from what he had been discussing the consensus was we should let it pass.

'After all things,' the Rabbi added, 'you all think God Himself got divorced.'

This was news to everyone around the table. 'All right, Rabbi,' Pinkerton said mischievously, 'let's have it. Who do we say God married and divorced?'

'Us,' the Rabbi said.

That one word, softly spoken with a Slavonic sizzle at the end, flattened the rest of us. There was no bitterness in the word though it seemed to me in retrospect that, voiced

140

by this black stick of a man, it somehow expressed the sorrow of millions.

Mr Probble coughed clerically. 'We were discussing – '

'A mixed-up marriage,' the Rabbi concluded for him. 'Suppose – God will forgive – my Edzia turn Christian. At the bed's side she kneel at night. "Are you sick, Edzia?" I say. "No, Zorach." "What have your knees done to you, Edzia," I say, "that you are trampling them under foot?" "I am praying, Zorach." Then perhaps my Edzia make the cross on herself. I jump fast to the door like a goat. "Why you frighten me like so, Edzia?" "I am praying, Zorach, in the name of my Saviour, Jesus Christ." "*Now* you remind me of your Saviour and his cross, Edzia," I say, "when I am trying to tumble asleep? That I want like an egg with blood in." '

The Rabbi's simple, domestic dialogue did far more for our cause than Fr Duddleswell's position paper or Mother Stephen's grasp of Church history.

The meeting broke up soon after that. 'Enchanting afternoon,' Mr Probble said, as he hastened to join the Gadarene rush of his colleagues.

'Father Duddleswell,' Mother Stephen said, 'I will pray before our Foundress's tibia for those unbelievers.' She stretched out an icy hand. 'I must congratulate you on the hard line you took.'

Fr Duddleswell touched the hand briefly as if he was afraid of frostbite. 'I will be content, Mother, if you simply tell the Bishop that I gave 'em Hell.'

'How better to help them on the way to Heaven.' The speaker was Billy Buzzle, the last to leave.

'As for you, Mr Buzzle,' Fr Duddleswell fumed, 'good riddance to bad rubbish and be sure not to come again.'

'Don't be like that,' Billy said in a conciliatory tone. 'I'm going next door this minute to tell my Pontius the good news.'

Fr Duddleswell steeled himself for a saucy remark. 'Oh, yes?'

'You've convinced me at last there's an everlasting fire.'

'I am glad of that, Mr Buzzle,' Fr Duddleswell said,

visibly warming towards his neighbour. 'But which of me arguments finally converted you?'

'No particular argument,' Billy replied. 'It suddenly occurred to me, if there's no Hell, where will you and Mother Stephen go?'

Rabbi Epstein made such an impression on me that the following day I spoke to Mrs Hughes' class of ten-year olds about the Jews.

'It's wrong to blame the Jews for Jesus' death on the cross,' I told them. 'Our Lord Himself was born a Jew, so was His Mother and all his disciples. Only a few Jews in the world ever knew Him and fewer still trespassed by rejecting Him. And yet, over the ages, many Christians thought it right to persecute Jews when, of course, they can't all have been responsible for crucifying our Lord.'

I'm no teacher and my language was obviously not simple enough. After I left, Mrs Hughes asked the children to write in their theme books what I had taught them. Later, she showed me what Robert had written: 'The Christians trespassed and the Jubes got prosecuted.'

Canon Mahoney, miraculously restored to the perpendicular after what I took to be a diplomatic illness, joined us for lunch at The Clinton Hotel.

After hearing Fr Duddleswell's account of how he had routed the Protestants with minor assistance from me and the occasional annoying interruption from Mother Stephen, the Canon heaved an audible sigh.

'It's more healthy by far, Charlie, to make a Novena to the Virgin for 'em. She has the patience, y'see. What is the flicking Bishop thinking of? He's Irish, he should know better.'

'Truth is, Seamus, Bishop O'Reilly never comes across Protestants, except in his prayers, like. He thinks they are reasonable craters like you and me.'

'They have heads on them as dark and empty as a church at night, Charlie.'

'That is no fiction but a plain fact.'

'No sense of the sacred, Charlie. Their sort would piddle on the Burning Bush.'

'They would, Seamus, they would.'

So far it was banter and little more, even though it annoyed me considerably. Then the Canon grew more serious.

'They didn't appear to grasp, then, Charlie, that if the theological issues are not settled before a mixed marriage they never will be.'

'I can just imagine it, Seamus. A husband and wife having a debate every night before they slip in between the sheets about what they are going to do there and what faith the kiddies will be baptized in.'

Canon Mahoney wearily pushed his wine glass towards me. 'Fill it up again, Sonny. We have to cheerify ourselves somehow.'

'At least the Rabbi was on our side, Seamus.'

'In the matter of mixed-up marriages,' I said.

'Excuse. I doubt that you remember me well, Father Boyd.'

In the murky hallway, I took in the slight figure of the Rabbi at a glance. The broad-brimmed black hat that seemed to be slipping off the back of his head; the bushy beard; the grey-tinged side-curls; the owl-like glasses; the black overcoat, smooth as the skin of a seal fresh from the sea, that dropped straight down and hid his shoes.

Even with six holes in the head, who could fail to remember well Rabbi Zorach Epstein?

I stretched out my hand to him. '*Shalom aleichem*, Rabbi.'

He took my hands and kissed them both. No words. His moist lips on my skin expressed better than words his thanks for my feeble effort at friendliness.

'Have you come to see Father Duddleswell?' I asked, a trifle embarrassed.

'You are young, Father,' he said inconsequentially. 'I once was young also.' He spoke as if had never a hope of making me believe it.

'Yes, I am, I suppose.'

Behind his glasses, the brown eyes twinkled. 'Only the old know the young are young. If the young knew it, they would never grow old.'

I murmured something about liking the sound of that.

'My mother, peace be with her, say that always, Father. Yes, I come for to see Father Duddleswell.'

I explained that he was out visiting the parish. He might be away for five minutes or an hour, he left no word.

'I make good watchman.'

I gathered he intended waiting so I invited him up to my room.

'How is your wife, Rabbi?'

'Edzia? Well. Perfectly now.' His eyes seemed to turn inwards at the mention of her name. 'She lives with me always.'

'Of course,' I said lamely. It took me a few moments to grasp that this was his way of telling me his wife was dead. Had she died since the Conference a week before?

This was his story as I pieced it together. His narrative was not wholly consistent nor his language clear.

Rabbi Epstein and Edzia had lived with their seven children in the Warsaw ghetto not far from the Vistula. In 1939, as the Germans threatened Poland, the Jews began to flee for their lives. No section of the population was more relieved than they when, on September 3rd, the British entered the war on Poland's side.

The Rabbi had joined the crowd outside the British Embassy in Warsaw soon after the Declaration. Everyone was chanting and singing, 'England is on our side. England is with us. Soon we will chase the Nazi barbarians from our land.'

When, a few hours afterwards, planes with Swastikas on flew low over the city dropping bombs the Poles could not believe their eyes.

Meanwhile, Rabbi Epstein had gone home, lit his kerosene lamp and called for salt pretzels.

He sat perched on his chair now as he remembered.

' "What is up and doing, Zorach?" my Edzia say. "Drink a glass of coffee, Edzia," I tell her. "Soon our salvation comes. Mr Neville Chamberlain say so. Mr Lord Halifax say so. Prepare the borscht for supper. And, Edzia mine, stop your crying like it is Yom Kippur." '

Next day, not realizing the danger, the Rabbi went north-west to visit a sick relative in a village near Palcz. The speed of the German Panzer advance was staggering. Polish horsemen with muskets took on tanks and armoured cars. The whole district was overrun. The Rabbi, fortunate to be sheltered by a sympathetic Polish family, was cut off from his wife and children.

All through the bitter winter of 1939/40, he lived in a cemetery. At night, his friends brought him food and drink and he was able to take exercise. During the day, wrapped in sacking, he hid in a tomb that had been hollowed out for him and furnished with a mattress, blankets and a small oil lamp.

By the Spring of 1940, the Nazis were satisfied the Jewish extermination in that area was complete. The friendly Gentile family further risked their lives by hiding the Rabbi in an alcove of their house. They walled it up, leaving only three loose bricks through which they passed food and water and he handed out his refuse.

There he learned his family's fate. Everyone of them had been killed in 'the camp'. He did not, and, I felt, could not name it. I remembered his words at the Conference, referring to his children, 'Filled the earth.'

The Rabbi had no details, except in the case of his eldest son, Samuel. The S.S. had tortured him to make him divulge his father's whereabouts. The lad of sixteen was hung from a butcher's hook. He dripped blood for hours but did not say a word, except to pray the psalms. Afterwards, the camp Commandant joked that Samuel was the first koshered Jew he had come across. If the rest of the family were hungry, let them eat him.

'A sergeant say, "But Herr Commandant, Jews does not eat swine." "Not even their own?" says the Commandant.'

The Rabbi removed his glasses. There was a deep weal

on the bridge of his nose. Without his glasses, he looked white-faced and blind like a statue. He wiped his eyes with the back of his sleeve.

'You know, Father Boyd, before I left home on my voyage, I had row with Sammy. "Sammy," I say, "mend your roads. Behave yourself or I not speak with you no more. Remember you are my firstborn son, Respect your daddy." I spoke wickedness without meaning wickedness, as fathers does. Sammy remembered. He respect his father and he did not even squeak.'

My room was dark now. Normally I would have put on the light but I dared not move.

'In the nights,' the Rabbi said, 'it is mostly in the nights, I cannot forget. I took long time to forgive God, you know?' I nodded. 'Not for Sammy's death.' I shook my head, not knowing why. 'Who cries for martyrs? But why did God not let me say to him only, "Sorry, Sammy"?'

Late in the war, the Rabbi's hideout was discovered by an Alsatian dog when a squad of soldiers were foraging for food. The Gentiles who had harboured him were immediately taken out into the yard and shot, among them a boy of fifteen. The Rabbi was put in a concentration camp for Jews and gypsies.

There he came across a teenage boy, Isaac Brader. Isaac's father was lucky; he died young. The boy and his mother had been hounded for years before being captured and imprisoned.

The camp was small, off the beaten track, and the Commandant, not of the S.S., was unusually kind. Perhaps one reason for this was that the war was going against Germany.

The Rabbi was not sent to the gas-chamber as he had expected and prayed for. The Angel of Death passed him by. Isaac's mother caught influenza. Unable to shake it off due to malnutrition, she died in Isaac's arms. The Rabbi said Kaddish for her and for a hundred other victims of the epidemic.

Isaac lived. He helped the Rabbi slowly to forgive God. And the Rabbi taught the boy what he knew by heart of the Torah, the Talmud and the Commentaries. He bar-mitzvahed him in the camp. It was overdue, the boy being nearly seventeen. They became as close as father and son.

'Even my Sammy, peace be with him, is not closer me than my Isaac.' He looked up to Heaven. 'Perhaps only a bit of a bit closer.'

After the war, when the camps were emptied, the Rabbi nursed Isaac till he was strong enough to travel.

'Between us,' the Rabbi said proudly, 'we had not one zloty. We was too poor to run a chicken but I mended my Isaac.'

They hitched lifts and, like thousands of Poles, made their way to England.

Isaac picked up the language easily, went to school and landed a job in a bank. At the Rabbi's insistence, he found a flat of his own while the Rabbi rented a room in a tenement building. It was very comfortable.

'Warmer than a grave and cleaner than a camp,' he assured me. 'God is good.'

His story concluded, he took out a big red handkerchief and blew his nose.

'God is good,' I said only because he had said it.

He sensed my reluctance to echo him. 'Everything we lost in Holocaust. But God camped with us, eh? We could not light Him one candle, but He stayed.'

I realized, dimly, that we Christians had the same belief.

'Yes, Father Boyd, God is a very funny chap.' The Rabbi laughed aloud at his own quaint use of English and, to compensate, muttered something, in Hebrew I think, which sounded as if he were swallowing soup with lumps in. 'If I meet God, I will put a pumpkin on His head with seven candles on and dance with Him.'

I felt sure God would be honoured.

The Rabbi blew his nose again even louder, tapped the side of it and said:

'In my synagogue, I am needing no *Shofar*. One ram's horn enough is, eh?'

* * *

As soon as Fr Duddleswell entered my room, Rabbi Epstein greeted him with:

'He góod rabbi, Father Boyd. He listen and say nothing, like God.'

Seeing that the Rabbi and I were on friendly terms, Fr Duddleswell invited us both to his study. Perhaps the Rabbi's unexpected presence unsettled him. Or he had a premonition of surprises in store and needed support.

'Coffee, Rabbi?'

Rabbi Epstein turned down Fr Duddleswell's offer with polite regret. I guessed it was something to do with Jewish dietary law.

'How can I help you, Rabbi?'

He replied inconsequentially as before. 'I am become *Na-v'-nad*, as we say in Hebrew, a wanderer. Jews are like fleas. They turns up everywhere. Always they give surprises. Unpleasant. Except to other fleas.'

'I must be a flea,' Fr Duddleswell said gallantly. 'You are very welcome here, at any rate.'

'In the world to come, says Talmud, you must answer triple questions: Did you buy and sell *in bona fide*? Did you study orderly? Did you lift up, no, pardon, did you *raise* a family? I have come about my son, Isaac.'

That shook me. Fr Duddleswell, for his part, naturally bewildered, said, 'You have?'

'I do not want Isaac to enter a mixed-up marriage.'

The Rabbi explained that his beloved Isaac Brader, like a son to him, had met a Gentile girl. She worked in the same bank as Isaac and he had told the Rabbi he intended marrying her.

'I know her?' Fr Duddleswell asked.

'Her name is Christine Hammond.'

The revelation of Isaac's fiancée gave me a great jolt. As for Fr Duddleswell, he went deathly white. For of all his parishioners, no one was nearer to his heart than Christine Hammond.

148

EIGHT

Christine and Isaac

Mrs Pring had told me Christine's story.

One night in 1940, Fr Duddleswell was firewatching when a string of incendiary bombs fell on York Street where the Hammonds lived. Risking his life, he entered the blazing building and rescued Christine from her ground-floor bedroom. He made further attempts to release the parents who were trapped upstairs but was driven back by the flames.

He spent two days in hospital after that with burns and respiratory troubles.

Christine's legs were badly burned. She was in and out of hospital for months and had several skin grafts. Every afternoon, except when she was being operated on, Fr Duddleswell visited her and took her for walks in a wheel chair.

'He worships the girl,' Mrs Pring had said.

'And I bet she's fond of him, Mrs P.'

She smiled reluctantly. 'There is a little bit of him that's worth saving, Father Neil.'

When Christine finally left hospital, she went to live with an aunt, Mrs Mabel Coyne. She was widowed when her husband fell at Arnhem. Mrs Coyne, a parishioner of St Jude's, brought Christine up as a devout Catholic.

'When Christine left school,' Mrs Pring said, 'she entered the novitiate of the Sacred Heart Sisters.'

'How long did she last there?'

'Only a year or less. Father D was upset when she left. But he realized she was really looking for security. She was only twelve, you see, when she was orphaned.'

Mrs Pring went on to say that Fr Duddleswell had seen Christine through the crisis in her vocation, pulled a few strings to get her a job in a bank and was with her when her Aunt Mabel died of leukaemia early in 1950.

I was quite moved by Fr Duddleswell's part in the story and joked, 'He'll be canonized some day, after all.' Mrs Pring had replied, 'If you melted old short-pants down you'd make half a dozen ordinary sized priests out of him.'

When Fr Duddleswell said to Rabbi Epstein, 'Christine Hammond. I know her well,' I understood something of the pain he felt. I wanted to tell him why Isaac Brader was so dear to the Rabbi but there was no opportunity.

The two men began to speak, haltingly at first and then with fluency, of the trials and tribulations bound up with mixed marriages. Especially between Jews and Gentiles.

How could it be otherwise? Christine, for example, believed that Jesus is God made man, while Isaac thought the idea blasphemous. For Christine, Jesus was the longed-for Jewish Messiah; for Isaac, the Messiah is still to come. For Christine, Jews are the people who reject the Way; for Isaac, Jews are the elect of God, the apple of His eye.

Between priest and rabbi there was complete accord. Even on a practical level, the differences were unbridgeable. Would the young couple marry at the altar before Fr Duddleswell or under the Jewish canopy in front of Rabbi Epstein? Would a boy-child be baptized or circumcized? Would they worship on Sunday or the Jewish Sabbath, in a church or a synagogue?

Marriage between Jew and Gentile entailed the mix-up of every possible gene and chromosome of race and creed. An unthinkable amalgamation. What hybrids would their children be?

Yet I must confess, as I listened to these two elderly men – each of whom seemed strangely older than their combined years – I saw through their differences to certain common factors. A plump Irish priest and a wafer-thin Jewish rabbi joined in some mysterious brotherhood?

It was absurd and still the conviction grew in me the longer they were together.

Two recent classroom incidents sprang ridiculously into my mind. 'Father,' George said, 'if a telegraph pole grew branches it would look just like a tree.' And Esther, the only Jewish child in Mrs Hughes's form, seeing a picture of Pius XII wearing his white skull cap like a *yarmulka*, gleefully called out, 'I didn't know your Pope was Jewish. When was the wedding?'

Priest and rabbi, as I remember them after the years, were both deeply religious. Religious at a level beneath that of 'religion' which is all that most men, myself included, ever reach. They were religious in the subterranean caverns of the spirit. There God flowed through them like clear spring water, spoke to them like music, cancelling all their doubts before there were words to voice them.

Their principles were of steel, but were they themselves bigots? I think not. Perhaps because their religion made them channels of love. Before their God, they did not exist; but everyone else did.

Yes, I was thinking even then, my beloved, bewildering, often fuddled Fr Duddleswell would give up his life for anyone in need as easily as he removed his shirt at night. And the Rabbi? I don't suppose Rabbi Epstein understood the meaning of death at all.

The two men got on so famously they were now on first name terms: Zorach and something that sounded like 'Charoly'.

'Well, now, Zorach, I suggest we meet these two young people and impress on them the utter impossibility of their marrying.'

A meeting with Isaac and Christine was arranged provisionally for Wednesday evening at the Rabbi's place.

When the Rabbi had bid Charoly goodbye, Fr Duddleswell was in a sombre mood.

'That Rabbi is an exceedingly holy man.' That from Fr Duddleswell was the highest praise. 'He seems very fond of that lad, right enough.'

Now that the opportunity presented itself, I did not repeat what Rabbi Epstein had told me. I felt, somehow, it was *his* story. If he wished to tell it, so be it. I would not.

I asked if I could attend the Wednesday meeting. Fr Duddleswell was none too keen but he said yes.

Why did I want to be there? It was not mere curiosity. More like pride. I fancied Rabbi Epstein and Fr Duddleswell saw things with such piercing clarity they were, in a sense, blind.

The door of 57 Russell Buildings was ajar. We knocked and, receiving no answer, went in.

The Rabbi, draped in a prayer shawl and wearing a *yarmulka*, was poring over an enormous, faded Bible. In the light of candles, I noticed that his fingers were tracing the words on the page which his lips were forming. Just above his right wrist was a blue serial number.

Back and forth he swayed as if in a trance, the tears pouring down his cheeks. He made no attempt to brush them away. They remained there, glistening like orange beads at the base of his beard.

The room contained only the bare essentials: divan bed, table, chairs, a sideboard and small cupboard, a gas ring, a two-bar electric fire and a book shelf. It smelt strongly of snuff, cloves, garlic, fish and incense. It was very cold.

'Charoly, may I be forgiven?'

The Rabbi leapt to his feet. Off came his prayer shawl and in its place he put on a black quilted jacket with frayed cuffs and lapels.

'I have no clock piece,' he said, apologizing. 'But what is time? Even God who invent it does not understand head nor foot of it.'

The Rabbi kissed his Bible, carried it across the room as if it were a silver salver filled to the brim with precious wine and placed it on the shelf. We sat down at the square oak table.

'Honoured,' the Rabbi said. 'Full is my heart. Like new moon in Yom Kippur.' He jumped up suddenly and lit the gas under a saucepan. '*Cholent*,' he exclaimed. 'You like?'

We managed to convey to him, tactfully, that we were not expecting a meal.

'You don't like?' He seemed hurt.

'We've never had it,' I explained.

'You *will* like,' he affirmed, and ran through the ingredients to whet our appetites. Butter beans, potatoes, onions, meat, seasoning and, he seemed proud of this, 'a famous dumpeling'. It came out as three syllables.

'You prepared it yourself?' Fr Duddleswell asked warily.

'In Poland we say, "Six cooks, no meal".' He fixed his eye on Fr Duddleswell. 'Your lady no give you *cholent*?'

'My lady?'

'Every man has lady, Charoly.'

'I do not have a wife, Zorach, as you know.'

'Ah, no. You do not marry your lady or she not share your bed, that is all.' He pointed an accusing finger. 'Mind, for turning down precious delights of the bed, God will accuse you very naughty at the Judgement. So say Talmud.'

'Nor do I eat with her,' Fr Duddleswell added for good measure.

The Rabbi did not pick that up at once. 'If all Catholics naughty like you, Charoly, soon no Catholics left.' He caught the remark made to him at the second attempt. 'You don't eat with your lady, Charoly?' He was astonished.

'No, Zorach,' Fr Duddleswell said, looking strangely pleased with himself.

'You eat alone, yes?'

'Not at all, I eat with Father Neil here.'

'But, Charoly,' – the Rabbi was finding the notion difficult to grasp – 'your unmarried lady, she not eat alone?'

Fr Duddleswell did not answer, none too happy to have to admit something which he had never questioned before.

Rabbi Epstein said, half to himself, 'Your lady live in your house, she work for you, she cooking for you, she serve you food – and she not eats with you?' The shake of his head indicated there was nothing in the Talmud itself quite as puzzling as that.

'Mrs Pring eats in the kitchen, Zorach.'

The Rabbi saw the light at last or thought he did. 'So your lady a Muslim and she eat with this Mrs Pring.'

'Mrs Pring *is* my lady,' Fr Duddleswell said, adding quickly, 'I mean, me housekeeper's name is Mrs Pring.'

'And what you call her, Charoly?'

'Mrs Pring.'

'How long she with you, one week, two week?'

'Twenty tedious years.'

'Twenty . . . And she no call you Charoly like me?' The Rabbi shrugged his shoulders as if he were squeezing out a mop. 'What you hold against this lady, tell me?'

'Nothing,' Fr Duddleswell said, flustered. 'Nothing you would understand, I mean.'

'You are good man, Charoly. A good man eat food with even his enemy also.'

'She is not me enemy, Zorach,' Fr Duddleswell said lamely, as if that might be sufficient reason for excluding Mrs Pring from his table.

'Is it not as I say before, Charoly?' the Rabbi said, smiling. 'Why you so right about the marriage business when you know lesser than nothing?'

The leg-pulling was interrupted by the arrival of the young couple. They were holding hands, a gesture of defiance directed at anyone who dared try and separate them. Instinctively, Isaac touched the *mezuza* by the door as a Catholic might dip his fingers in the holy water stoup in the church porch.

I already knew Christine by sight. A tall, slim, pretty brunette with big almond eyes and fleshy quivering lips. She wore thick woollen stockings. As soon as she came in, without a word, she put her arms round Fr Duddleswell's neck.

Isaac surprised me. I was expecting a youngster of slight build, in the mould of the Rabbi. Instead, there stood this

154

broad-shouldered young man of about my age, dark, handsome with long, somewhat pointed features.

As he removed his overcoat, I saw he was wearing a broad leather strap on his right wrist. I found myself thinking: *he* was starving in a prison camp while *I* was living comfortably in a seminary.

At the table, Christine and Isaac continued to hold hands. They listened in silence, first to Fr Duddleswell and then to Rabbi Epstein who sat opposite them.

Fr Duddleswell explained gently but persuasively that it's not possible to stop being a Catholic. A Catholic cannot deny that Jesus is the Christ and Son of God. He cannot, as the New Testament puts it, go back from light to darkness, from truth to shadows.

'A Catholic like Christine,' he said, 'might go her own way and marry a devout Jew without prejudice to her own faith. But what about the children? Can a believing Catholic mother compromise the faith of her unborn?'

Rabbi Epstein explained that a Jew is a Jew. One of God's chosen. How can a Jew reject Torah, the covenant, the promises to his fathers? How can a Jew, especially one who has felt the lash of persecution, turn his back on his own persecuted people?

This last point, far from impressing Isaac, aroused him to wrath. He released Christine's hand and brought his fist down on the table with a crash.

'Enough, Rabbi. I have had quite enough of this pious verbiage.' His accentless English contrasted strongly with the Rabbi's flawed and halting diction.

This outburst brought fully half a minute of pained silence. The only sound was of the *cholent* simmering and bubbling in the pot. For the first time, I noticed its suffocating smell filling the room.

Isaac, gently touching the Rabbi's wrist, broke the silence. 'I am not even sure I believe in God any more, little father.'

'Sammy,' the Rabbi whispered, horror-struck, and, realizing he had mixed up the names of his beloveds, found no more words for a while. 'Isaac, Isaac,' he said at length, 'if there is no God how comes He sends Jews so much sorrow?'

'Oy, oy, oy,' Isaac cried in a plaintive voice. 'You throw sorrows at me again. God shows He loves Jews because He sends us more sorrows than He sends Gentiles! In the War, God let one mad Gentile kill six millions of us to prove He loves us. What a pity, Rabbi, He didn't let Hitler slaughter *twelve* millions of us to prove He loved us twice as much.'

'I no sure we had twelve millions, Isaac. Perhaps.' The Rabbi swallowed with difficulty. '*Avinu Malkenu*, Our Father, our King, be graceful to us,' he chanted. 'But your mother and father, Isaac. Your uncles and aunts. Your old granniemother.'

Isaac sealed his lips, so that the Rabbi was forced to ask, 'Am I a letter that you no answer me?'

'Rabbi, Rabbi,' Isaac moaned, 'should foxes be proud of being foxes just because dogs are good at tearing them apart? Did we win prizes for going to the gaschamber? Must I remain Jewish because my family, peace be on them, were turned into soap?'

The sound of *cholent* hissing and bubbling again, the smell of it so strong it nearly spoke to us. The light from the candles washed back and forth across two Jewish faces, as in a Rembrandt painting, inviting each in turn to speak.

The Rabbi, at last, took up the offer. 'Blood, my Isaac,' he said, as if apologizing for mentioning something so obvious. 'Blood.'

Isaac let out a heart-rending sigh as if a blow, long awaited, had fallen on him, crushing him.

'Blood, blood, blood. The blood of the Jews. Centuries of Jewish blood pumped in and out of Jewish veins. Seas of Jewish blood wetting the earth. From the time of the Patriarchs to you and me.'

The Rabbi nodded. 'That is the true. History I did not invent.'

'Rabbi,' Isaac pleaded, 'can't you see it's just a myth? An old Jewish myth?'

'Myth, myth, what is myth?' The Rabbi understood as Isaac was on the point of explaining. 'Ah, yes, *myth*.'

'Can't you see,' Isaac said, 'the Nazis had the same myth? They stole it from *us*. They turned it inside-out, that's all. The Nazis said *they* were the chosen people, not us, and Hitler was their Messiah.'

The Rabbi held up his hands as if all this was incomprehensible to his old brain but Isaac did not relent.

'We gave the Nazis the myth that killed my father and mother, and your wife and children. Now that the Nazis are finished, the Gentiles have repented and given the Jews their myth back. And with that same myth you, Rabbi, are wanting to kill . . .'

He pointed a finger at his heart but the last small word proved too much for him. Christine stood up, put her arms round his shoulders and kept kissing the top of his head until his shaking ceased.

After a while, Isaac, dry-eyed, signalled Christine to sit again. And she, needing to defend her love, rounded on Fr Duddleswell. 'You're no better than him, Father,' she said, indicating the Rabbi. 'You have your religion, you don't need people.'

'Christine,' Fr Duddleswell said.

'No. You have your comfortable creed, you don't need truth,' she blazed. 'You have your dogma, you don't have to listen any more.' She drew in a violent breath before saying stertorously, 'you have your prayers, Father, you don't even need God.'

The outburst was the more pitiful for having been so obviously rehearsed any number of times inside her head.

Fr Duddleswell was silent. From the shape of his mouth it was easy to see he was biting the inside of his lip.

'Well, Father, what do you say to that?' Christine's challenge was petering out. 'Please, Father, say something to *me*, Christine.'

Bowing his head and beating his breast, he simply said, 'Through my fault, through my most grievous fault.'

'Oh, Father,' Christine cried, 'that's no answer.'

Isaac took hold of her hand again, the stag and the hind, wounded both and hounded, defending each other. A man and a woman, almost archetypal, I thought, loving

157

each other passionately and, in their way, loving the God of love.

Also two godly men who loved them above all ordinary love and, in Love's name, urging them to part.

A question flashed across my mind, piercing, rebellious: Does the love of man and woman for each other count for so little? And as I asked it, I had the strong impression that there were colossal centrifugal forces at work threatening the very room we sat in with disintegration. Not reason but forces disguised as reason were in operation, primeval forces that had increased rather than diminished over millenia and become focused to two nail points in the black, candle-lit figures of a rabbi and a priest.

Isaac was threateningly calm now. 'You have ears, Rabbi, listen. I have the right you should listen to me because you kept me alive. You gave me food from your own mouth.'

'No, no, no,' the Rabbi protested.

'It is true. Yes, yes, yes. Do you think I did not know that in that accursed camp you gave me more than half your food? You lived for months on air . . . and on faith and prayers.' Isaac had to add that, though it weakened his case. 'I *know*, Rabbi.'

The Rabbi broke in, speaking rapid Yiddish. Isaac held up his hand to silence him as though he feared some magic in his native tongue.

'Listen to me, Rabbi. You are a scholar. You learned Polish because you were a *cheder* boy and went to a rabbinical seminary. I was fourteen years old before I learned a word of it. Imagine, for 800 years we Jews lived in Poland and hardly any of us spoke Polish.'

The Rabbi said something in a language I could not grasp.

Isaac again silenced him with a gesture. 'Eight centuries of solitary confinement, Rabbi. A ragamuffin in the port of Alexandria will pick up a smattering of German, English, French, Italian, Greek – any language you care to mention. And we lived in Poland for eight centuries and

158

most of us could not even say, "*Dzień dobry*".'

'Was it our fault, Isaac mine, if Gentiles would not wish us "Good day"?'

'I picked up Polish,' Isaac said, ignoring the Rabbi's intervention, 'first in a barn and then in a cupboard. My mother –'

'Blessed be her memory,' the Rabbi said.

'My dear mother could not, *would* not learn it. It was like dirt in her mouth. The Gentiles who saved our lives were the first I had ever spoken to. I blushed because I could not even say "thank you" in words they understood.'

'They understood, my Isaac.'

'Please, Rabbi, do not keep interrupting me. Not even "thank you". Do you know what that means? In a barn and in a clothes cupboard, I had freedom for the first time.'

The Rabbi held up his hands. 'Freedom,' he sighed, as if to say, Was that ever a problem?'

'Not the freedom you had, Rabbi, lying in your grave and talking endlessly with the God of Israel. The freedom I tasted was being a man, a human being. In a barn and in a cupboard, Rabbi, I was for the first time in my life outside the ghetto. Not our Warsaw ghetto, you hear me?'

'I hear you, Isaac, why you talk no sense?'

'For the first time, Rabbi, outside the ghetto of race and religion, outside crippling prejudice.'

'Who builded the blasting walls, Isaac, tell me that?'

'And, Rabbi, *I am not going back*.' Isaac stopped to look, misty-eyed, across the table at Rabbi Epstein who had taken to muttering Hebrew prayers as though he were munching a carrot. 'Not even,' Isaac added in a whisper, 'for you, little father.'

'Tell me,' Christine said, facing Fr Dudleswell, 'if I marry Isaac in the Register Office or in a synagogue, will I be living in sin?'

Fr Duddleswell turned away sharply without replying.

'I won't be allowed to go to confession and communion any more, will I, Father?'

'Please, Christine,' Fr Duddleswell said, 'do not let us talk about it.'

'Father,' Christine insisted, 'I want the truth.'

'All right, Christine.' He spoke drily like someone reciting the catechism. 'Your marriage will not be a true marriage in the sight of Almighty God. You will be denied the sacraments until you put your marriage right.'

'What does that mean?'

'Exchanging vows before me after you both promise that your children will be Catholics and the Bishop has granted you a dispensation.'

'Now you, Rabbi,' Isaac said.

'What did I teach you, my Isaac, in the shadow of the death?'

'I want it from your lips *now* when you are teaching me about *me*.'

The Rabbi shook his head wearily. The task was too big for him. All he could say was, 'Hear, O Israel.'

'Rabbi,' Isaac said, 'for Jews, our church is our home. Only the child born of a Jewish mother is really a Jew, isn't that so? If I married Christine in a Register Office or a Catholic church you would turn me and my children out of the House of Israel.'

'Not I, Isaac.'

'God, then, with a face like yours?'

The Rabbi shook his head once more. 'Not the God of Israel even can stop a man walking out the House of Israel.'

Isaac pushed his chair back a few inches, noisily scraping the bare boards.

'Priest and Rabbi,' he began, for all the world as if he was delivering a judicial decision, 'you tell us we should not marry because our religions are different. We have the same God of love but not the same religion. How can that be?'

No answer came.

'What do we have in common, then? Flesh and blood. What every man and woman who love each other have in common. More, we have in common that our parents were killed by the same enemy, our families incinerated. We have in common that we were both branded by the same

160

Beast. But that is not enough for you. You are religious men.'

The last words were spoken not ironically, as I would have expected, but almost with veneration. Isaac waited a moment before adding:

'Priest and Rabbi, if you force me to choose, I choose Christine for my family, my race, my creed, my religion, and if you say I am defying Him above, I choose her for my God.'

Blasphemy, but it seemed more like a prayer.

All the same, there was one other common factor that Isaac failed to mention: both he and Christine had had their life saved by the minister of their respective religions sitting at table with them.

After a long silence, Fr Duddleswell suggested another meeting at St Jude's.

'What d'you say? Why not wait a couple of weeks till the pair of you have had time to pray about it and think things through?'

It was agreed.

Walking home with Fr Duddleswell, I was troubled by the feeling that we had forgotten something important. What could it be? I snapped my fingers.

'What is the matter with you, lad?'

'No *cholent*,' I said.

Late one evening, I found Mrs Pring in her kitchen almost in tears. She was reading a book. She held it up for me to see the title: *Kosher Cooking*.

'A Jewish cookbook, Father Neil.'

Fr Duddleswell, to atone for our bad manners in not eating the *cholent*, had invited the Rabbi to lunch with us on the day of the next meeting. He had promised the Rabbi that Mrs Pring would prepare the food in the orthodox Jewish manner. *Kosher Cooking* would provide the guidelines.

'The book must tell you what Jews can eat and what they can't, Mrs P,' I said, trying to buck her up.

She nodded. 'They can't eat pork, eagles, vultures,

161

crocodiles, polar bears, camels, lions, rats, reptiles, snakes, horses, and pachyderms in general.' She looked up from her list. 'What's a pachyderm?'

'I think it's a four-legged animal with hoofs that doesn't chew the cud. But what *can* they eat?'

'Chickens, goats, cows and things,' she answered, sniffing sadly, 'provided there's no blood in it.'

'What about fish?'

'Anything with fins and scales.'

'Not oysters, then. That's a relief.'

'Not shrimps,' she read, 'lobsters, frogs, snails, octopuses, squids, mussels.'

'Give us plaice and chips,' I said, as if I were in a restaurant, closing the menu.

Fr Duddleswell appeared clutching a letter.

'What is bothering you, Mrs Pring? You have a long face on you like it has been through the mangle.'

'I can't cope with Jewish cooking, Father D, and that's the God's honest truth.'

'Where is the trouble, woman? Pick out a recipe and follow it.'

Mrs Pring looked obstinate. 'Did you know that Jews keep meat and dairy products separate?'

'I knew something of the sort,' he said vaguely.

'Well, it means special utensils and dishes for different courses. The money for it won't come out of my pocket.'

He pretended to shudder. 'Send me the bill.'

'Listen to this,' she said, and she read from the book. 'Meat is not kosher if the animal is not slaughtered by the instantaneous severance of the carotid arteries in the neck.'

'Where *is* the problem, Mrs Pring?' Fr Duddleswell had the face of a man who slaughtered animals every day at the altar.

'I don't know what a carotid artery is.'

'Plaice and chips, Mrs P,' I repeated. 'I bet you fish don't have arteries.'

'Do your best,' Fr Duddleswell said cheerfully. He showed her his letter. 'The Rabbi has accepted me invitation. But he requests that you, Mrs Pring, sit at table with us.'

Mrs Pring firmed the line of her jaw. 'I'll not sit down with you at table, Father D,' she said, 'not even in the Kingdom of Heaven.'

Mid-morning and our three guests arrived together.

'Come in and kindly welcome,' Fr Duddleswell said.

This meeting began in a calmer atmosphere than the first. Everyone seemed determined to listen rather than argue. But argument was not long in breaking out.

The Rabbi said, 'It is not easy to be member of the chosen race.'

He intended it, I'm sure, as an expression of sympathy for Isaac in his predicament. That is not how Isaac saw it.

'The chosen race,' he snapped in derision.

'Isaac, my son,' the Rabbi said, soothing him, 'I always tell you Israel was not chosen because she is special but –'

'Special because she was chosen,' Isaac concluded for him. 'Words, Rabbi, words.'

'True words, my Isaac.'

'Dangerous words,' Isaac said. 'If we are chosen, others are not chosen. They will resent us thinking they are not chosen and hate us for it. As they always have.'

'We were only chosen to serve, Isaac.'

'It doesn't matter, little father,' Isaac said in a weary voice. 'Does it make any difference what we were chosen *for*? Even if we were chosen to suffer and die for the rest of the world that makes us *special* and the rest of the world won't thank us for that. And can you blame them?'

'My God,' the Rabbi said ironically, 'you want I dance on Good Friday? What I do, Isaac, convert? Tell me and I turn today.'

'Do you want me, Rabbi,' Isaac retorted, 'to wear a long gaberdine, a tiny hat, grow earlocks like woodshavings and pray to the east wall? Do you want me to be always one of the *zydy*, one who is chosen to be in exile always and everywhere? Don't you think I have burdens enough?'

'Shoulders are not for carrying only heads, Isaac. Anyways, everybodys is chosen for something.'

Isaac sighed deeply before his features loosened and he adopted a rueful smile. 'You mean God chose everybody else not to be Jewish, Rabbi.'

'Excuse.' The Rabbi did not grasp the point.

'Everybody else is personally chosen by a sensitive God *not* to be a member of the chosen race.'

The Rabbi still looked bewildered. 'Isaac, what you want I should do? Preach we are *not* the chosen? What sort of teaching is that for a Jew and a rabbi? If I blink the facts, they will say me, "Who you try kidding, Rabbi?" '

Isaac banged the table. 'That is my point. It's got to stop. It's going to stop with me.'

The Rabbi shook his head vigorously.

'Yes, Rabbi. I refuse to say I'm a member of the chosen race even if that phrase means nothing more than that God chose me to have my Jewish head knocked off for His sake.'

The Rabbi was shaking nervously. 'Nobody will believe you, Isaac.'

Isaac conceded that *that* at least was true.

'Everybodys else believe we are chosen, Isaac.' Isaac nodded. 'Even your fellows Jews, they will say, "Why Isaac Brader say he not chosen, why he think he so special?" '

This amused me so much, I felt relaxed enough to make my first contribution.

'You *are* chosen, Isaac.' He was startled to find I could talk. 'And you know you are chosen.'

'Tell me more,' he said, recovering from the shock.

'However much you protest, you believe that you have been chosen out of all mankind.'

'I do not,' he said, his spirit rising at this Gentile interference in a specifically Jewish squabble. 'I wouldn't be so *arrogant*.'

'It's not arrogance but humility.'

'What are you, Father,' Isaac said, 'a secret member of the Hassidim?'

I spoke slowly and carefully. 'You believe, Isaac, in all

164

humility that you were chosen, yes, *you*, out of all mankind' – he tried to silence me but I insisted on finishing – 'by Christine.'

Isaac collapsed. For the first time he smiled, showing a perfect set of teeth. Even that made me choke. Hell, I complained inwardly, he smiles and it's sad. Lack of vitamins in the camp must have been responsible. Only in his twenties and he had false teeth.

'Father . . .' He was searching for my name.

I helped him out. 'Boyd.'

'Father Boyd.' He raised his left hand, curling it from somewhere around his ear until it was flat, palm upwards, above his head. There it rested as if it was asking God a question on its own. A thoroughly Jewish gesture. 'When stones speak, Father Boyd, you should expect what you least expect.'

A strange noise emerged from the Rabbi's throat. Yiddish was my guess. It sounded like a cockney sparrow with a speech defect trying to speak German. It went on for fully five minutes. Several times Isaac attempted to stop the flow and, in the end, decided to wait until the Rabbi ran dry.

'What you think, Isaac?' the Rabbi said, at last.

Isaac slowly shook his head. 'We will put you out of your agony, little father.'

Fr Duddleswell sat bolt upright in his chair. 'You will tell us what you have decided?'

Isaac and Christine spoke together as they must have planned it. 'What we have *done*.'

There was a stunned silence before Fr Duddleswell, in a daze, asked, 'You are married already?' He turned to the girl who was like a daughter to him. 'Christine?'

Christine blushed and nodded. Isaac was left to explain.

'It was obvious after the last meeting that you two could never agree. So we decided to marry in the Register Office. Yesterday, in fact.'

Had I tried in advance to imagine the effect of such a disclosure I would have been hopelessly wrong.

Fr Duddleswell almost ran to Christine, crying, 'Congratulations! Me little girl married.'

Christine looked up, wide-eyed. 'Aren't you upset, Father?'

'Of course,' he said, and I knew that a part of him must have felt blasted like a tree in a storm. 'But Christine a bride? Congratulations a hundred thousand times.' And he put his arms around her.

'But, Father,' Christine said, overcome, 'mortal sin. I'm living in sin.'

Fr Duddleswell put his fingers to her lips to silence her and when she kept murmuring about the Church's law and marrying outside the Church he knelt before her and held her tight.

'Never let me hear you talk so of someone I love, d'you hear me speak to you? The Church tells us what is a sin. Even she does not know who the sinners are, nor the saints.' He smiled weakly. 'Only God knows such things.'

'But, Father . . .'

Still holding her, he leaned back to look at her and brushed her tears away. 'What will you be wanting for a wedding present? Bed linen? Cutlery? You tell me, now, and I will see you get it.'

'Father, Father,' was all she could say, 'Father.'

He rocked her in his arms, whispering things I could not hear.

I averted my gaze only to see the Rabbi holding Isaac's hands in silence and shaking his head with deep emotion and from time to time kissing first his right hand, then his left.

'Rabbi,' Isaac managed to get out, 'I have left the path of righteousness.'

'*Leben.*' The Rabbi kissed his right hand. '*Leben,*' now it was the left. 'You want I call a special meeting of the Sanhedrim and have you punished? No, no. You suffer too much before in a tiny life, *Leben.* Grief should be on holidays. Grief not yours to know, no more.'

Isaac was a little boy again, dependent on his only friend and comforter.

'What now, little father. Can even you sort out this trouble?'

'Wait till Elijah come,' the Rabbi said. 'What else he paid for?'

'What about the God of Abraham, Isaac and Jacob?'

'He hold six crows by the tail if He want.'

'What will He say?'

'He recover, Isaac mine. He take smelling salts with His snuff. Besides, He is patient, He has lived long times.' The Rabbi peered optimistically into the future. 'You have two Sabbaths a week, lucky fellow and chap. You will live twice as old as any Jew, living and dead. *Mazel Tov.*'

Isaac was really taken aback. 'How can you wish me Good Luck, little father?'

The Rabbi shrugged as if he amazed himself at the incredible things he was capable of.

'Should you not rend your clothes in mourning?'

'I should be but look, my clothes already mourned themselves dead.'

'You always said *you* wanted to read the *Ketubah* for me under the wedding canopy.'

The Rabbi was not listening any more. He blew his nose, called out, laughing, 'New Year's Day, Isaac,' and searched around till he found what he wanted.

Fr Duddleswell had placed a sherry bottle and five glasses on his desk. Rabbi Epstein grabbed a glass and put it on the carpet by Isaac's feet.

'Trod this for me, Isaac.'

'But,' Isaac objected, 'that is the priest's glass.'

'So? Is there such a thing as Gentile glass for you?'

'I mean the priest might not like it.'

Rabbi Epstein turned to Fr Duddleswell. 'Charoly?' and Charoly gave his consent.

'Come here over, Isaac, you are groom. Trod it for me. For my joy. And then we drink toast, "To Life".'

'I can't do that, little father,' Isaac said, sharply tipping the emotional see-saw once again. 'Because it's not true.'

'What is not true, my Isaac? I am so happy. Can you not see my heart is full as moon on a night of great festival?'

167

'I mean,' Isaac said solemnly, 'we are not married.'

We all sat down again, the breath squeezed out of us.

Isaac, holding Christine's hand, told us that, after the previous meeting, they were so confused they agreed, like Solomon, to put priest and rabbi to the test.

'You took such a cruel line,' Isaac said, 'or so it seemed to us, that we made up our minds to pretend we'd married in the Register Office.'

'But why . . .?' Fr Duddleswell asked.

'Which ever one of you accepted our news more charitably, we would ask *him* to marry us.'

Not a bad test, it seemed to me, if a test was needed. Christine and Isaac wanted to marry in the faith and obedience of the minister who represented the more merciful God. But whose God had won?

'We know we lied,' Isaac said, 'but so did the pair of you.'

Fr Duddleswell and Rabbi Epstein shook their heads simultaneously.

'Oh yes, you did. You roar like tigers beforehand and then love like lambs. You threaten us with damnation and when we commit our unforgivable sin you reward us with the promise of paradise.'

'We are a discredit to our religions,' Fr Duddleswell said, which left all but himself and Rabbi Epstein laughing loudly.

We three ministers of religion sat down to wash our hands, Jewish style. Fr Duddleswell stopped himself from making the sign of the cross over the table in the nick of time.

Mrs Pring, unexpectedly cheerful, served a sort of vegetable soup. After the first mouthful, I decided God did not choose the Jews for their cooking.

'One day,' the Rabbi said, 'you, Charoly, must eat *Pesach* with me.'

'The Passover?'

'I will invite all you both to my next *seder*.' Before Fr Duddleswell could decline the invitation on conscientious grounds, the Rabbi said, 'Jesus a good Jew. He celebrate *Pesach.*'

'That,' Fr Duddleswell said, gulping, 'was before – '

'He converted?' I said.

'Before He . . . died.' Fr Duddleswell himself could not restrain his mirth at his unintended joke. He changed the subject with an apology. 'Not much of a meal so far, I am afraid.'

'I have not before taste food like this,' our guest said ambiguously. 'It has interested flavourings.' He took another mouthful and rolled it round his tongue. 'For me, a crust and an onion is paradise. If I eat here twice a week I weigh as much as five tons of coal.'

'The dumpling is exceedingly hard to eat, Zorach.'

'An absented dumpeling is harder to eat, still.' The Rabbi was no doubt harking back to his war-time experiences.

Fr Duddleswell tried unsuccessfully to spike his dumpling with a fork. 'If Moses were here with his rod, now, he would get a stream of water from this, that's for sure.'

'Moses?' the Rabbi said, glowing. 'Blessed be his name.'

'D'you know, Zorach,' Fr Duddleswell said, mischievously leaning over the table, 'you are almost – almost, mind – nice enough to be a Catholic.'

'Thanks you, Charoly. And if you ever decide to become Jew, – '

'Yes?'

'I will see you circumcized for free.'

Fr Duddleswell ceased attacking his dumpling. 'One thing,' he muttered benignly, 'how can you Jews be the chosen people when everybody knows we Catholics are?'

The Rabbi replied with something which I had vaguely felt but was unable to express. He began:

'You are like me, Charoly.'

'How so?'

'You are *Na-v'-nad*, too.'

'A wanderer,' I translated, as if Hebrew was my native tongue.

'Irishmans are all emigrés, you agree, Charoly?'

'True for you,' Fr Duddleswell said. 'For us, everywhere outside Erin is Egypt.'

'Even,' I said wryly, 'when Egypt provides you with work and food.'

'You even speak the English like me, Charoly,' the Rabbi said sympathetically. 'Funny foreign talk. More fluidly, of course.'

Fr Duddleswell smiled graciously and intoned, 'There by the waters of Thames I sat and wept when I remembered Ireland.'

'Thames or Vistula or Tiber or Volga,' the Rabbi said. 'It all the same thing. *Diaspora*. We are dispersed, you and us, no?'

Fr Duddleswell nodded. 'Like members of the dog family.'

'And, see, we joke the same, Charoly. We know how to laugh like drains because we suffer.'

Fr Duddleswell agreed philosophically. 'Mirth and sadness, as I always say, Zorach, are the same to us.'

Mrs Pring, his most proximate and unrelenting source of persecution, came in. She removed the dirty dishes and was serving the second course when she made an admission.

'I brought in a firm of Jewish caterers, Father.'

Fr Duddleswell, not in the least upset, smiled gratefully. 'You are a very wise woman, Mrs Pring, despite appearances. 'Tis better to call in the experts, after all.'

He went on to chide the Rabbi good-humouredly for the plethora of Jewish dietary laws, for the weird things they had to do with their food and drink. One clear case at least, he suggested, of Jew and Irishman going their separate ways.

'D'you think, Rabbi,' he said, 'Almighty God really intended folk to get so steamed up about culinary matters?'

Before the Rabbi could answer, I touched Fr Duddleswell's wrist. 'Father.'

'What is it, lad?'

'The next course is chicken.'

'So? Fowl is kosher, isn't that so, Rabbi?'

'Today's Friday,' I pointed out.

Fr Duddleswell pushed his plate from him, making it plain that, whatever suited the Rabbi, *he* wasn't under any circumstances going to eat meat of a Blessèd Friday.

'Mrs Pring!' he roared.

Three weeks later, we received by post a small packet containing a slice of wedding cake. The accompanying letter informed us that Isaac and Christine had plighted their troth in the Register Office.

NINE
The Pilgrimage

The first hint I had that Fr Duddleswell was feeling foot-loose and fancy free was when I caught him reading the travel section of the Catholic press.

'God Almighty,' I heard him exclaim. 'I was hoping for a trip to the Holy Land this year but look at the prices.'

I had a glance and shook my head to indicate it was well beyond a curate's means.

'It seems to me, lad, that only those who are not disciples of Christ can afford to follow in the footsteps of the Master.'

'Never mind, Father, remember the last thing it says about our Lord in the Gospel: "He is not here, He is risen." '

A few evenings later, I heard Fr Duddleswell and Dr Daley reminiscing about their 1937 pilgrimage to Croagh Patrick.

'It's a great high mountain in Connaught,' Dr Daley said for my benefit, 'overlooking the fairest of the fair hills of Ireland. Nothing as beautiful did I ever see with my two eyes, not before or since.'

I refilled his glass.

'With that one exception,' he added, his small eyes twinkling. 'Did I ever tell you, Father Neil, you are the very pink of a gentleman?'

'You are speaking the blessed truth about Croagh Patrick, Donal, even if you are a long way down the cork-screw road.' Fr Duddleswell had the look of one standing tall on a mountain peak. 'Two and a half thousand feet below us the blue waters of Clew Bay. North, the mountains of Mayo. South, Joyce country.'

'*My* country,' Dr Daley put in proudly. He gestured with a sweep of his arm. 'See them there, the twelve Pins of Connemara.'

'Westwards,' Fr Duddleswell went on in a lyrical vein, 'the Atlantic that swallows up the evening sun like a firefly and further yet the capital of Connemara.'

When I registered surprise, Dr Daley said, 'Boston, Massachusetts, Father Neil.'

'A green land no different from when the great St Patrick saw it,' Fr Duddleswell said, and Dr Daley added, 'As the good God made it.'

I was told in detail how St Patrick fasted throughout Lent in 449 on Croagh Patrick. After which an angel promised him he would not rest in Heaven till all the wicked Saxons were driven from Ireland.

'St Patrick,' I ventured to say, 'must be tossing and turning in his grave.'

'The saint insisted, too,' Fr Duddleswell went on, ignoring me, 'that on the Last Day he would be the judge of all the men of Ireland.'

'A hard man, right enough,' Dr Daley said.

Without difficulty, Fr Duddleswell squared the circle of his jaw. 'Men of charity always are.' When Dr Daley held out his glass again, he repeated himself and sighed, 'Donal, surely you see a life of drink always ends in disillusionment.'

'Oh it does, Charles, certainly, but think of the alternative. To be disillusioned all the way through.'

'Have you ever given serious consideration to taking the pledge?'

'Oh I have. And every time I have come to the conclusion I'd be better off alive.'

'The weakness of the flesh, Donal.'

Dr Daley thrust out his hairy hand with the empty glass in it. 'If you ever had a thirst on you like mine, Charles, you wouldn't talk any more about the *weakness* of the flesh.'

'I am giving serious consideration to making another

173

pilgrimage, Donal,' Fr Duddleswell said, pouring him the milk of human kindness.

'Safe journey,' the doctor said, toasting him. 'But what is your holy intention this time?'

'Two-fold. Firstly,' Fr Duddleswell said, inclining modestly, 'I want to become a better person and a holier priest.'

Dr Daley slowly shook his head. 'Dear, dear, dear, Charles. Take away from you your vices and there'd be nothing lovable left.'

'Secondly, to get *you* unhooked from the liquor.'

'Have I ever caused trouble or messing through the drink?' Dr Daley enquired heatedly.

'I've always been as the histories describe St Pat himself: a steady and imperturbable man.'

'Mind you, Donal, oftentimes your tongue sounds as if it has been stung by a whole swarm of bees.'

'I can't deny,' Dr Daley agreed, 'that I am well in with the drink.' He glanced upwards at an unseen Observer. 'My God, my God, why haven't you forsaken me?'

'Good, Donal,' Fr Duddleswell said excitedly, 'so you will come?'

Dr Daley there and then grounded his glass and stubbed out his cigarette. 'I will.'

'Father Neil?'

'Can I come, too, Father?' I had a lightning presentiment of a pleasant trip abroad. To Fatima, perhaps, or Rome or Compostela.

'Indeed, you can. We will be going to Becksbridge.'

'Becksbridge!' Dr Daley and I echoed in unison.

It was to be a parish overnight to Becksbridge on the southern tip of Lincolnshire. Our Lady is supposed to have appeared there to the wife of an inn-keeper in 1321. The statues of our Lady of Becksbridge, squat and blue, always reminded me of Toby beer jugs.

Henry VIII, in his youth, made a pilgrimage to the Benedictine Abbey of Becksbridge and worshipped the statue of our Lady in his stockinged feet. Years later, grown into a gross heretic, he issued orders for the same monastery to be sacked. All that remains of it is a beautiful Gothic arch, once part of the chapel transept, and the outline of the monk's refectory.

Fr Duddleswell announced the pilgrimage from the pulpit. Immediately, many parishioners wanted a place in the char-à-banc, among them Mother Stephen, the Superior of the convent.

I heard Fr Duddleswell say to her at the church door, 'That will be three pound for yourself, Mother, and three pound for your companion.'

Mother Stephen agreed to pay only ten shillings for the fare since she was not wanting accommodation in the local hostelry.

'We will be staying at a convent nearby, Father.'

'And the purpose of your visit, Mother?'

'To ask our Lady of Becksbridge to see to it that our Foundress is canonized at her earliest convenience.'

'Very good, Mother. But I trust you will keep your intention private, like.'

Mother Stephen straightened up so that she towered over him.

'I am heading this pilgrimage, Mother, and I do not want you distracting me people from devotion to Mary by diverting their attention to your Foundress's tibia.'

'This is not Ireland, I would have you know. This, Father Duddleswell, is a free country.' She turned to her companion, Sister Perpetua. 'Follow,' she said and stormed out.

'Dear God, Father Neil,' he said, 'that woman has a face on her would trip a duck.'

'I don't know why you allow it, Father.'

'Allow what?'

'You let her slap you up and down as if she's painting a wall.'

He did not like the suggestion that she had bested him. 'St Columba had the right idea, lad. When he founded the monastery of Iona, he would not allow so much as a cow on the island. "Where there is a woman," says he,

175

"there is bound to be trouble." '

'If I were you,' I said, ready with advice if not support, 'I'd assert myself on the bus on the journey there.'

'How so?'

'Don't let the old Crow make any decisions about when to stop for lunch, when to recite the rosary – that sort of thing.'

'I promise you one thing, lad. There will be no conflict of authority on that char-à-banc.'

Neither was there. Fr Duddleswell, Dr Daley and I decided at the last moment to travel by car.

We waved goodbye to Mother Stephen and companion, the two Miss Flanagans, Mrs Rollings, my only convert, and a whole busload of pious parishioners. Then we finished off our packing.

'Travel light,' was Fr Duddleswell's advice. 'Do not take the kitchen sink. Mind you, 'tis always wise to take a thick pair of trousers to keep your cylinders warm.'

Into my small hold-all I put only one luxury: a mouse-trap and a piece of cheese to work it. We might, after all, be sleeping in a thatched cottage and I'd heard tales.

Fr Duddleswell appeared weighed down by three enormous battered suitcases which we only just managed to squeeze into the boot. Then came Dr Daley with only a toothbrush sticking out of his top pocket. It was obvious he hadn't even a packet of cigarettes or a hip flask.

'Goodbye to you, Mrs Pring,' Fr Duddleswell said, his head sticking out of the window of his old Chrysler.

'I hope you don't miss my cooking, Father D.'

'I've never eaten it for fun, that's for sure,' he said, grinning. 'Bless you, I will pray for you at our Lady's shrine.'

'Don't threaten me,' she said.

'All right, Mrs Pring, I will pray only for meself that I reach Heaven.'

'If you succeed, do let us know so we can warn others.' There were tears in her eyes as she said it. She didn't like to see us go even for one night.

I looked through the rear window and waved until Mrs Pring was out of sight.

'Ah, Charles,' Dr Daley was saying, 'I'm going to pray at Becksbridge for a weeshy bit of Home Rule for parish priests.'

'Indeed, Donal, you would fancy that herself introduced tea and tobacco into Ireland.'

'God, Charles, traffic should be forbidden.'

We were having problems wending our way through suburbia. The pile-up of cars surprised us. I was sitting in the back with a map on my knee, relaxed, ready to navigate once we found ourselves in less familiar parts. In the meanwhile, I was content to listen to my elders and betters. Their philosophizing, nostalgia and occasional jibes.

'Never mind the crush of cars,' Fr Duddleswell said, 'this is a pilgrimage and we must show charity.'

Dr Daley was dubious. 'Out of charity, Charles, I loaned my neighbour my lawn-mower, garden shears, spade and rake.'

'Very commendable, Donal.'

'Not at all. Now my own garden is like a jungle and he won't even talk to me.'

'Nothing like charity to turn a friend into an enemy, you mean?' Fr Duddleswell tooted his horn angrily at a car that wouldn't let him pass. 'Holy God, this is hardly like the roads of Connemara.'

For Dr Daley it was a magic name, conjuring up the smell of meadowsweet and sea-weed used as manure and the tangy smell of the peat fire. He turned round in his seat to talk to me.

'Peat isn't like wood at all, it gives no sparks. Neither does it break up like coal. It glows gentle like all things Irish.'

'Bloody fool,' Fr Duddleswell cried, as a car nearly went into our rear bumper.

'Turf,' the doctor continued, 'gives no red hot cinders, only white ash.'

'And you put it to sleep at night,' Fr Duddleswell contributed, 'just by covering it up with another blanket of turf.'

'Do you remember, Charles, in that Summer of '37 when we climbed the Holy Mount. An American asked us, "How do you light a peat fire?" and he pointed at the golden glow in the pub grate.'

'Do I remember?' Fr Duddleswell chuckled. 'I told him, "How should I know how to light a peat fire? Nobody round here knows." And the Yank looks real puzzled and says, "What about that fire there, isn't that peat?" and I says, "Oh, 'tis, but, y'see, that fire was lighted before the Spanish Armada." '

'It's true what our parish priest is telling you,' Dr Daley insisted. 'There were fires alight when Columbus set sail from Galway that are still burning there today.'

'They have pulled houses down,' Fr Duddleswell said, 'and rebuilt 'em round a still smouldering turf fire. By the God that's over me, I'm not lying to you.'

'Ah, Charles,' Dr Daley reminisced, 'it all comes back to me. All nineteen of us in a small cottage and I but a scrapeen of a boy at the time with a mouth wide as a church door.'

'The life did you no harm, Donal.'

'The school was just as crowded. Seventy-five in our class, of all ages. And didn't we learn our prayers and catechism.'

'Else you got a whack from a stick, I bet.'

Dr Daley nodded the truth of that. 'No Irish spoken in school at that time, except when the master swore at us. And we paid him a penny each Monday morning for his tutoring. Or a jug of milk or two eggs or a sod of turf.'

'Oh for the good old days,' Fr Duddleswell sighed.

'Myself,' Dr Daley responded with a laugh, 'I'm still waiting for the good old days to arrive.' He swiftly changed his tune, though. 'No, you are right, Charles. I remember the dodges we got up to, when, for instance, we wanted to sell a sheep. At the fair, we'd put the scraggy little feller on some eminence so he'd look bigger and more important than he was. Like yourself in the pulpit, Charles.'

'Thank you for the kind word.'

'D'you know, Charles, what my mother, God rest her, did to sell a few pounds of butter she'd made? She'd be up at three to walk eighteen miles to market, trade the butter for eggs and bacon and be back at dusk to milk a farmer's cow.'

'A saint she must have been seventeen times over,' Fr Duddleswell murmured appreciatively.

'And *her* mother's mother, that's another story again. I remember her when she was nearly up to a hundred years. The mill of her mouth was empty with all the grinders long ago gone.'

'I have dropped a tooth or two meself along life's way, Donal.'

'But my great grandmother, she could crack hazel nuts with her gums to her dying day. And could she swallow the poteen!'

'It runs in the family, then, like noses and little legs.'

'Nearing the end, Granny says, "Before the shovels throw clay over me poor eyes for ever and ever, give me an eggshell of poteen." And Father Pats anointed her and handed her what she asked and she says, "Thanks, Father dear, but isn't death a damned nuisance sometimes." She sits up, drains her glass conscientiously and expires with the sweetest smile that ever adorned a face.'

'She died happy, then, Donal, with even her old throat anointed.'

'I couldn't ask for a happier exit myself. And someone said, "Didn't she die well?" And another, "So well, you'd never guess she'd not done it before." And still another, "She should be congratulated all right," and he slapped her on the shoulder, saying, "Well done to you, Missis." ' The doctor's eyes were swimming. 'Oh,' he cried, 'the laughter that was on us.'

'Tell him about Michael McCarney, Donal.'

Dr Daley lifted his head as if he wanted to examine the car roof. 'God, what a man was Michael McCarney.' He fixed me with his gaze again. 'A real peasant, Father Neil. The first time he saw a double-track railway he thought he was drunk. Anyway, Michael had never a shilling to bless himself with. But one day, he came into ten pound and bought himself a buck goat. "And where will you be keeping him?" asks Father Pats. "Under me bed, Fairther," says he. "Shure the smell will be powerful bad, Michael," says his Reverence. "May be, Fairther," says Michael, "but the goat will have to get used to it." '

An old chestnut, I was sure, but I rocked with laughter all the same.

We hadn't made much progress when we stopped at The Saracen's Head for a late lunch.

'I am ready to drink me shilling's worth of wine,' Fr Duddleswell declared at table, licking his lips. 'It'll help shorten the road.'

'Not for me, Charles.'

'I am sure I beg your pardon, Donal.'

'Don't let me ruin your pleasure, Charles,' the Doctor said lugubriously, 'but remember I'm a reformed character.'

Fr Duddleswell coughed with embarrassment. 'So you are, Donal.' He looked at me, hoping I would strengthen his hand for a drink. 'How about yourself, lad?'

'If the doctor's eating dry, so will I, Father.'

After that, he could scarcely go it alone. 'A pilgrimage,' he said morosely, 'is not meant to be an alcoholiday.' He stood up, went and banged his belly up against the bar, demanding, 'A carafe of water, if you please.'

'Don't drink it for my sake, Charles,' the doctor said on his return. 'If the Almighty had wanted us to drink the stuff, wouldn't He, in His wisdom, have given some taste to it?'

Fr Duddleswell changed his order to three lemonades.

'God,' Dr Daley said, looking sourly at the fizzy drink, 'my whistle is dry as the bed of a summer's river and I'm condemned to swallowing this.'

'You look like a hurler without a stick,' Fr Duddleswell said sympathetically.

We weren't long into the afternoon when Fr Duddleswell called over his shoulder accusingly, 'We seem to have lost the big road, lad.'

It was true. Lately, we had been travelling on narrow winding lanes, dodging potholes and stray sheep.

Dr Daley came to my defence. 'There are no signposts hereabouts.'

'They are rarer than nightingales or courting couples in Ireland,' Fr Duddleswell was forced to admit.

Dr Daley's head nearly hit the roof as we came across a particularly vicious hole. 'Jesus my Lord,' he cried, 'this road could do with a spot of darning.'

Fr Duddleswell pulled up and peered incredulously through the windscreen. 'And what, pray, is that river doing rushing across the road?'

'A ford, I think, Father.'

His tone turned nasty. 'Is it marked on the map?'

'I don't know, Father. I'm not sure where we are.'

'Dear God in Heaven, you are babbling away like a bloody Protestant. Whoever heard of a major river bisecting a road and not being marked on an Ordnance map? Get away out of here and try out those rapids ahead.'

The water was above my knees and in a moment would have reached my rolled up trousers when Fr Duddleswell had mercy.

'Come back here, lad,' he called. 'I cannot risk me old banger floating downstream.'

He reversed without looking and by the time I reached the car one of the rear wheels was turning wildly in a ditch.

By building a kind of raft with fallen branches we managed to get the car back on the road. It took a curse-crammed half an hour.

'God turn a deaf ear to your maledictions, Charles,' Dr Daley said.

Fr Duddleswell was apologetic. 'You know how 'tis,

181

Donal, a good curse cleanses the soul like a good spit does the bronchial tubes.'

'On a pilgrimage, Charles?'

Fr Duddleswell thought about that and came up with, 'I am a skunk and that's all there is to it.'

'We'll think none the worse of you for that, Charles.' Dr Daley patted his arm forgivingly. 'Only Mary is immaculate, my dear friend.'

'I am a skunk, a rat, a worm and a louse.'

'Well, Charles,' the doctor sighed, 'if it makes you feel better to say so. Even though you don't believe a word of it.'

As Fr Duddleswell drove off to anywhere but the river he was cheerful again. 'I know I am a hypocrite, Donal, but at least I don't boast about it.'

I began to realize what A Kempis meant in *The Imitation Of Christ*: 'Those given to much travelling are rarely the holier for it.'

'Get out and shoo them cows aside, Father Neil.'

I carefully studied the herd that was blocking the lane. 'They are *not* cows, Father.'

'So,' Fr Duddleswell said ironically, 'you are become now an expert dairy farmer.' He sounded his horn malevolently to no purpose.

The great square-faced creatures came slowly towards us, like American tourists chewing gum. As interested as a congregation listening to one of my sermons.

'They have no horns, Father Neil. They are cows, I'm telling you, and 'tis cow time.'

'The lad's right, Charlie,' Dr Daley said. 'They're bullocks.'

I rattled my map and examined it in order to pay back Fr Duddleswell in his own coin. 'I can't find them on this map, Father. Surely a herd this size ought to show up on an Ordnance map.'

'Get out and move 'em on, Father Neil.'

'They're probably going home for milking, Father, don't you think?'

'I tell you,' Dr Daley said, leaning out of the window, 'they are bullocks that have been neutered till they are almost as harmless as curates.'

Fr Duddleswell, losing patience, banged the outside of his door and started a stampede. The herd rushed up the bank and tried squeezing past us. One of them slipped and his flank brushed against the off-side wing making a colossal dent.

'Heavens, Father,' I exclaimed, amazed at the damage. 'That could have been me.'

When the dust had settled we drove on. After half a mile we came across a hamlet with a pub, The Green Dragon.

'Anyone care for a drink?' Fr Duddleswell pleaded. 'I'm paying.'

'Don't let me stop you, Charles,' Dr Daley said prohibitively. His drinking had never annoyed Fr Duddleswell like his abstinence.

'Nor me,' I added. 'Toss one back for both of us, Father.'

He drove off in a fury. A hundred yards further on, I called out imperiously, 'Stop!' and he jammed on the brakes.

'A signpost,' I explained. I had to get out to examine it because it had gone to ground. 'Would you believe it, Father. It says, "Becksbridge 43½ miles" on it.'

'Which way is it pointing, lad?'

'Downwards,' I said.

'It must be an Irish signpost,' Dr Daley put in. 'Over there they all point in that direction.'

'They were all knocked askew deliberately to confuse the Black and Tans,' Fr Duddleswell said by way of excuse.

A half mile further on, a milestone said '43 miles to Becksbridge'. We were feeling cheered until the next sign post, a mile after it, also said, '43 miles to Becksbridge'.

'Now there's two explanations for this,' Dr Daley decided. 'First, either one or other or both these signs is misleading. Or, second and more likely, Becksbridge has just flown a mile northwards like the holy House of Loretto.'

'Things have got to get better soon,' I suggested, 'because the bad has nowhere else to go.'

'You *are* an optimist, young feller,' Dr Daley said.

In the distance I could see a man sitting on a stile. I proposed that we drive on and consult him.

He was a long, thin person, meticulously dressed in black corduroy jacket, black trousers and white open-necked shirt. A brushed bowler was on his head. He had a small nose and huge, bifocal-looking eyes.

'You're lost, ain't you?' he said in a strange dialect before any of us could open our mouths. 'As soon as oi sees you I knows. Only lost people are clever enough to foind this ould lane. Pretty, ain't it?'

'Very,' Fr Duddleswell said politely. 'Would you mind telling us where this road goes?'

'Roight to the end, Reverend. Roight to the very end.'

I realized immediately that he had escaped from somewhere.

'We are going to Becksbridge,' Fr Duddleswell said, not yet cottoning on.

'Oh, Bucksbridge,' the stranger said.

'You know it?'

'No, oi can't say oi've ever 'eard of Bucksbridge. Where's that?'

'I hoped you might know,' Fr Duddleswell said, beginning to have suspicions.

'Oi was 'aving an evening sit-down on this ould stile. I didn't expect no one to ask me about no Bucksbridge. If you asked me the way to 'The Tin Kettle' I could tell you where tha' is.' He peered through the rear window. 'Ain't you got no map, then?'

'I have,' I said guiltily.

'But where *are* we?' Fr Duddleswell asked. 'What is this place called?'

'This place? I ain't 'eard no one ever call it by no name. It's just the ould lane, i'n't it? It ain't Bucksbridge, I can telly you that.'

184

'Well, thank you kindly, sir,' Fr Duddleswell said, preparing to restart the engine.

'Wait, now, Reverend,' the man on the stile said. 'If oi were you oi'd go to the crossroads.'

'Where is that?'

'Go on for two moile or so, then left, then roight, then roight again by the ould church and then ask where you is.'

'That is very helpful,' Fr Duddleswell called out, as he put the car in motion.

'Oi'm a stranger in these 'ere parts moiself,' the man said finally. 'Oi've only lived 'ere these past fifteen year.'

'Dear God,' Fr Duddleswell said when we were on the road, 'if I wasn't lost before I asked I am now. Did you get the directions to the crossroads, Donal?'

'In a word, Charles, no.'

In common with the other two, I had left it to someone else. Besides, it was a classical case of not knowing whether 'right' meant his right or ours.

'You will find navigating a little easier in three hours time, Father Neil.'

I waited for an explanation.

'Because then,' Fr Duddleswell said, 'the bloody stars will be out.'

A police siren sounded behind us. We must have been exceeding the speed limit without realizing it.

Fr Duddleswell cursed incoherently and drew in. The police car stopped behind us and a constable alighted and, leaden-footed, came alongside the driver's seat. He had a notebook in his hand.

'I must warn you,' he said, as if he was in a movie, 'that anything you say will be taken down and used in evidence against you.'

'Right, Officer,' Fr Duddleswell replied, far too mischievous for my liking, 'stop hitting me like that.'

The constable looked as bewildered as Dr Daley or I.

'Will you write *that* down, Officer,' Fr Duddleswell insisted. 'Both Dr Daley and me navigator here are witnesses that I said, "Stop hitting me, Officer." '

'Very well, sir,' the constable said compliantly. 'I'll just make a note of that for the court.' Then a sudden transformation. 'Father Duddleswell,' he cried, 'what a joy to see you again. What're you doing in these parts?'

'Gerry, I had no idea you were operating in this nick of the woods.'

'I'd recognize your old Chrysler anywhere,' the constable said.

Thank God they were on friendly terms. It was fortunate for us that the constable was a former parishioner of St Jude's.

He was able to direct us without difficulty to Becksbridge. To make sure he drew us a detailed map.

'You can't miss it,' was his final remark.

When Fr Duddleswell was sure we were on the right road, he handed over the wheel to Dr Daley, 'Seeing, Donal, you are as dry this day as a baker's oven.'

Dr Daley obliged while Fr Duddleswell and I settled down to finish off our day's Office before we reached our destination.

'Hasten slowly, now,' Fr Duddleswell advised, 'and you won't meet sorrow.'

In spite of the warning, Dr Daley drove at a tremendous lick. Twenty minutes later, I chanced to look up and the lane was strangely familiar. When I saw the yokel come into view still sitting on his stile I was quite certain.

'Stop, Doctor,' I said.

Fr Duddleswell emerged from deep contemplation with, 'Are we there already?' as we shuddered to a halt.

I pointed to our guide, philosopher and friend.

'You're lost, ain't you?' the man said to our new driver.

'Not at all,' Dr Daley replied bravely. 'I am sight-seeing in the lovely lane where I was before.'

TEN
A Night to Remember

'That journey, Father Neil, was almost as endless as an Irishman's prayers.'

We had made it at last. The stars came out, too late to be of help.

Becksbridge was a cool, quiet Lincolnshire village of miniature stone houses, winding streets and wandering dogs up to no good. We had dropped Dr Daley off at a house on the outskirts where he was staying the night with a former colleague. Fr Duddleswell and I had found a friendly pub that served us sausage rolls and sandwiches washed down with pilgrim's orangeade. Now we were combing Becksbridge for our digs.

At the door of 'St Paul's Shelter', as our hostel was called, Miss Eccles was waiting for us.

A member of the local quality, Miss Eccles was a convert to Catholicism who took a great interest in our Lady's shrine. She was a charming, intelligent woman in her mid-forties and obviously wealthy. She courteously waved aside our apologies for being late and showed us to our rooms. The Shelter was made up of several stables recently converted into a hostel. It was spotlessly clean, whitewashed throughout, though on the small side.

'Your rooms are at the top, Fathers, second floor.' On the first floor, Miss Eccles paused to whisper, 'Two maiden ladies called Flanagan have these rooms.'

Our accommodation was comfortable enough for a one-night stand. No running water in the rooms but a wash basin and big china jug filled to the brim. An iron bedstead with a soft mattress, a cupboard for clothes,

187

a desk and chair and a black metal fireplace. There was, fortunately, a bathroom to each floor.

'If there's anything you need,' Miss Eccles said, 'give me a ring at the Old Rectory and I'll come and help.'

She wrote her phone number on a piece of paper which I slipped in my jacket.

'When and where will we celebrate Mass tomorrow, Miss Eccles?'

'At nine, if that suits you, Father Duddleswell. The only place I could fix up was in the public house next door. Many priests prefer that.'

Fr Duddleswell, I knew, had declined the offer of the High Anglican clergy, guardians of the shrine, to celebrate at their altar.

Miss Eccles left for a dinner appointment. We smartened ourselves up and went for a stroll before turning in for an early night.

'A word of advice in your ear, Father Neil.'

'Yes, Father?'

'If anyone knocks you up in the night, do not answer the door.'

I said I wouldn't but would appreciate it if he told me why.

'It'll only be one or other of the Miss Flanagans wanting you to hear her confession.'

I promised to take no notice and wished him goodnight.

'Sleep that knits up the ravelled sleeve of care,' was his parting remark. It was 9.15.

I tried saying another round of the rosary but sleep still eluded me. I could have sworn I heard scratchings in the fireplace.

Imagination, I told myself. To make sure I laid my mousetrap, sacrificing a sizeable lump of cheese.

I had no sooner returned to bed than I heard a snap. 'Damn it,' I said aloud. I got out of bed to reset the trap more carefully this time when horror seized me. What should be in my mousetrap but a mouse? It was still twitching and its black pin-head eyes stared accusingly at me. I found myself saying, 'Forgive me. It was only self-defence.'

When the mouse's twitchings had ceased, I gingerly picked up the trap, carried it to the open window and released the metal bar. After a couple of shakes, the broken-necked mouse disappeared into the night.

Only with the relief of bidding the rodent goodbye did I become aware of voices below me.

'What was that, Kathleen?' An Irish voice. A Miss Flanagan voice.

'Something hit me on the head, Maura. Right here.'

'Let me have a see.'

When I heard the screams, I nose-dived into bed and stayed there for five minutes. The bloody corpse of the mouse must have become entangled in Miss Kathleen's silver locks.

Plucking up courage, I stepped out of bed, closed the window quietly and set my trap again. My hand was trembling so, the bar whipped down on my index finger almost breaking it.

'Oh, my God,' I screamed, forgetting momentarily my predicament.

Having recovered, I set the trap again more carefully. Back to bed. I heard the Miss Flanagans debating whether the creature which had attacked them was a mouse or a bat. Then, snap again. Once more, investigation revealed a furry, blood-stained victim.

Since that night, I have recounted this story a hundred times. Only one old farmer has ever believed that I caught fifteen mice in my trap in the first hour. The fireplace was strewn with their corpses when I gave up the unequal task, stuffed paper in my ears and pulled the sheet over my head.

At an unspecified hour of the night, when I was in that uncomposed twilight realm between waking and sleeping, I was interrupted by a sharp knock on my door. It came as a relief from the dream I was having at the time. A mouse the size of a bullock with eyes like saucepan lids was having his teeth cleaned by Dr Daley with his toothbrush.

The teeth gleamed menacingly like swords. Dr Daley was saying, 'Here's the lad that did all them murders in the grate, sir. See you catch him fast.' I plunged into a river and began swimming madly with the giant mouse in hot pursuit, gaining on me fast.

Following Fr Duddleswell's advice, I snuggled down further in the bed. Miss Kathleen Flanagan might want me for more than hearing her confession.

Another knock and another, accompanied by a familiar voice: 'Father Neil, will you open this bloody door.'

He stood there in the light of the landing in his pyjamas and dressing gown.

'Is it time for Mass already, Father?'

'It is only a quarter after eleven.'

'Ah,' I said, disappointed and rubbing my eyes. 'Have you had trouble with them, too, Father?'

'The Miss Flanagans?'

'No, the mice, Father.'

He pushed past me into my room. 'I am in diabolical trouble, lad.'

I pointed to the pile of fur by my fireplace. 'Me, too,' I said.

'Will you keep quiet about your bloody mice and listen while I speak to you.'

His problem was simple but ruinous. He had gone to the toilet and while he was away the wind had blown his door shut. He had forgotten to put it on the latch with the result that he was locked out.

'You can share with me, Father.'

'I do not intend sharing a room even with me guardian angel, Father Neil. Besides, me razor and all me clothes are in there.'

I still hadn't gathered my wits about me but I put on my dressing gown and rooted out my penknife.

'I'll see if this will do the job,' I said, without a hope in hell. I have difficulty opening a can of beans with a can opener.

He followed me out and no sooner were we both on the landing than my door slammed too.

Fr Duddleswell looked at me, fearful and wide-eyed. 'Father Neil, you haven't – ?'

'I'm afraid,' I began.

'You leather-head,' he snarled, 'you gaping booby.'

'Don't pick on me,' I retorted angrily. 'Didn't you do it first?'

'Indeed I did but you had the benefit of my experience.'

'Tell me what to do,' I said miserably.

'Do not stand around like an Irishman waiting for the pub to open, use the knife.'

I tried the knife on both doors in turn. It was no use. Each was fitted with a brand new yale lock.

'We will have to phone Miss Eccles, Father Neil.' He saw my furtive look. 'Don't tell me. The number is in your jacket pocket.'

I nodded. 'Shall I knock up the Miss Flanagans, Father?'

He turned his head away in disgust. 'Are you wanting me to lose me license as a priest? That pair'll tell the parish and then run to me after, to confess they are guilty of spreading scandal.'

'What are we going to do?'

'I tell you one thing, lad. I do not intend taking turns sitting on the toilet all night. I am off looking for a ladder.'

We crept downstairs past the Miss Flanagan rooms and into the back garden. It was cool and cloudy but there was no rain.

I felt something soft brush against my leg and recoiled in horror until I heard the thing meow.

The moon appeared long enough for us to find a big ladder but its trustworthiness was a bit suspect. Besides, it was nearly twenty feet up to my bedroom ledge and the route went past one of the Miss Flanagan rooms.

Fr Duddleswell put the ladder against the wall. 'Stop gaping like a crocodile, lad,' he whispered hoarsely, 'and up with you.'

'I'm not feeling too well, Father.' I was speaking the truth.

'Nonsense. You are as healthy as a haddock. I will hold the ladder for you.'

191

A light appeared in one of the ladies rooms. Fr Duddleswell grabbed me and hauled me to a section of the garden in shadow.

The Miss Flanagans put their heads out of the window.

'Kathleen,' one of them said, 'a ladder.'

''Twasn't there a little while ago, Maura. D'you think – ?'

'I don't know what to think.'

'Sacred Heart of Jesus!'

They withdrew hurriedly, closed the window and locked it, no doubt wondering whether to call for help. If they knocked on our doors they were in for a nasty shock.

In the ladies' highly emotional state, it was too dangerous for us to return to our landing. We decided to look for an old shed. Without success.

But there was a glimmer of light coming from the window of 'The Plough' where we were booked to say Mass next morning.

'Our only chance, lad.'

I agreed and followed the foreman.

We silently approached the side door of the pub. Near the window through which light was filtering we heard sounds of muted revelry.

'A family gathering,' I suggested.

'Knock the door, lad.'

I obliged and there was utter consternation inside, chair scrapings, loud stage whispers and glasses clinking. Someone called out:

'It's all right, Officer, my wife and me were just off to bed.'

'Dear God,' Fr Duddleswell said hoarsely, 'he thinks we are the Peelers checking up on after-hours drinking.'

He signalled to me to knock again. I did so, only louder. Another light went on inside the pub, the bolts were drawn on the door and a head peeked slowly round it. It was like the head of a walrus: round, sad, with big drooping moustaches.

Seeing us standing there in pyjamas and dressing gowns, the Walrus let the door swing open on its hinges.

'God Almighty,' he said.

'Is it that nice policeman, Tom?' a woman, presumably his wife, enquired.

'No, love,' the publican stammered.

'Who is it, then?'

'It's, um, I'm not quite – ' His powers of description failed him.

'We're from next door,' I said, smiling to show we were friendly.

'They say they're from next door, Iris.'

'But that's a lock-up shop,' Iris said, referring, I supposed, to the other side of them.

One of the illicit drinkers must have come out of hiding, for a man called out conspiratorially, 'It's a couple of loonies,' and another asked, 'From St Bernards?'

St Bernards was clearly the local mental hospital.

'Whoever it is,' his wife called out, 'ask them in and close that door, Tom.' She was a big woman with red hair and a white blouse. Seeing our appearance for the first time, she gulped loud enough to be heard. 'Wait a sec, ask the nice gentlemen what they want, Tom.'

'What was it you were wanting? We're closed really.'

'We have been locked out,' Fr Duddleswell told the Walrus.

'No offence meant,' the Walrus replied, getting agitated. 'Licensing laws, you know. It's after hours.'

'Locked out of our place,' Fr Duddleswell said.

'I can ring up if you like,' Iris offered.

'Ring up where?' I asked.

'Wherever you came from,' Iris said diplomatically, 'or where you want to go to.'

'You do know where you're from?' the publican asked.

By this time, the pub's patrons were squeezing past us, nodding with nervous politeness and bidding, 'Good night, Tom,' ''Night, Iris.' The publican did his best to keep a few of them back for support if needed with, 'Have a last drink on the House' and 'One for the road'. But no use. Soon it was only the four of us.

Fr Duddleswell, speaking through the departing

throng, informed Iris that we were from the Shelter and wanted to go back there.

'Is there something stopping you, darling?' Iris said. 'Afraid of the dark, are you?'

'We're the two priests from London,' I managed to say. 'And we've locked ourselves out of our rooms.'

Iris was transformed. 'Come in, Fathers,' she said welcomingly. 'We're Catholics ourselves, of a sort.'

I nudged Fr Duddleswell. 'The truth is so simple,' I whispered. 'You should try it sometime.'

We followed a relieved Walrus into a bar reeking of tobacco smoke and the thick smell of booze. We explained our predicament in detail to the kindly couple. They sympathized but had little means of helping. They didn't know Miss Eccles's number and it wasn't in the book. When we phoned the operator, she told us the number was ex-directory and it was against the rules for her to give it to us.

'Nothing for it, Fathers,' Tom said cheerfully. 'You'll have to stay here the night. The wife'll rustle you up a few blankets and pillows. Meanwhile,' he winked, 'how about a snifter before turning in?'

Pilgrimage or no pilgrimage, we needed a pick-me-up after what we had been through.

'Whisky neat,' Fr Duddleswell ordered and I asked for a brandy to inject some life into my aching limbs.

We had been poured a generous helping and the landlord was filling his own glass when there was a rat-tat on the door.

'Not again,' the Walrus moaned, forgetting that the first intruders had been us. Without a word, he grabbed our glasses and poured the contents into a jug on the bar counter.

Another knock and an authoritative voice: 'Open up, do you hear me, Landlord?'

'The law,' Tom mouthed in our direction as he went to open the door.

A middle-aged police Sergeant with a fierce face was let in. 'You do know it's next to midnight, Mr Foyle?'

194

'I do, Sergeant,' the publican said. 'But, as you see, there's nobody here.'

'What about that crowd of harem-scarems who just nearly knocked me off my bike? Where have they been living it up, then, eh?'

'I think you'd better ask *them*,' the publican said politely. 'I was having a quiet conversation with these gentlemen here.'

The policeman nodded to us. 'It's all right, you. You can go off upstairs to bed.' When he saw us hesitate, he added, 'You are guests here, aren't you?'

'No,' I blurted out.

'You happened to be passing, eh?'

'That is exactly right, Officer,' Fr Duddleswell said, no doubt hoping that truth would do well by us again.

The policeman was flummoxed. 'In your sleeping clothes? D'you go out regularly on the tiles at midnight in your sleeping clothes?'

Fr Duddleswell resented the tone and contents of his remark. 'We are on a pilgrimage, I would have you know.'

The publican said, 'These here gentlemen are priests, Sergeant. Catholics like you and us.'

'That's a good 'un,' the Sergeant said. 'Best I've heard in a long while.' He poked Fr Duddleswell in the chest. 'Come for the rosary, have you, Father?'

'I tell you they are priests,' Tom insisted.

'Seen their papers, Mr Foyle?'

'No.'

'Rung up their Bishop or something?'

'As a matter of . . .' For the first time since we had disclosed our identity the Walrus was having doubts.

'Look here,' the Sergeant said, 'are you two from St Bernards?'

'St Jude's,' I said.

'Where's your brains, Mr Foyle?' the Sergeant whispered to the publican on the side but perfectly audibly to us. 'A couple of dafties walk in here at midnight in their sleeping clothes and you entertain 'em because they say they're Catholic priests. Priests, Napoleon, what's the difference?'

The publican scratched his head. 'Well, I don't know,' he said.

Another whisper from the policeman. 'Lucky for us they don't seem too dangerous.'

Iris came in with a couple of sleeping bags and an armful of pillows. She sorted the situation out in no time.

'Say Mass for us, Fathers,' she said.

'We cannot until the hour before dawn,' Fr Duddleswell replied, quoting canonical regulations.

Iris smiled. 'I meant the *words*.'

Fr Duddleswell, catching on, intoned, '*Introibo ad altare Dei*' in his best ministerial manner, and I responded with, '*Ad Deum qui laetificat juventutem meam*' – and so on to the end of the introductory psalm of the Mass.

Afterwards, the Sergeant wiped his forehead. 'Pour us out a glass of water, Tom.'

The Walrus handed all of us a liberal dose of something stronger and the Sergeant gave us a toast, 'To Mother Church.'

We were on the point of swallowing when the clock in the village square chimed midnight. We priests knew that if we were to celebrate Mass next morning, not a drop of anything must touch our lips.

'You're the genuine article, all right,' the policeman said.

'I hope you'll be very comfortable here, Fathers.'

'Thank you, Iris,' Fr Duddleswell said, casting a miserable glance around the bar.

'You don't happen to have mice,' I said.

'Have a heart, Father,' Tom replied.

'Of course, living in the country, we have had the occasional rat,' Iris contributed, out of a mistaken sense of honesty. 'But not for fully six months.'

Tom promised to call us at eight, then he and Iris left us. We settled on where to park our sleeping bags. The most secluded spot was under the billiard table.

I placed a towel from the bar counter under my hip,

knowing from experience that the hip hurts a lot after a night on a wooden floor.

'Goodnight again, lad, and may you sleep like a sack in a mill.'

Not much hope of that. It was well after midnight and, as Fr Duddleswell had wryly observed, 'Perhaps the Holy Family were lucky there was no room for them in the inn.'

I lay awake for what seemed like hours, listening to the distant hooting of owls and any suspicious scrabblings on the floor around me. I could tell from Fr Duddleswell's restless movements that a long day was ahead of him as well.

Against all expectations, I slept. I was awakened all of a sudden by pounding feet and hushed voices. It can't be morning, I thought. It's not light yet. Am I dreaming? Where am I? It dawned on me that I was under a billiard table in a bar with the curtains drawn. I groped around for Fr Duddleswell. Not there. He had deserted me but why?

The pilgrims, I could tell, were already assembling in the bar for Mass. I could make out the shapeless legs of the Miss Flanagans and the habits of Mother Stephen and Sister Perpetua as they placed the altar stone on the counter and laid out the Mass vestments. My watch showed 8:50. I prayed devoutly that Fr Duddleswell would come back soon and fish me out of this mess.

I listened intently. What was that sizzling sound over my head? Could it be himself? I crept to the far side of the billiard table and raised my head. There on the green surface was the prone figure of Fr Duddleswell, his lungs swelling and shrinking in sleep.

I poked him awake rudely with thumb and forefinger. When he had taken in the unpromising situation, he slid silently over the edge and joined me beneath the table.

'That bloody publican,' he growled, 'has overslept himself.'

Like us, I nearly said. Instead: 'You can't say Mass in here, Father.'

'And why not?'

'Because,' I joked, 'canon law says the one place you can't offer Mass is a bedroom.'

From the look on his face he was swallowing swords. 'D'you want me to close your ogles for you?' he hissed, holding up his fist.

The publican who appeared then must have been reading the same canon as myself. He said:

'Not in here, ladies and gentlemen. Mass will be next door in the private bar.'

As the congregation trooped out, we heaved a sigh of relief, especially when we heard Tom Foyle adding, 'Leave the vestments, Mother. The Father will be vesting at the bar there.'

Moments later, the Walrus poked his head under the billiard table.

'Thank you kindly, Tom,' Fr Duddleswell said. 'Have you asked Miss Eccles for the spare keys?'

'She's had to go home for them, Father. It'll take her about a quarter of an hour.'

'Why don't you start Mass, Father?' I said.

Fr Duddleswell thought it a good idea. Tom snatched the vestments off the counter while the pilgrims were busy singing the Lourdes hymn and carried them to the Gents. Fr Duddleswell followed him on his belly like the serpent in Genesis and emerged three minutes afterwards ready to celebrate. The only thing likely to give him away was his slippers and the ends of his pyjamas protruding below the alb.

He preached an impromptu sermon of prodigious length for my benefit, only bringing it to an end when he saw that Miss Eccles had returned with the keys.

The publican slipped them to me but I waited all the same until Fr Duddleswell reached the consecration. When the congregation was bowed in adoration, I rose from my hiding place. Using my sleeping bag as if I was in a sack race, I hopped quickly out of the bar without attracting attention.

Unfortunately for me, outside the pub, sitting under a coloured table canopy, was Miss Kathleen Flanagan.

'I was feeling faint, Father,' she explained. I didn't doubt her, poor soul. Not with the memory of a bleeding mouse falling on her head.

'I'm just doing my usual penitential exercises before Mass, Miss Flanagan,' I lied.

She rubbed her forehead. 'I do think you're a good and holy man, Father Boyd.'

I thanked her for the kind word and hopped smartly home.

I had hardly finished shaving and dressing when Fr Duddleswell hammered on the door. He unvested in his room and dropped the vestments on the landing. 'Get your harness on for Mass as fast as you like, lad,' he ordered.

I hurried down to the pub and celebrated the second Mass for the pilgrims with Dr Daley as the acolyte. The Doctor joined us for breakfast in the local Hotel and, after that, we met up with the rest of the pilgrims in the square. Off we marched to the small Catholic shrine a mile and a half outside the village.

Fr Duddleswell was in high spirits after our narrow escape. As he was to say later, 'I do not mind being humbled, Father Neil, but I take exception to being humiliated.' He never explained the difference.

The sun was shining on cornfields still surprisingly green, fat pigeons heaved themselves like Abbots out of the oaks, sparrows and jays were chattering in the hedges lining the route, there was a flavour of cow in the air and trees showed up bright green against the blue.

'Is not this a newly minted morn?' Fr Duddleswell fairly sang. 'The dew thick as butter, you could put it on your bread.'

Then he switched to a bellow: 'First Joyful Mystery of the Holy Rosary, the Annunciation. Our Father who art in Heaven.' And we were launched on our prayerful way.

We reached the half-mile mark. The tradition was for all pilgrims to remove their shoes at this point and walk the last mile unshod. I was feeling so much under the weather, I demurred. But Fr Duddleswell insisted that we priests should set the people a good example. 'If Mother Stephen and Henry VIII can walk on naked feet, so can we, lad.'

Dr Daley was muttering to himself, 'My father, God rest him and give him peace, never wore shoes till the day he wed.'

'Perhaps he only married,' I suggested, wincing, 'to ease the pain in his feet.'

'I shouldn't wonder.'

We set off again, less spiritedly and much slower. 'Hail Mary, full of grace –' Fr Duddleswell broke off in mid-prayer. 'Bloody hell,' he let out with a strangled cry.

The procession came to a halt as the leader collapsed on to the seat of his pants.

Dr Daley, bare-footed, with his trousers rolled up to his shins, knelt down by his side, concerned.

'''Tis me foot, Donal. I have trodden on a bloody nail.'

'Dear, dear, dear,' the Doctor said soothingly. 'Wouldn't you think a nail had something better to do than start crucifying our parish priest?'

Ever the professional, he took out a bottle of disinfectant and a bandage. He cleaned the wound and bound it up for him as the patient sat grimacing on the grass verge.

'Only four more holes, Charles, and you will be rivalling the stigmata of Padre Pio himself.'

'Reminds me of King Aengus, Donal,' Fr Duddleswell said, gritting his teeth as the disinfectant was applied.

'King Aengus?'

'Indeed, Father Neil,' Dr Daley explained. 'St Patrick baptized the royal feller in the Golden Vale of Cashel. St Pat was on the downward slope of life at the time, so he digs his crosier into the ground to support himself.'

'Not too tight, now,' Fr Duddleswell complained.

The Doctor nodded. 'Well, Father Neil, after the christening, St Pat saw blood reddening the grass. And then his own holy face reddened when he realized he had driven the spike of his crosier clean through the king's foot. "Why did you not say something?" says St Pat to the king. "Well, first, St Patrick, sir," says the king, "did our Blessed

Lord, the King of kings, cry out when He shed His blood for me? He did not. And, second, St Patrick, sir," says he, "I thought it was part of the ceremony." ' Dr Daley tied a knot in the bandage. 'How's that, Charles?'

'Ouch,' Fr Duddleswell replied with a grin and proceeded to put his shoes and socks on.

'That's cheating,' I said.

He looked up at me indignantly. 'Haven't I a martyred foot and all?'

Dr Daley was busy rummaging around in a ditch until he found a suitable stick. 'Here, Charles,' he said, offering it, 'a third leg for you twenty years or so ahead of your time.'

'Thank you, Donal. More like a crosier, isn't that so? 'Tis fitting for me, the Lord's anointed, to continue guiding you all heavenwards.'

Our heavenly guide promptly wriggled this way and that like someone about to fall into an apoplectic fit.

'What ever is the matter with yourself, Charles?' Dr Daley asked anxiously. 'Even if the nail was poisoned, gangrene can hardly have set in as soon as this.'

Fr Duddleswell, holding his backside, managed to point to the anthill he had been sitting on. 'A fairy mount' was his word for it.

'It must be red ants,' Dr Daley declared. 'The black ants only eat Protestants.'

The procession was held up for another twenty minutes while Fr Duddleswell 'went behind' a convenient haystack. There he divested himself of his clothes and got rid of the ants.

'God,' Dr Daley said when Fr Duddleswell was restored to us, 'isn't Providence a queer business altogether?'

'How is that, Donal?'

'With the entire world to feed on, them ants preferred to take bites out of your tough little bum.'

In my heart, I felt the incident had answered one of my mother's constant teasers: 'Why did God in His wisdom make such horrible things as ants?'

* * *

'I insist, Father Duddleswell.'

Fr Duddleswell was stiffly refusing to accept Mother Foundress's tibia encased in its golden reliquary. 'I will not allow veneration of that thing at our Lady's shrine,' he said shrilly.

'Then, Father,' Mother Stephen said, 'to use a vulgar expression, I will spill the beans.'

'What d'you mean, Mother?'

'I think the Bishop will be most interested to know that one of his senior parish priests spent the night of a pilgrimage carousing.'

'Carousing?'

'In a drunken debauch.'

'Mother,' Fr Duddleswell spat out, 'I have not so much as had a drink taken in the last twenty-four hours.'

'Then why did you sleep on a billiard table with parts of you bared — ?'

'Which parts?'

'In a public bar,' Mother Superior concluded.

'I can, um, explain, Mother.'

'I am listening.'

When it came to it, he found he could not explain. Not at the shrine of our Lady of Becksbridge with some of his most devout gossip-mongers within earshot.

'Perhaps you will also be kind enough to tell me, Father Duddleswell, why you celebrated Sunday Mass in your bedroom slippers and pyjamas, having first put on the sacred vestments in the Gentlemen's, I can hardly bring myself to say the word, *lavatory*.'

'That is a long story, Mother.'

'And, doubtless, a tall one. Did you know that those vestments are the property of our convent?'

'I had not realized you had loaned them to us, Mother,' Fr Duddleswell said humbly.

'Will I be able to see them used at Mass again without them conjuring up the most unholy associations?'

Fr Duddleswell took the tibia of Mère Madeleine and kissed the reliquary containing it as an example to all his parishioners.

'Did I ever tell you, Mother,' he said, squaring his jaw, 'of the intense devotion I have in me heart's core for your holy Mother Foundress?'

The winds and tides of fortune turned. Or perhaps we had merely exhausted our ration of ill-luck. We returned home that Sunday evening with the minimum of incident, Fr Duddleswell both driving and navigating. He had slowed down, it is true, as we passed almost every pub but his silent appeal left us unmoved.

Dr Daley shared a light meal with us which Mrs Pring had prepared. Fr Duddleswell was hobbling. I was aching in every limb from impending 'flu. As for Dr Daley, he was as spry as a sparrow.

Mrs Pring had been unpacking Fr Duddleswell's suitcases. She came to ask where his dressing gown was.

'In the Gents of a public house,' he said.

'And I was hoping,' she sighed, 'the pilgrimage would do you good.'

After the meal, the leader herded us into his study. He rubbed his hands enthusiastically.

'Well, now, Donal, the days of penitence are over and I can offer you a drink.'

'Thank you, Charles. No.'

'No?' It was the most poignant appeal yet for clemency.

'I have decided, Charles, to be as brave as your holy self. While you abstain, I will not permit a cigarette or sup of whisky to defile my lips.'

Fr Duddleswell's left cheek twitched irritably. 'Father Neil?'

'In the seminary, Father, the spiritual director advised us not to take whisky till we're forty. That way, he said, we'll be sure not to bury our youth.'

'He did, did he?' was all he could reply to that.

'Yes, Father, I believe he once had a priest friend who killed himself with drink. At about your age.'

'A clear case of euthanasia,' Dr Daley said, his hand on the door. 'Thanks for the lift, anyway, Charles, and for your towering example.'

He went and we heard the front door close after him.

'So there, Father Neil, it was all worthwhile if it has made Dr Daley go on the wagon.'

'He went home as pious and sober, Father, as if you'd just anointed him for life everlasting.'

Fr Duddleswell laughed hollowly. 'I have had a rough time of it, what with a night spent on a billiard table, a puncture in me foot and then being cannibalized by a nest of ants.'

'Have you?' I said, not encouraging him.

'There is nothing,' he murmured, steaming towards his cupboard, 'like a quiet drink in the heel of the evening.'

He poured himself a double whisky and was about to drink it when in marched Dr Daley, his eyes gleaming gratefully and a cigarette already alight in the corner of his mouth.

ELEVEN
Little Sinners and Little Saints

Corpus Christi, one of Fr Duddleswell's favourite feasts, was fast approaching. In his study, he outlined plans for first Communion, always held at St Jude's on the Sunday nearest the feast.

Each child was to have his picture taken individually with the girls dressed up as little brides and the boys sporting white blouses with white shoulder bands and grey flannel trousers. Each would receive a certificate, a rosary and a prayer book.

'The kiddies are the best evangelists in the parish, Father Neil. Lapsed parents come to church to see their little ones make their first Holy Communion. We can even expect a convert or two.'

'That's good, Father.'

'Of course,' he said, rubbing the side of his nose, 'in preparing for this great event, you will take a hand at the churn.'

I promised I would do my share.

'Fine, fine. Kind of you to offer.'

'Tell me what to do.'

'I suggest you instruct God's darlin' little ones in the sacraments of penance and Communion.'

'Who will hear their first confessions?'

'The experience will do you good.'

'What will you do, Father?'

'I will distribute first Holy Communion, naturally.'

He beamed as he said it, aware that nothing had been shared out so unevenly since the lion ate with the lamb. Not that I minded. Giving seven-year olds their first

Communion was the parish priest's privilege. In the years ahead, my turn would come.

I had recently attended the lectures of a nun, a specialist in religious education, on preparing children for the sacraments. Her common sense approach impressed me and I was keen to put her teaching into practice.

'Would you mind, Father, if I heard the children's confessions in my room?'

Fr Duddleswell was as shaken as if I had said I was turning Jewish or wanted to open a bordello.

'Educational psychologists,' I explained, 'think it's better for children to confess in an informal atmosphere to someone they know and can see.'

'Is that so?' he said defensively.

'In my room, they won't be afraid of the dark. They can relax and tell me what is really worrying them and not just rattle off sins their teacher's taught them.'

'Look, lad,' he said grimly, as if the balmy days of tame curates was over, 'the darkness of the confessional guarantees them anonymity. Penitents do not *want* you to know who they are.'

'Even though you boast you do.'

'They think I *don't* know, that is the point.'

'I see,' I said ironically, 'you prefer them to talk not to a person but to the dark.'

'They are not meant to be confessing to you, lad, but to our Blessed Lord.'

'He heard confessions in a box, did He? Or just the children?'

'Why are you at me throat today like a weasel?' he complained. 'Our Lord did not hear in a box but He was the Son of God. If we are to take His place in forgiving sins, 'tis essential we keep ourselves in the background.'

'I suppose you're right, Father,' I said, continuing the vein of irony, 'we mustn't take children's sins too seriously, must we?'

He nodded his head with annoyance. 'There is something in that, too. We take the kiddies' sins seriously enough to hear the confession of each and every one of them. But not so seriously that it worries 'em to death.'

He was parish priest not I. 'All right, Father. Have it your way.'

''Tis not my way but the Church's way.'

'That's consoling, isn't it, Father? Saves us having to think for ourselves how to improve things.'

'There is such a thing as tradition, lad.'

'Dead wood, Father. Dead wood.'

'I will show you what tradition is, Father Neil. Look.' He pointed through the window into the garden. 'The silver birch tree. See the stake 'tis tied to?'

'Yes.'

'Dead wood, lad. 'Tis that piece of dead wood, as you call it, that makes the living tree grow straight and tall.'

'How nice,' I said, beginning to retaliate. 'Did you ever hear the story, Father, of the boy who planted an acorn in his garden?'

'I cannot say I ever did.'

He must have, really, because the image of the acorn germinating was a common one for the growth of faith.

'Anyway, Father, this little boy planted his acorn and went away for fifty or sixty years.'

'And?' he asked, smiling pleasantly, convinced he knew the end of the story.

'When he returned home after all that time, what did he find in his garden reaching up into the heavens but this enormous . . . acorn.'

He humphed and left the room.

A couple of hours later, I apologized.

'Jasus,' he said, 'you are getting to be as bad as I was.'

'If that's meant to be a compliment, Father, thanks a lot.'

He grinned. 'So you will behave as a Catholic priest, after all.'

'On one condition, that I don't have to hear the confessions of all 35 kids in 35 minutes.'

He looked apprehensive again. 'You can take a full hour, if you like.'

'I want to take a week.'

'I'm sure I beg your pardon.'

'I will hear seven children a day during their religion lesson. That will give me at least five minutes with each one.'

'Twill be a massacre,' he warned, 'and you will make a cod of yourself.'

I told him I'd risk it.

He didn't seem to be worrying unduly. 'Only make sure you see they are good for saying their prayers to our Lady.'

I reminded him that I was an Englishman and England's proud title was once, 'Dowry of Mary'.

Not to be outdone, he told me that Irish was the only language in which there were two words for Mary. *Maire*, a girl's name, and *Muire*, the name reserved for the Mother of God.

'I must tell you the tale,' he said, 'of when Cromwell's army took Cashel.'

'Must you, Father? Carry on, then.'

'A drunken soldier grabbed a statue of our Blessed Lady –'

I interrupted him. 'I didn't know the Puritans drank?'

'This feller was mouldy drunk, anyway. He picked up a handful of food and stuffed it in the mouth of the Virgin, much to the amusement of his drunken comrades –'.

'Who also drank a lot.'

'It seems so. And the soldier called out, "Now, now, Mary of Ireland" – a beautiful title, incidentally – "Mary of Ireland, let us see you eat peas." ' He bit the inside of his cheek in grief at the blasphemy. 'Mind you, Father Neil, it had a wonderful happy ending.'

'The Puritan soldier became a Catholic.'

'No, no, no. Better by far. A while after, a big brick fell off a roof on to his head.'

'And killed him on the spot.'

He looked surprised. 'You have heard it before?'

The sevens were in Miss Gregson's class. She was a teacher of the old school. With her steel-rimmed spectacles, hair in a bun and generally well-laundered appearance, she was calculated to put the fear of God into God.

'I have warned them, Father, that they must tell the priest in confession all their sins, especially the mortal.'

I had it from various sources that Miss Gregson had a fixation on mortal sin.

'They know it's a sacrilege to keep back a mortal sin in confession.' She challenged the class to contradict her. 'Don't you, children?'

'Yes, Miss,' came back from thirty-five throats.

'How is it a sacrilege, children?' A forest of arms went up. Miss Gregson chose one at random. 'Yes, Donald.'

'Because, Miss, it's telling a lie to the Holy Ghost in making a bad confession.'

'Very good, Donald. Sit. A *terrible* sacrilege.'

It seemed to me that the sacrilege being committed was not the one Miss Gregson had in mind.

I explained to the children that I was intending to hear their confessions in a leisurely way. I wanted them to look on me not as their judge but as their friend and helper.

Then, in lighter mood, I told them a story once told me by my grandmother. A circus boy was making his first confession. Afterwards, he was so happy at having his sins forgiven that he went cartwheeling all round the church. The next child to confess said to the priest, 'Father, please don't give me cartwheels for a penance because I can't do them.'

Not a flicker of amusement on any child's face.

Miss Gregson thanked me coldly for my visit and I left the classroom in embarrassment, once again convinced that humour is not my strong suit.

At lunch, Fr Duddleswell asked how I was making out in preparations for the feast.

'So-so.'

'A grand crowd of kids, Father Neil. Only yesterday, I told 'em the story of a little circus lad making his first confession.' He proceeded to relate the story I had just come a cropper with.

At the end, while blaspheming inwardly at his interference on my patch, I forced myself to titter. 'Very funny, Father.'

'That's what the kiddies thought. Even Miss Gregson nearly died laughing.'

'Pity,' I said.

Preliminaries were complete. It was Monday morning and the first batch of seven children, unshepherded at my request, were waiting in church.

'Pray, Father, give me your blessing for I have sinned.'

I gave my blessing.

'This is my first confession and these are my sins. Have you told lies? Have you been greedy? Have you been cheeky to your mummy and daddy?'

'Stop, please.'

'Have you fighted with your brothers and sisters?'

'Will you please stop.'

'Is that enough, Father?' the child said.

'Quite enough, dear.'

'Thank you, Father.' And before I could say another word, the child had left unabsolved and another had taken his place.

So much for Miss Gregson's method of teaching, I thought. My record so far, was one confession without absolution. I turned my attention to the second penitent.

'I told lies,' the child said in a piping voice. 'I was greedy. I was cheeky to my mummy and daddy.'

I groaned inwardly. Miss Gregson's catalogue of sins again. 'What did you say to your mummy, dear?'

The child seemed surprised at being interrupted before the list was complete. 'Nothing, Father. I just shouted at her.'

'Why?'

"Cos she shouted at me.'

I felt we were getting somewhere at last. 'She must have had some reason for shouting at you.'

'No, she just likes it. My dad says she experts at it.'

'Does she?'

'And she's very good at crying, too. She says it helps pass the time.' I let it go. 'She smacked me, Father.'

'What for, dear?'

'For hiding, Father. But I knew where I was. And she smacked me for playing my favourite music.'

A chance of establishing some kind of human relationship with my tiny penitent kneeling alone in the dark.

'What's your favourite music, dear?'

'Loud, Father.'

'I see.'

'Mummy smacked me too for not giving grandma a kiss but it was worth it.'

'Do you live with your grandma?'

'No, she lives with us. In her house, though.'

'You surely love your grandma, dear.'

'I don't, Father.'

'Have you brothers and sisters?'

'Worse luck.'

'I bet they love your grandma.'

'They don't. Nobody loves her.'

'Why is that?'

'I think it's cos she keeps saying nobody loves her.'

'Well,' I said encouragingly, 'I'm sure you are doing your best.'

'No, I ain't doing my best 'cos I can't.'

I felt that here at least was a child not given to lies.

'This is a big day for you, dear. Your first confession. I want you to promise our Blessed Lord you will *try* to be a good boy.'

'I can't try, Father.'

'Why not?'

'Because I'm a girl, Father.'

That's one mistake I wouldn't have made, I thought as I gave her absolution, if I'd been allowed to hear confessions in my way.

'Pray, Father, give me your blessing for I have sinned.'

A real croaky voice this girl had. Was it a girl? Yes, it definitely wasn't a boy. I blessed her.

'I told lies, Father. I didn't say my prayers.' The laundry list again, I was thinking. When: 'I committed adultery twice, Father.'

I smiled at the echo from the past. I had dealt with this very 'sin' in my own first confession as a priest.

'What did you do, dear, steal two pennies from mummy's purse?'

'*No*, Father.'

'Well, then, dear, tell me exactly what you did.'

'Er, Father, er, I got into his bed –'

Panic shot through me. 'Wait. You *do* belong to Miss Gregson's class?'

'No, Father. I was doing my morning shopping and I popped in and when I saw the confessional was open –'

I heard out this housewife-intruder and sent her back to the shops.

'This is my first confession, Father.' The new penitent hesitated. 'I've done the worst sin there is, Father.'

After the housewife, I could hardly wait to find out what it was. 'Yes,' I said encouragingly.

'With my spaghetti.'

I feverishly racked my brain to find any sin in the book that sounded like 'spaghetti' but came up with nothing. Having given up, I said:

'With spaghetti.'

The penitent confirmed that that was his sin.

'What did you, um, do with your spaghetti?'

'I cut it up with a knife, Father.'

I suspected there was far more to it than that. I said, 'Is that a sin?'

'My dad says it's the worst sin he knows to turn good spaghetti into confetti.'

'Is he Italian?'

'No, Father, he comes from Sicily.'

'Anything else?'

'My mum, Father, gets sinful milk.'

'*Sinful* milk?'

'She's not a Catholic, that's why.'

I was intrigued by this and wondered if 'milk' was a euphemism in this child's family for an alcoholic beverage, say, gin or whiskey. 'What does sinful milk look like, son?'

'It's white, of course.'

'Have you ever tasted it?'

'I put it on my cornflakes.'

I could only think that the boy's mother must have a habit of stealing milk. 'What's sinful about it, son?'

'It's stelirized.'

'Sterilized.'

'That's right. And Miss Gregson said it's a sin for Catholics to do with stelirized.'

The next penitent was a budding sadist.

'When I went to the circus, Father, I saw this man walking on a piece of cotton, thousands of feet up.'

I waited for the sin.

'And I prayed 'ard 'e'd fall off.'

'That's not nice, is it?'

'Not for 'im, Father,' my penitent chuckled, 'but I thought it was a smacking good idea.'

'God doesn't answer prayers like that.'

"E did, Father. The bloke fell right orf.'

'Did 'e? I mean, did he?'

'Yeah. God don't usually say yes to my prayers. I know 'E can but 'E don't bother much.'

I felt it incumbent on me to correct this pagan view of God. 'I'm sure the man did not fall off just because you prayed he would.'

'You mean God would've knocked 'im orf any'ow?'

'Not exactly.'

'What, then?'

Rather than spend half an hour giving him an answer which neither of us would have understood, I distracted him with, 'Was there a safety net?'

'Yeah, a big one.'

'There, you see,' I crowed, 'God is good, isn't He?'

'The bloke missed it, Father.'

Together we said the 'Out of the Depths' for the repose of his soul. Afterwards:

'My dad punched my ear, Father. In church, Father. For talking. That was wrong, wa'n't it?'

It was not my job as a confessor to arbitrate between

father and son when they sinned against each other. 'Why were you talking?'

'I was bored. My dad says to me, "Billy boy, everybody's bored in church. That's why we go. But that's no excuse for talking." Then 'e punched my ear. Is that right, Father?'

'Um.'

'Dad says it's the best thing to be bored. Jesus was. Always bored 'E was but 'E didn't care. If you get real bored like a stick of rock, dad says, God will love you a very lot.'

'Uh huh.'

'If you talk in church, people can't be bored properly and they won't feel they've been to church at all.'

This was such a novel rationale for churchgoing I stored it away in my mind for reflecting on in a quiet moment.

'Anything else, son?'

'My stone broke a winder. Is this okay for confession? Miss Gregson didn't say.' Before I could speak, he added, 'But I didn't shut it, did I? 'Is winder. Any'ow, Father, if Mr Ross didn't want me to break 'is winder, 'e should 'ave put a notice up.'

'Mr Ross?'

''E lives next door. 'E's got cherry trees.'

I am almost as fond of cherry blossom as the Japanese. 'Do you like cherry trees?' I asked hopefully.

'I think they're the best invention God ever did.'

'You like the pink and white blossom?'

'Nah, the cherries, Father. Mr Ross is an 'orrible bloke. 'E won't let us pinch 'is cherries.'

'Is that why you broke his window?'

'I didn't think of it. Nah, I was aiming for 'is cherries.'

'What would your father say if he knew?'

''E was there. 'E says if I 'it Mr Ross on the 'ead with a brick 'e'll give me a tanner.'

When I dismissed the lad I asked him to tell the other children to calm down. They were beginning to make an appalling noise.

After I had gained the confidence of the next penitent,

he said, 'I know what sin looks like, Father.'

'You do? Would you mind telling me?'

'Like my brother.'

'How does your brother look?'

'Black and ugly.'

I smiled. 'He can't look as bad as that.'

'Worser.'

'But you love him all the same,' I said optimistically. When the boy didn't answer, I added, 'Christians are supposed to love everyone. Even their brothers.'

'If you loved everyone,' the boy said, 'you wouldn't have any friends, would you?'

'Well, son, ask our Blessed Lady to help you love your brother.'

'Father,' the penitent said confidingly, 'when I kneel down by the side of my bed at night-time, my mum thinks I'm saying my prayers.'

Before I could stop myself, I asked, 'And what *are* you doing?'

'I'm really talking to God.'

I was glad of that.

The sixth penitent came in, noisy and breathless. After the preliminaries: 'Damien's a dirty rat, Father.'

'Why, dear?'

'After I shot him he pretended he wasn't dead.'

'I see.'

'He always laughs at my jokes, though, cos I'm twice as big as him.'

'Do you share things with Damien?'

'I do when I ain't got none.'

I was in the process of saying we should be kind and charitable always but the noise was so terrific outside the confessional, I opened the top half of my door and yelled, 'Will you kids shut *up*!'

That was when I realized that the whole church was ablaze with light. Someone had lit a candle in every candle-holder. There must have been over a hundred burning.

I rushed out of my box and extinguished them, with my

215

fingers until I scorched them, and then with my breath. The children thought this was more fun than a birthday party. One called out, 'All in one puff, Father,' and another, 'I'll huff and I'll puff and I'll blow your house down.'

When I was finished puffing I demanded to know, 'Which joker did this?'

Johnny Steele put his hand up.

I rounded on him in a temper, 'I hope you tell this in confession.'

'I've already been, Father,' he said.

'I'll charge this up to your dad,' I said.

'I ain't got a dad, Father.'

That and the temporary lull in the chaos sobered me up. I returned to my box and continued where I had left off.

'Where were we, son?'

'You was saying, Father, that I've got to be kind and charitable to everyone.'

Before I had finished with this little fellow, the noise in church was once again at a deafening pitch.

As he went out, the lad said to the morning's last penitent, 'Your turn, big-head.'

'I'll blacken your bleedin' eye for you,' the other lad returned.

'You and who else? When you come out of that box, come round the corner and I'll pin your ears to your ugly fat head.'

The last penitent knelt down and, in a pious voice, asked for my blessing which, as Christ's representative, I was obliged to give.

'I called my best friend a big-head, Father.'

'I know. I just heard you.'

'That wasn't my best friend, Father. That was Jimmy Kane, my second best friend.'

This lad specialized in problems of personal hygiene. 'My dad keeps telling me off for wiping my nose.'

'Why?'

'On my sleeve, Father. What grown-ups don't understand is my nose likes being wiped on my sleeve.'

I was almost at the end of my tether. 'Anything else?'

'I don't like washing my hands, Father. I wouldn't mind if they didn't have so many fingers sticking on.'

'Anything else?'

'I broke some eggs but that was God's fault. If He made 'em in tins like baked beans it wouldn't have happened.'

'Anything else?'

'I put my tongue out at teacher when she wasn't looking. Fifty-three times, Father.'

I was very interested. The boy could count and was brave, besides.

'Once I was caught, Father. Miss Gregson saw me.'

'Bad luck,' I said involuntarily.

A tennis ball thudded against the glass top of my box. I gave the lad his penance and absolution and rushed out into the side aisle.

'Who did it?' I cried.

Damien stepped forward with the ball in his hand. I snatched it from him and threw it towards the exit.

'Get out, you rascals, all of you.'

Only when they had scrambled did I see Fr Duddleswell framed in the doorway of the sacristy.

'Problems, Father Neil?' he said.

'How were the little ones today, Father Neil?' Mrs Pring asked.

I had just returned from instructing Miss Gregson's class on Holy Communion.

'Not so bad, Mrs P. One little fellow wanted to know if the church burned down would I risk my life getting the hosts out of the tabernacle.'

'What did you say?'

I grinned. 'If the fire brigade were standing by.'

'I hope he doesn't set the church alight to test you out.'

'Then there were the usual questions about fasting before Communion. One said if he could put his breakfast on top of the host why not underneath.'

'I've often wondered that myself.'

'Another said, what's so special about the tongue that

it can touch the host when the teeth can't.'

'Ah,' Mrs Pring said, 'that was my Helen's problem. When she made her first Communion, she accidentally bit the host. She was heartbroken because she thought she'd hurt Jesus.'

I smiled at a child's way of thinking until I saw how upset Mrs Pring was.

'After that, Father Neil, Helen wouldn't go to Communion again for a whole year. Even Father D couldn't persuade her. She was afraid it would happen again.'

'I'm sorry,' I said.

'It's not uncommon that sort of thing,' Mrs Pring said. 'There's a lad in this parish who won't clean his teeth on a Sunday morning in case he swallows toothpaste and breaks his fast. His mum told me.'

'Molly Jenkins is a problem,' I said.

'The little girl who's lost her daddy?'

I nodded. Her mother had written me a note to say that she only had a part-time job and she couldn't really afford a white dress for her daughter.

Mrs Pring's reaction was, 'I've still got my Helen's first Communion dress. I'll pop round and see Mrs Jenkins. Maybe she'll let me alter it for Molly. After all, we're both widows, aren't we?'

Mrs Jenkins was delighted. When, a couple of days later, Molly came for a fitting, she looked very pretty in her long, white dress. I led her into Fr Duddleswell's study and his eyes lit up. He noticed at once that Molly was wearing his beloved 'niece's' dress.

Not all parents were as sensible as Mrs Jenkins.

I dropped them a line about the Feast, asking them to be sure to give the children a good meal the night before. Children were not used to the long fast and I didn't want them to faint in church in the morning.

Mrs Kane, Jimmy's mother, a non-Catholic, was very aggressive. She regarded my note as a personal insult and a slur on her concern for her darling's welfare.

'I don't need *you* to tell me how to feed my Jimmy,' she said angrily, her hair standing up on her head like a cos lettuce. 'Nor did I like the idea of my Jimmy having to tell you his sins when he hasn't got any.'

Mrs Kane then proceeded to shed light on Jimmy's sanctity which no one in my acquaintance had ever suspected.

'Where in the name of God is Ronan's baptism certificate?'

'It should have arrived by now, Father.'

'That's what comes of leaving you in charge of preparations for Corpus Christi, Father Neil.'

Ronan Carrol had been born and baptized in Columbus, Ohio, towards the end of the war. Miss Gregson told me she had received a letter from the American parish priest saying he would send me the certificate directly. It hadn't come.

This was the Thursday before the great day. Next morning, I was at the door when the postman made his delivery. Seeing my worried expression, he said:

'Expecting something important, Father?'

I told him I was hoping for a letter from America.

'None from the U.S. today, I'm afraid.' He thought for a moment. 'Funny, but I delivered a letter from there to Mr Buzzle only yesterday.'

'A long white letter with a seal on?' I was clutching at straws.

'Come to think of it, it was.'

I popped round to Billy's place, hoping against hope that my letter had been wrongly addressed. Billy didn't answer the bell. Mrs Pring told me he was on a week's holiday in Torquay.

'Well, Mrs P, if that letter does contain Ronan's baptism certificate, it's too bad. The poor lad won't be able to receive first Communion with the rest now.'

Mrs Pring must have mentioned it to Fr Duddleswell because in a few minutes he was in my room, flapping.

'We will have to get that letter, lad.'

'Do you know Billy's phone number in Torquay?'

'I do not.'

'Well, then?'

'Break in, Father Neil.'

'I don't mind seeing if he left a downstairs window open,' I said.

I tried them all without success. I noticed, though, that Billy's upstairs bathroom window was slightly ajar.

Fr Duddleswell said, 'I've no objection to you getting in that way, lad, provided you wait till 'tis dark.'

I reminded him that this wasn't my idea.

'Look at the shape of me, Father Neil. Are you wanting me to break my neck?'

For answer I didn't answer.

When dusk fell, I propped our ladder against the side of Billy's house. A gale was blowing.

'Dear God,' Fr Duddleswell exclaimed, holding on to the ladder for dear life, 'that wind will be shaking the barley tonight.'

I climbed up and squeezed through the bathroom window. I managed to find my way by torchlight to the front door when I heard the ominous sound of a police siren.

I thumbed rapidly through the pile of letters on the floor. Near the top was an official-looking letter with a U.S. stamp on it, addressed to 'The Incumbent, 10 Chindell Road.' I stuffed it in my pocket and beat it.

'Hurry, lad, hurry.'

I hurried so much I twisted my ankle on the last rung of the ladder. Forced to abandon the ladder, we clambered over the fence as fast as we could, only a few seconds before a policeman appeared in Billy's back garden flashing a torch.

Five minutes later, our front door bell rang. I hobbled downstairs to answer it. There stood two policemen. I was getting to know every copper in the district.

'Evening, sir.'

I smiled at the spokesman. 'How do you do?'

The senior policeman explained that he and his colleague were responding to an emergency call. Someone had broken in to Number 10. 'You didn't see anything suspicious, sir?'

'Like what?'

'Like someone breaking in.'

'No, Officer.'

'Would you care to come with us, sir?'

'Believe me, Officer,' I said, shaking, 'I wouldn't steal anything belonging to Billy Buzzle. He's my friend. I like his dog. There's no need to take me to the Station.'

'We were wanting you to come round to the back, that's all.'

I agreed to go with them.

'Is this your ladder, sir?'

I pretended to have initial difficulties seeing it. 'Good heavens,' I said, at length, 'no doubt about it. We keep it in our garden shed.'

'Have you used it recently?'

'Yes,' I admitted. 'Only this evening.'

'Well, sir, it was used a few minutes ago in an attempted burglary.'

'Extraordinary.'

The policemen left a few minutes later, not knowing quite what to make of it.

When the coast was clear, Fr Duddleswell came out of hiding. 'Well done, lad. Now where is the letter?'

I handed it over. He ripped it open and out dropped a cheque for $500.

'Gambling debts, Father Neil.'

'Poor Ronan.'

I was pleased to hear Fr Duddleswell say, 'Leave him to me, lad. I will handle this.'

I was in the school at 8.45 on the Sunday morning overseeing final preparations. There was a carnival atmosphere. Children scrubbed as clean as nuns. Mothers putting the finishing touches to the girls' white dresses and the boys' blouses.

Marisa, a Neapolitan girl, was decked out in bright angel's wings that opened and closed when she pulled the strings. The wings had small, Christmas tree lights sewn on them and her mother was telling Marisa to switch them on just before receiving Communion. I pretended not to notice because I didn't want any argument with that swarthy, muscular mama.

Some older children were carrying jam jars filled with poppy leaves, rose leaves, lilac and laburnum blossom. The flowers were to be strewn in the procession to the church.

'Very nice,' I said to one of the boys.

'Yeah,' he replied, 'we nicked 'em from the park, Father.'

Miss Gregson brought Molly Jenkins to see me in her white dress, accompanied by her mother who was in tears.

'Molly, Father,' Miss Gregson said brusquely, 'cannot go to Holy Communion.'

'Why not, Miss Gregson?'

Molly said, 'I put a sweet in my mouth before I went to sleep last night, Father, and when I woke up it was still there.'

'A boiled sweet?' I asked. Molly nodded. 'What a terrible pity.'

I knew from my seminary training that to eat anything nutritional broke the fast. The only apparent exception was swallowing things like wasps and bluebottles which wasn't the same as eating them. Also, chewing bits of wood or swallowing liquid parafin, the latter being judged by moralists to go right through the digestive system without nourishing it at all. Fortunately for me, Fr Duddleswell was close by and again took it on himself to sort things out.

I found the sacristy full of processional banners, woven with mottoes like *Panis Angelicus* and *O Bread Of Heaven*. The servers were scrambling around trying to find cassocks and cottas to fit them and arguing about who would carry the torches and lanterns. In the *mêlé*, the cotta of one of the boys caught fire. Luckily I noticed it and was able to tear it off him before he did a Joan of Arc.

The ceremony itself was flawless and full of quiet joy. My own peace of mind was disturbed by the thought that Molly and Ronan were unable to receive.

Fr Duddleswell was beaming, especially when he

222

preached to the first communicants and gave them our Blessed Lord in the Eucharist for the first time. Including Molly and Ronan. It would have melted the stoniest hearts to see 'the little saints in all their finery,' as Fr Duddleswell called them. No one left the church before Mass ended. Not even the dozen or so Irishmen who regularly knelt on one knee at the back as if they were under starter's orders, only waiting for the last blessing so they could sprint away.

When it was all over, Fr Duddleswell was heard boasting that not even the Italians at Sutri near Rome, with their festival of 'A Carpet of Flowers', ever put on a show like ours.

'Mrs Pring,' Fr Duddleswell said, 'for your performance today I will award you an ear.' And he gestured as if he were about to sever one of mine.

Mrs Pring had brought us in our nightly cup of cocoa. Because of all the celebrations it was much later than usual.

'Why, Father D?'

'Little Molly looked a treat in Helen's first Communion dress, so she did.'

Mrs Pring blushed and left for bed in a happier frame of mind than for many a long day.

'As for yourself, lad, you look puzzled.'

I decided to come clean. 'You broke all the rules in letting those two children receive today.'

'I did and I will probably fry for it.' He beat his breast three times like a drum. 'But you knew, surely, that I was going to do it.'

'Yes. And I'm pleased you did. Even though I wouldn't have had the courage for it.'

'Courage?' he said, laughing. 'What did our Blessed Lord say about the Sabbath observations?'

'That the Sabbath was made for man not man for the Sabbath?'

'Indeed. The same is true of the sacrament of sacraments which contains the Lord of the Sabbath, does it not?'

'I agree, Father, but what about the Church's laws?'

'They are to be kept.' He smiled broadly. 'With the utmost vigour when you can and provided it doesn't harm the little ones. After all, lad, when the apostles received Holy Communion at the Last Supper, were they baptized?'

'I don't know.'

'Neither do I, but does it worry you, lad?'

'Not in the least.'

'And were the apostles *fasting* before their first Communion?'

I shook my head. 'I still don't know what the canonists would think about this.'

'D'you know, Father Neil, me dear old father, God give him peace, had a little maxim. It has meant more to me over the years than all the wise talk I ever heard from moralists or canon lawyers. "The man who deals but bare justice is just as bad as an unjust man." '

I made him repeat it and, after pondering a while, said, 'That's not true.'

'Of course not, Father Neil. 'Tis something better. 'Tis a wee saying that encourages a man to strive for something more than justice. Magnanimity.'

I had another sip of cocoa. 'Sorry for my jibe about the enormous acorn, Father.'

He waved the apology aside as if it were long ago forgiven and forgotten.

'You're about as old-fashioned as next week,' I said.

'Kind of you to say so, Father Neil.' He looked at his watch. 'Now down that cocoa before it strikes midnight,' he said sternly. 'Else you will not be able to celebrate holy Mass tomorrow morning.'

TWELVE
Goodbye to St Jude's

Hugh Drummond was a thief. Why was Fr Duddleswell refusing to admit it?

Twice I had caught Hugh with his hand in the Sunday collection. He pretended he was putting in his own contribution whereas I was sure he was helping himself.

'Hugh stealing from the till, Father Neil? Never. He is as honest as yourself.'

I took measures to find out which of us was right. With a nail, I scratched a mark on a half-crown and asked Don Martin to put it in the Sunday Collection for me. After that Mass, the coin was still there. I tried again the following week. When I came to count the money, my half-crown was missing.

The same trick the following week gave the same result. This was proof enough for me and should be enough even for the blindly loyal Fr Duddleswell. I didn't want to accuse Hugh Drummond of stealing but God alone knew how much he must have pilfered over the years. Still I hesitated. Why? Firstly, because I liked Hugh. He was a gentle, affable old fellow in his mid-sixties. Not an enemy in the world, as far as I could tell. And he had taken up the collection at St Jude's for as long as anyone could remember.

The second reason for holding back was Fr Duddleswell himself. In the past few months, he and I had not seen eye to eye on a number of issues. Many a time he had brought his fire-power to bear on me and I had fired back. I did not want to risk falling out with him further.

It was only after considerable thought and prayer that I ventured to say:

'Father, I'm very sorry to have to tell you but I have proof that Hugh is a thief.'

He regarded me with tolerant amusement. 'I have known Hugh for twelve years, lad, and I tell you he is not.'

I laid my reasons on the line. After which, he said enigmatically:

'You mustn't think that Hugh is a thief just because he helps himself to a few bob.'

His explanation, as I had come to expect, was not of the usual sort. For the last three years, he told me, Hugh's wife had been a patient in a distant mental home. Her departure coincided with Hugh's retirement. His twice-weekly visits to his wife cost him £2 and he couldn't afford it. Hence, he helped himself to four half-crowns from the collection each week.

'But isn't that stealing?' I demanded.

'Not at all, Father Neil. I have often told the good people from the pulpit here that to take what is absolutely necessary for existence is not stealing, especially when you take from someone or some institution that can afford it.'

Fr Duddleswell saw the baffled look on my face.

'Listen, lad, Hugh realizes he is entitled to that money. Five shillings for his rent and five shillings for his beer and baccy.'

'Why doesn't he *ask*, Father?'

'Would you, lad? You surely do not want me to embarrass the poor old chap? Besides, he has contributed to the collection for years.'

'I suppose he knows you know.'

'Of course. He would not do it otherwise.'

'And he never takes more than ten shillings?'

'Never. He is completely trustworthy is Hugh.'

On reflection, I realized once again that however circuitous Fr Duddleswell's way of thinking it was invariably kind.

This is why when I caught him out in an act of blatant unkindness it was all the harder to bear. He said to me casually at breakfast one morning:

'I have suggested to Mr Wilkins that he resign.'

Mr Tommy Wilkins was the Headmaster of St Jude's secondary school, a man of outstanding dedication.

'He has been under a lot of strain lately, Father Neil.'

I had noticed that Mr Wilkins had been looking jaded. 'A nervous breakdown?' I asked.

'He is on the point of it, at any rate.'

'Too much work.'

'Probably.'

'Can't you arrange for him to have a few week's sick-leave, Father? You could easily persuade Dr Daley to give him a certificate.'

''Tis for his own good, Father Neil.'

I didn't like the way Fr Duddleswell presumed he always knew what was best for everyone. 'Whatever's the matter with him,' I said, 'sacking him is bound to make him worse.'

'Who said anything about sacking him?'

'Call it what you like,' I said, 'as the strong man among the school governors, you can do more or less what you please.'

He resented my biting tone. 'I have not consulted the governors about this and I insist I am not sacking Tommy Wilkins. Merely suggesting to him that it is best for himself and the school if he goes of his own volition.'

I knew Mr Wilkins's altruism. The slightest hint that the school would benefit from another Head would automatically induce him to resign. I said no more, simply bit savagely into my toast to show what I thought about Fr Duddleswell's autocratic behaviour. He, in turn, spoke words to me in Irish which I felt privileged not to be able to understand.

A few days after that disagreement, Mr Wilkins committed suicide.

The Coroner's verdict was that he had taken his own life while the balance of his mind was disturbed.

Fr Duddleswell admitted in open court that he had suggested to Mr Wilkins that he resign. He claimed not to have put any undue pressure on him. But had he known how near the edge Mr Wilkins was he might not have acted so hastily.

He went out of his way to praise Mr Wilkins for his professional integrity, his irreproachable family life and his dedication over eight years as Head of the school.

Afterwards, I heard Mrs Wilkins, accompanied by her three teenage daughters, thanking Fr Duddleswell for his immense kindness to her husband and family.

Fr Duddleswell patted Mrs Wilkins on the arm. 'Your husband was a grand man, Sheila. He worked himself to death for others. I will see he has a plaque erected in his memory.'

Inwardly, I was fuming. He should have been confessing, if not his guilt, at least his astounding folly. Instead, he was lapping up praise from the widow whose husband he was instrumental in sending to an early grave.

I had the same ill feelings towards him on the day of the funeral. He had prevailed on the Bishop to allow Mr Wilkins to have a full Catholic burial because his mind was disturbed when he committed suicide. The Mayor attended as did the school governors and a number of the older pupils. Pictures were taken by the local press. Once more, Mrs Wilkins and her daughters were profuse in their gratitude to Fr Duddleswell. I was not. Not a single word of regret or sorrow for his part in the tragedy escaped his lips. He seemed not to grasp the irony of their thankfulness.

He noticed my sullenness at lunch that day but said nothing except to deliver himself of a few words of Irish again. I brushed them aside.

When I broached the subject with Mrs Pring she put me off with, 'In matters like this, Father D is usually right.'

'If he sold your soul to the devil,' I retorted, 'you'd find some reason for excusing him.'

She smiled wryly. 'I suppose I would, Father Neil. I suppose I would.'

This takes the biscuit, I thought. He's got the whole damn parish in his pocket.

At the evening meal, he brought the subject up. 'I did

me best for him, Father Neil,' he said somewhat shyly.

'I'm glad you didn't do your worst.'

'Discipline in the school was beginning to break down and exam results last year were on the decline and –'

I butted in. 'He's dead, Father. Don't you understand Mr Wilkins whom you pressurized to resign is dead?'

He munched on for a few moments before: 'Why do you not accept what I say?'

'You suggested he should resign.'

'I did and nothing more.'

'Was anything more needed for a man as dedicated as Mr Wilkins?'

'He realized I was right. He said so.'

I nearly choked on my food. 'How can you go on insisting you were right? I repeat. Mr Wilkins is dead and he has a widow to prove it.'

Fr Duddleswell looked at me, a mixture of sorrow and kindness, and lapsed into Irish again.

'Do me a favour,' I said. 'Don't treat me like a child.'

'If they gave degrees for ignorance, Father Neil,' he snapped, 'a cockeyed curate like yourself would have first class honours.'

'Thanks very much.'

'If Mrs Wilkins does not blame me, why should you?'

'Because,' I replied, 'she is a better Christian than I am.'

He pushed his chair back, rose and stalked out, muttering, 'The best hurler on the field is always the feller on the fence.'

I called out after him, 'He can at least see better when a foul has been committed.'

He turned back to glare at me, opened his mouth, closed it without speaking and left me to finish supper on my own.

I took the phone call. It was from the Vicar General requesting Fr Duddleswell to come and see him as a matter of urgency.

While Fr Duddleswell went to Bishop's House, I visited Mrs Wilkins. I went to offer my sympathy but also, I have to admit it, out of curiosity. Why did Mrs Wilkins bear no animosity towards the man who was instrumental in her husband's death?

She had received through the post that morning a plan of the proposed plaque to her husband's memory. She was very moved by what Fr Duddleswell had arranged. Not wishing to stir up any rancour in her mind, I sat sipping tea while she expanded on her husband's virtues and her good fortune in having Fr Duddleswell as parish priest. I left her even more amazed than before at her generosity and simple Christian faith.

Fr Duddleswell did not return for lunch. At tea time, he came in and said, 'After seeing the V.G., I went on to visit Father Abe. He sends his love.'

'Thanks,' I said.

He put on his most impish smile, repeated his oft-quoted Irish phrase and closed the door on himself before I could object.

The next day was my day off. I decided to visit Father Abe for myself and tell him of my growing unrest at St Jude's.

The old priest was sitting in his cassock with a blanket round his shoulders.

'Come in and kindly welcome, laddy,' he said.

'I'm sorry if I woke you, Father.'

'Not at all. It was only a fox's sleep I was having. I can't seem to keep my head up these days. The flower's getting too big for the stem, I suppose.'

'Do the nuns look after you well, Father?'

He nodded appreciatively. 'I am better watched than a dead man's possessions, laddy.' When I laughed, he said, 'Sometimes I think that nuns is the best thing the Catholic Church ever thought of.'

I handed over a packet of cigars which Don Martin had asked me to give him. The old priest's eyes gleamed.

'Will you be sure and thank him kindly for me, now? I only have cigarettes left.' He took out a cigar and sniffed the end of it like a connoisseur. 'I cannot get used to smoking nicotine straws, laddy. White tunnels of filth, I call 'em. Oh, it's distressing watching the glow and smoke of them racing towards your nose like an express train with every little puff.'

He lit up and instantaneously the room was filled with the aroma of cigar.

'Now, tell me, laddy, what's on your mind?'

I pretended nothing was.

'Holy God,' he whistled, 'will you stop acting as if you wanted to buy my pig and come to the point. It's little Charlie, isn't it?'

'It is.'

'Out with it, what has the little divil been up to?'

I explained his recent behaviour over Mr Wilkins' death and how he kept swearing at me in Irish.

'What did he say to you, laddy?'

'I don't know exactly. It sounded like *Acushla agus* . . .' I couldn't continue.

'*Acushla agus asthore machree.* Was that it?'

'That's it.'

Father Abe shook his head and tut-tutted. 'The pair of ye should be ashamed of yourselves. You must have fallen out something drastic and no mistake.'

'I'm thinking of asking the Bishop to move me to another parish.'

Father Abe was very put out by that. 'A desperate measure, laddy, when you have to bring in Sponger.'

'Things *have* become desperate lately, Father. I can't see I have much choice. What's the point of two priests ministering in a parish when they're at one another's throats?'

'But little Charlie and myself were never any different, always squaring up to each other like a couple of tinkers at the fair of Knocknagree. And all the time, his soul was within me and mine within him.'

I smiled ruefully. 'Perhaps the pair of you were better able to take care of yourselves.'

Father Abe blew a mighty stream of smoke into the air. 'We Irish overdo everything, laddy, it's our generous nature, y'see. Do you realize, in the days of duelling, the

231

Irish were the only people in Europe who always blazed away at each other with *two* pistols?'

I laughed. 'Really?'

'It is so. And sometimes, when the duellists' seconds joined in, they made it a foursome, firing from all points of the compass.'

'I can believe it, Father.'

'We both know little Charlie has his faults but he has a big banquet hall of a heart and his charity is seamless as the blue sky.'

I promised Father Abe I wouldn't ask the Bishop for a move until I had thought about it longer.

'I'll come back and see you next week if I may, Father.'

He winked at me and blew a farewell cloud in my direction. 'Shut the door when you leave, laddy. That blasted wind would shave a gooseberry.'

The next week brought no improvement at St Jude's. I was seeing right through the long, white summer's nights. Fr Duddleswell and I had lost the power of communication. I was waiting for him to admit some responsibility for Mr Wilkins's death, he seemed to expect me to voice my support for him. The result was a stubborn, awkward silence.

Mrs Pring sensed the atmosphere. 'You two fallen out?' she enquired once at breakfast.

Neither of us could even say yes or no.

I gathered that Fr Duddleswell had visited the V.G. again but he did not report to me what was said. That was unusual in itself. Since he came back moroser than ever I suspected he had asked the Vicar General to give him a change of curates – and been refused.

Very well, the next step was mine. On his last visit to St Jude's, the Bishop had said that whenever I felt like a move I had only to contact him.

It was Tuesday. Later that afternoon, I was to visit Father Abe again. In preparation, I sat down at my desk and wrote to the Bishop asking to be transferred to another parish. I stressed that Fr Duddleswell had done his best to make me feel at home but that a change of scenery would benefit me, him and the parish.

I ended the letter, 'Your Lordship's obedient servant, Neil Boyd,' and sat in front of it for a whole hour, moping.

How sad to have to admit failure so soon. It was coming up to my cotton anniversary, as Fr Duddleswell called it, the first anniversary of my posting to St Jude's.

I could hardly bear the thought of saying goodbye to the parish and the close friends I had made there: Mrs Pring, Dr Daley, Billy Buzzle – even Mother Stephen – and a host of others. Most of all it hurt me that, after so promising a start, Fr Duddleswell and I had reached the stage of not being able to talk to each other. Perhaps divorcees feel the same awful isolation.

I was, as I thought, at my lowest ebb when the phone rang. I picked it up.

'Don Martin here, Father.'

I did my best to sound perky. 'Yes, Don?'

'It's our Neil, Father. He's just died.'

I tried to speak but couldn't. It was as if all the words until that second at my command had sunk to my feet. I wanted to lift a few of them to use but there was no strength in me.

'He was sleeping after his midday feed, Father. And when we went to look, he was –' Don sobbed openly. 'Will you come?'

I couldn't even say I would. I gurgled something and he interpreted it as meaning yes. He put the phone down and I heard the purring in my ear.

I was furious. Furious with myself for my loathsome self-pity. I threw the receiver against the wall, splintering it, and went to the drawer of my cupboard to take out my most precious possession. Then I ran down the stairs three at a time.

Mrs Pring was standing at the bottom, a tray in her hand. 'What's up?' she exclaimed.

'It's baby Neil.'

'Yes?'

'Died in his cot.'

Tears sprang into her eyes. 'Oh.' It was long and drawn out. 'I'll tell Father D.'

Having reached the bottom of the stairs in a flurry, I stood still for a few seconds as if all movement was denied me. I was *afraid*. What a terrible thing to have to visit a family whose baby had just died. While I stood there, fearful, vacant, wounded to the heart, there came a loud moan from Fr Duddleswell's study. Never had I heard such a desolate sound. Jesus on His cross must have sounded like that.

It went through where my mind should have been that Fr Duddleswell was a real father to his parish. After all these years, he could still cry in anguish over the death of a child. His grief gave me the strength to open the door and cross the road to the Martins' house.

I placed my grandmother's white-beaded rosary round little Neil's cold head. The crucifix rested on his breast. His face was slightly blue. That apart, he looked like any baby sleeping. I had promised my grandmother the day before she died that I would never part with her rosary. I knew she'd understand.

Dr Daley had gone and I was left alone in the child's bedroom. There was nothing for me to do. No absolution to be administered, no anointing, no final blessing. I signed the still, white form with the sign of the cross and tried to pray.

'Little Neil, Lord, never knew anything but love. He didn't know bitterness or cruelty or loneliness. He died and never knew death. For that I thank you.'

But my heart wasn't in it. A human being is entitled to all things human, even pain, sorrow, loneliness, his own death.

I gave up praying. What was the point?

'Why? *Why?*' If I had voiced the words they would have been heard from one end of the parish to the other.

Here was the only child I had ever seen born, the child who bore my name, and he was lying dead. I had seen him before his father and mother, and held him in my arms as

234

if he were my own. Dead. For the first time in my life I experienced anger, *real* anger. And it was more frightening than sex could ever be. My diaphram weighed a ton, an earthquake threatened my chest and, like Mephistopheles, I could have annihilated a world. I was *angry* and it made a man of me. Like Rabbi Epstein, I ranted against God for His inhumanity and it made a priest of me.

Inside me, a part of my soul detached itself from the rest and screamed, 'It's not fair, God. It's not bloody fair.'

I knelt down, listening to the sobs of the family downstairs and the puzzled questions of the boys. Danny said, 'Is Neil sick, daddy?' 'He's gone to Heaven,' came the reply. 'I told you,' Francis said, 'we won't be able to play with him until tomorrow.'

A couple of times, Jane came into the bedroom, dazed, talking to herself. 'He's not. He can't be.' Then she went out, shaking her head.

I was waiting for Fr Duddleswell to come. Why didn't he come? He had only to cross the road. Where was he? He can't have cared so much after all. It was outrageous.

How long I stayed there I do not know. My knees hurt when I rose.

I promised Don I would offer Mass for the family next morning, hugged Jane and returned to the presbytery.

'Where is he, Mrs P?' I was angry again. With myself, with the world, with *him*.

Mrs Pring's eyes and face were red from weeping. 'He's gone for a walk.'

'Gone for a walk!' I was staggered. Is this his priestly, fatherly devotion? I asked myself sarcastically.

'You see, Father Neil,' Mrs Pring explained, 'I was all upset and when I told him baby Neil had just died he thought I said –'

'*Father* Neil.'

Mrs Pring nodded.

It was clear to me all of a sudden. The only thing that was clear to me in the thick fog that was engulfing me. His cry of dereliction was his keening of me. He couldn't visit the Martins yet and sympathize with them because he was relieved that it was not his Neil who had died but theirs. When he had recovered, he would cross the road and see them. Not before. It wasn't decent before.

'What a mess,' I said. I was still angry but each time I learned something new, the reason for my anger and its object changed.

I put on my jacket and set out for the priests' home. I was on the point of dropping my letter in the pillar box when I caught sight of a blackbird nesting in the hollow of a wayside tree. The female bird did not move. Her yellowy beak was lifted as was her black, forked tail. Seeing her there at the mercy of every passerby, silently pleading to be left alone, to be allowed to bring her young to birth, I thought better of it. I thrust the letter into my pocket and jumped on the bus.

Before I got off, my letter of resignation was in shreds.

'So, laddy, you decided to stay with little Charlie, after all.'

'Yes, Father Abe.'

'I'm pleased. He tells me you're the best Simon of Cyrene he ever had. But as a matter of interest, why?'

I looked down from my height on the white-haired, white-bearded old priest in his armchair. 'Why?' I sighed deeply. 'I don't understand him and he can't make himself understood but – '

'He loves you.'

I winced at the word. 'I suppose so.'

'He made you understand that, laddy?' I nodded. 'He's not doing so bad, then.'

I shrugged to show Father Abe that he was right. I went on to tell him about Neil Martin. Afterwards, I wished I hadn't. He looked so distressed.

'Poor little emigrant,' he whispered, 'angel of the Lord. Here am I still holding on *per omnia saecula saeculorum*, so's you'd think the Grave-digger had mislaid his spade. While a baby dies and is sent back to the Manufacturer almost as soon as born.'

'It's not fair, is it?'

236

'Ah, but I'm thinking, the wee mite must have had the wind of God's mercy at his back.'

We were silent for a few moments. Each of us was thinking back, I felt sure, to Neil's christening: the baptismal garment new and for ever white, the light of his candle that would never go out.

Father Abe showed he remembered. 'Did I not bless him, laddy, and say, "May he never sin"?'

'You did, Father Abe. And they laughed at you.'

'Will you tell his dear father and mother that I will say Mass for them tomorrow?'

I promised.

'And now, laddy, I can let you into the truth about little Charlie. I couldn't have told you, mind, if you hadn't decided to stay.'

I was interested but apprehensive.

'You won't breathe a word to the wall about this because I'm betraying a confidence, y'see, and that's a terrible sin. Well, it would be if I weren't so old and past it.'

I smiled.

'You see, laddy, that Headmaster who put an end to his life –'

'Yes?'

'Little Charlie saved him.'

So Father Abe was himself under the spell. 'Saved him?' I said. 'How?'

'Mr – what was his name? – Wilkins, wasn't it? Mr Wilkins was on the edge of a breakdown.' I tried to intervene. 'Wait, now, laddy,' Father Abe insisted. 'Part of his illness was that he was, how shall I say? interfering with some of his pupils.'

'Girls,' I gasped.

'Boys, laddy. There was proof in the form of letters written to two of them by the Head. The parents found these letters and gave them in strictest confidence to little Charlie.'

Father Abe had no need to continue. Fr Duddleswell, in suggesting to Mr Wilkins that he resign, was allowing him to leave his post with honour. The alternative was to be sacked, disgraced and even incriminated. Yet before the Coroner, Fr Duddleswell had apologized for acting too hastily and being too hard on the Head.

'His wife knows, I suppose, Father Abe?'

He nodded. 'But not the daughters. Little Charlie swore he'd not tell *anyone* in the parish.'

'Not even me.'

'Seems so. Mrs Wilkins will bless little Charlie till her dying day for salvaging her husband's reputation, not to mention her own and her daughters' happiness. It would have broken little Charlie's heart to throw the Head before the courts, not after all his years of devoted service. And especially when he was really only a sick man.'

To keep my tears in check, I became sharply angry again but this time the anger was pure, emotionless, without any object. It was like screaming in a vacuum, eerie and soundless.

'Why did he swear at me in Irish, then?' I blurted out.

'*Acushla agus asthore machree?*'

'Yes.'

'I taught him that. Don't you know, it means, "You are the beat and beloved of my heart".'

I scratched my head and rubbed my face all over with both hands as if I was washing it.

'I thought he had gone to the V.G.,' I said, 'to get me moved to another parish.'

'He did.'

'So I was right.'

Father Abe smiled. 'How wrong can you be?'

'Tell me, please.'

'The Vicar General summoned him. He wanted to persuade little Charlie to take on this new and bigger parish. Charlie, the vain blighter, had had his eyes on it for years. He'd be made a Canon in the bargain.'

'And?'

'He asked if he could take his curate with him, and when the V.G. said no —'

'He refused.'

'Never known such a thing before in all my life.'

I took in a deep breath of air.

'You should realize, laddy, that little Charlie doesn't blame you in all this. On the contrary, he says you are quite right on the evidence you have. He admires you immensely, y'see.'

I stood up and asked Father Abe for his blessing. He gave it and said:

'Little Charlie is a good priest, laddy. He is nailed to his trade. As to yourself, trust in Christ.' He drew his blanket tight across his shoulders. 'Our trust, our dreams, too, are safe with Him.' He closed his eyes. 'Love and long life to me little Charlie.'

Our meeting was over. His white head dropped and he relapsed into an old man's sleep, effortlessly.

I murmured goodbye and went homewards. Back in the parish, I wandered around aimlessly for a whole hour, ashamed, wondering what to say to Fr Duddleswell when we met.

In the hall, I was met by Mrs Pring. She still looked badly shaken.

'He's back, Mrs P?'

She nodded.

'Is he completely better?'

Mrs Pring shook her head sadly. 'Go to him, Father Neil.'

Fr Duddleswell was at his desk, his discarded glasses in front of him. He rubbed his eyes with the back of his sleeve as I entered.

'I'm sorry,' I began, troubled to see him so upset over me.

'Father Abe, lad. He's gone.'

'But,' I gasped, 'I was with him less than a couple of hours ago.'

Through my head went a torrent of thoughts. What a foolish thing to say! Does it take an old man two hours to die? There were no cigar fumes in the air. Did the news about baby Neil finish him off? Did I watch him go and not realize it? He didn't die like an Italian tenor, after all.

Fr Duddleswell looked up at me, not seeing anything. 'I had a phone call, Father Neil.'

I repeated Father Abe's last words: 'Love and long

239

life to me little Charlie.'

He shook his head gratefully and the tears flowed. For the first time I saw him without clouds or smokescreens of his own making. There he sat like any other man, hurt, vulnerable, undefended.

As I leaned over him and rocked him in my arms, he was mourning Father Abe.

'*Ahir, vick machree,*' he kept saying, '*Ahir, vick machree.*'

How could I have guessed then the paradoxical meaning of that refrain: 'O father, son of my heart.'

Bishop O'Reilly came up trumps. In response to Don Martin's request, seconded by Fr Duddleswell, he allowed baby Neil and Father Abe to be buried together. The Bishop adapted the liturgy himself to make this possible.

No funeral was ever quite like it. Father Abe's coffin with its black drapes, adorned with his biretta and sack of Erin's soil, alongside the white coffin of a baby with its wreath of white roses.

Not one of the 120 priests or the congregation who crammed the church sensed anything incongruous in the ceremony. Not even the fact that Neil's two brothers were wearing white blouses and his mother was proudly wearing a white hat.

So, it came to me, Father Abe is proving to be a legend right to the end. We're burying an 86-year-old priest with the last child of the many hundreds he must have baptized in his long priestly career.

The Bishop himself presided, Fr Duddleswell celebrated Mass with me assisting him. Fr Duddleswell's sermon, one of the shortest yet the most moving I ever heard him preach, ended with the words:

'Hand in hand they go, unsullied ones, into the Kingdom of Light.'

THE END
GOOD FRIDAY 1979